Blood In, Blood Out

The Violent Empire of the Aryan Brotherhood

by

John Lee Brook

www.WorldHeadpress.com

Blood In, Blood Out

The Violent Empire of the Aryan Brotherhood

CONTENTS

FOREWORD

THE FIRST TIME I became aware of the Aryan Brotherhood was
in jail, standing in line to get clean laundry. A deep voice behind me
said, "I know who you are."

I ignored the voice, because I was nobody. Whoever the guy was
he wasn't talking to me.

"I know who you are," said the voice again. Only this time the voice
wasn't behind me, it was over me. Turning, I found myself staring
at somebody's chest. A chest that was about one inch from my nose.
Taking a step back, I looked up. The guy stood about six feet four
inches and had a shaved head. And, from the muscles that adorned
his body like ornaments on a Christmas tree, it was obvious he came
from good breeding stock. Unlike myself.

"I read about you in the paper," he said. "You're famous."

Sighing, I replied, "Infamous is more like it."

He thought about that for a second and grinned. Then he held
out his hand, which was attached to an arm as big as my thigh. His
forearm was covered in a spider web tattoo. So was his other forearm
and everywhere else. I shook his hand.

He told me his name was T.Rex. His real name was Charles Kemp,
but everyone called him T.Rex.

"Why do they call you T.Rex?" I asked.

He paused, thinking about it. Then he shrugged. "I dunno."

Because wise men don't go where angels fear to tread, I didn't say
anything. I just nodded.

He said he'd just arrived. He was being transported down south
from up north, where he'd been at Pelican Bay prison. I nodded and
turned back around. In jail, you don't ask too many questions. If you
do, it could mean you're a snitch.

viiiBLOOD IN, BLOOD OUT

Thirty seconds later, T.Rex growled and said, "This is bullshit, man." Putting his hand on my shoulder, he stepped out of the line, taking me with him. He then marched—with me in tow—to the front of the line, where the Trustees were doling out clean laundry.

In jail, cutting the line was tantamount to a mortal sin. Anyone stupid enough or crazy enough to try it was immediately challenged by a bevy of angry voices. And since the owners of those angry voices were armed robbers and murderers, persons who didn't think twice about stomping someone, they usually got their way. The line cutter would "get back in the fucking line!" and wait his turn like everybody else.

But not this time. No one said anything.

"Whaddaya need?" asked the Trustee.

T.Rex looked at me, raising his eyebrows. "Large," I said.

"Size large for my dog here," pronounced T.Rex. "An' triple-X for me."

The Trustee tossed two bundled rolls of clean clothes at us.

As I walked away, I marveled at T.Rex's brashness. I figured it was his sheer size and badass attitude that accounted for the episode. I was wrong. It wasn't T.Rex's size and attitude that caused the other inmates to bite their tongues. It was what he was.

Later, I found out T.Rex was a member of the Brand, which was a nickname for the Aryan Brotherhood. They were also called the AB or Alice Baker. Whatever they were called, they were royalty in the pecking order of prison, where gangs ruled supreme. Their royal status came from the fact that they were—to paraphrase Psalm 23— the "meanest motherfuckers in the valley of the shadow of death." Which meant they ran the show in prison.

Which probably explained why T.Rex was in protective custody. Protective custody is jail inside of jail. It's where they segregate the baddest of the bad guys from the ordinary bad guys. "You gotta keep 'em separated," a classification officer told me, or somebody's going to get hurt. This is because the culture of jail revolves around gangs. And gang affiliation is based on skin color.

There were Crips, Bloods, Joe Boyz, Nortenos, Surenos, MS-13, and Nazi Low Riders, just to name a few. Then there was the Aryan Brotherhood. And the truth about the AB was this: no matter where the powers-that-be put them, the Brotherhood did as they pleased. They found a way to reach out and control their environment. Wherever the AB was—inside prison or outside prison—they prevailed. The way they did that was simple: fear, macho violence, and death.

After I found out who and what T.Rex was, I kept my ears open. Anytime anyone spoke about flagrant events in prison, the Aryan Brotherhood was mentioned. To me, it soon became evident that these guys—the AB—were the Real McCoy. They were the definition of 'Machiavellian function,' because they took care of business. They didn't posture, they didn't negotiate, and they didn't hesitate.

I became fascinated by the Aryan Brotherhood. I didn't want to be one, but I did want to understand how they operated and why they were the way they were.

The purpose of this book is to view the remarkable role that the Aryan Brotherhood has played in the largest and most densely populated prison system in the history of humanity—the penal system of America.

When I was released from jail, I began toying with the idea of writing about the Aryan Brotherhood. I wanted to tell the story of the AB from the inside. To tell how they did what they did. To that end, I started doing research. I contacted acquaintances I had met in jail and asked them to hook me up with AB members willing to talk. I also contacted members of law enforcement agencies.

The AB has a code of silence, which each member vows to abide by. Their motto is "lie or die." In other words, never say anything about the inner workings of the Brotherhood. If you do, you die.

Most law enforcement agencies have a similar code. Only without the death clause, of course. Leaking confidential information is frowned upon, especially for active agents. It is considered a breach of faith and a conflict of interest. So mum is the word.

There were—as is always the case—individuals who were willing to talk. Some were bitter. Some were whistle-blowers. Others just wanted attention. But almost all insisted on one thing: anonymity. They would only talk if they remained unnamed or—in some cases— if their names were changed. Members of the AB feared retaliation or incarceration. While members of law enforcement agencies didn't want to lose their jobs or become pariahs. And active correctional officers had a very real fear of reprisals from prison inmates.

Of the two groups—good guys and bad guys—the bad guys were motivated by a lust for approbation. They wanted attention. They wanted the world to know how tough they were, how smart they were, how they beat the system. So they agreed to be interviewed, as long as they could hide behind an anonymous wall.

For example, Arturo Colano, who is my favorite character in the book, had never been arrested or interrogated by the authorities. Oh, they knew he existed, but that's all. They had no name, no description and no photograph. Zilch. In my opinion, when Arturo agreed to be interviewed, he did so out of a need for recognition. Like Zorro he wanted to leave his calling card, his mark. Yet at the same time, he realized that removing his mask would end his career. And he thoroughly enjoyed his career. So he insisted that his real name not be revealed.

In other instances, high-ranking gang members spoke openly about gang activities. They agreed to do so only if their names were withheld, which was their way of taking the Fifth Amendment. They didn't want to incriminate themselves. Under the circumstances, a portion of what they said was possibly embellished, amplified, enhanced and sensationalized. However, it's also likely that there's more here than meets the eye. Since they were speaking anonymously, why wouldn't they speak with accuracy? Which means the Devil may be just as black hearted as he says he is.

In any event, the text tries to carefully reproduce their words. These interviews form the primary sources for the book.

Without the interviews of Sam Sauter, Arturo Colano, Wolf Weiss, members of the Aryan Brotherhood, members of the Nazi Low Riders and others, including US marshals, DEA and ATF agents, correctional officers, officers of the court (attorneys), and FBI agents, the story would have been bereft of flesh.

While much of the dialogue and background in the book is taken directly from court transcripts, newspaper and magazine articles, and depositions, in many cases it is based on conversations with the actual participants.

It should be recognized that trial testimony and interviews sometimes produced conflicting versions of events. Where such conflict existed in testimony or recollection, I sought to provide a version of the facts which was in my opinion the most plausible.

Roger Poppen, who was—once upon a time—a crackerjack investigative journalist, performed a number of interviews during the big federal trial of the Aryan Brotherhood that took place in 2004 through to 2006. Access to those unpublished interviews provided extremely valuable information.

Court transcripts report what was said. The veracity of what was said is open to debate. Most of the television documentaries relied on former members of the AB, who had an agenda. Their agenda included applauding themselves. According to them, they had seen the error of their ways and had gotten out of the Aryan Brotherhood for one reason or another. More often than not, that reason was opportunism. They became informers in exchange for reduced prison sentences.

Due to the Freedom of Information Act—often called 'sunshine laws'—certain bureaucracies released files relating to the Aryan Brotherhood. For the most part, the files were highly redacted. Which means they were bankrupt, as far as providing any concrete information about the inner workings of the AB.

All that being said, writing about the Aryan Brotherhood was simultaneously frightening and exhilarating. For absolute evil has among its constituents a subtle hallucinizer. The observer is hypnotized by that which his senses cannot comprehend. Pure, unadulterated, raw violence is beyond the understanding of most people. It is as alien as little green men from outer space.

That's what separates the Aryan Brotherhood from the rest of humanity. And in the end, it's what sets them apart from other prison gangs.

John Lee Brook

ONE

The Baron And The Hulk

December 2002

THEY CAME FOR THEM while it was still dark. Shortly after four in the morning, a convoy of vehicles turned off the main highway. US Marshal Clarence J. Sugar sat in the passenger seat of the lead vehicle. A tall, heavily muscled man, Marshal Sugar carried himself with a swagger, and an air of menace hung from him like a cloak. Today he was strapped to the max: pepper spray, a Taser, and a Glock 9mm all rode on his Sam Browne belt. In his lap rested a Mac-10 machine gun. Next to his right leg, an M-16 assault rifle rested against the door of the SUV. Black body armor encased his upper torso making him appear even broader than he was.

Spread out among the other vehicles, Marshal Sugar had a total of nineteen deputy marshals accompanying him. All of them wore black fatigues and body armor, and carried fully automatic weapons. All of them were hard men who knew how to handle themselves in a combat situation.

It was cool and damp outside. A faint ribbon of blue arose from the western horizon to meet the darkness. Marshal Sugar looked out the window of his vehicle and shook his head. Even California had a Siberia, he decided, and this was it. 'It' was a remote forested area near a town called Crescent City, in Del Norte County, California. Up ahead he noticed the white glow that signified the huge, lighted compound ahead. Around the perimeter of the compound, spread out over 275 acres, he could see miles of curlicue razorwire. Outside the wire stood electrified fences that would fry anyone who touched them.

The massive gate of the main entrance slowly opened. As the convoy roared inside, guards armed with high-powered rifles looked down from their watchtowers. Reaching a complex of white concrete buildings—that formed a series of X's when viewed from above—the convoy screeched to a halt. The twenty US marshals jumped out, moving in formation to the main door of the complex.

Once inside the building, the small army of marshals moved down a long gray corridor, observed by an array of surveillance cameras. They passed through a series of barred doors, which thunked closed behind them, before arriving at their destination: The Security Housing Unit of Pelican Bay state prison. SHU for short, or the Hole by those who worked and lived in it.

The SHU was a prison built inside a prison.

Pelican Bay state prison was California's supermax prison. The place where California caged its most ferocious human animals. Some people called them criminals, others prisoners or inmates. But they were beasts of the jungle, men so savage and so dangerous they had to be separated from the other violent men.

Marshal Sugar and his deputy marshals were here to pick up and transport two of these men.

Arriving at the first cell, Marshal Sugar slammed the butt of his Mac-10 against the steel door. Inside the cell, a man jumped up from his bunk where he had been asleep. Standing in his white boxer shorts, he glared at the cell door, as if trying to burn a hole through it with his vision.

"Assume the position," said Marshal Sugar. "You're being moved."

"Fuck you," snarled the inmate. This was Barry Byron Mills, but no one called him that. Everyone called him the Baron or McB. The name Baron was in reference to his power and authority over other inmates. Those who called him McB did so because he was like McDonald's, worldwide and everywhere.

"Assume the position," repeated Marshal Sugar. This command meant the Baron should place his back against the inside of his cell door and put his hands through a slot in the door, so that his hands could be cuffed behind his back.

"No," said the Baron. Then he smiled and added, "Make me."

Marshal Sugar stepped aside and nodded at the corrections officer who stood beside him. The CO put his key in the doorlock, heavy pneumatic bolts snapped back, and the CO pulled the door open.

The Baron looked at Marshal Sugar. "Who the fuck are you and what do you want with me?" he asked.

Marshal Sugar noted the man's massive muscles, tattoos and gleaming bald head. "US marshals," said Sugar. "And like I just told you, you're being moved. And we're moving you right now. We can do it the easy way or we can do it the hard way." Marshal Sugar then smiled. "Or we can do it the semi-easy-hard way. The choice is yours."

Narrowing his blue eyes, the Baron asked, "What's the semi-easy-hard way? I'm not familiar with that one."

"The easy way is that you act like a civilized human being and we'll treat you like one. The hard way is that my deputies rush you and take you by force. Sometimes—in the chaos that occurs in this particular method—you get a little roughed up," explained the marshal and gave the Baron a fat smile. "The semi-easy-hard way is that I simply shoot you with this thing"—he held up his Taser—"and after you do the funky chicken for about thirty seconds, we search your body cavities and bundle you up."

Marshal Sugar shrugged. "I don't really care how we do it, because in the end the result is the same." With a dramatic flourish, he raised his forearm up to his eyes and looked at his wristwatch. "You have ten seconds to decide."

The Baron clenched his fists, as if checking his energy levels. After a few seconds, he winked and turned around, clasping his hands at the small of his back. Deputy marshals quickly surrounded him. One cuffed his hands, while the others probed his ears and nose with flashlights, in search of anything that might be used as a weapon or as a key to unlock handcuffs.

"Open your mouth, please," said one of the marshals.

The Baron opened his mouth wide and a flashlight was shined in it. "Touch the roof of your mouth with your tongue, please," said the marshal, peering into the Baron's mouth.

"Okay. Thank you." The marshal stepped back and the Baron snapped his mouth shut, thrusting his head forward a little bit like he was a shark biting into flesh.

A deputy marshal pulled from a bag a yellow jumpsuit, stenciled across the back of which, in bold, black letters, was the word PRISONER.

"Put these on, please," said the deputy marshal, holding the jumpsuit out to the Baron. "But before you do, please squat down three times. Then we'll remove the cuffs so you can dress."

The Baron hissed a little between his teeth, shaking his head. If he had a shank—which was a crude, handmade knife—hidden inside his rectum, squatting three times would cause the shank to move and probably pierce his intestines. He squatted three times.

His hands were then uncuffed. While he pulled on the yellow jumpsuit, three deputy marshals pointed their Tasers at him. All three were big, beefy men, who gazed at him flatly. Then they cuffed his hands behind his back, and shackled his feet. The final touch was a waist chain, like a steel belt, which they threaded through his handcuffs and locked snugly around him.

"What about shoes?" demanded the Baron.

"You'll get socks and slippers once you're in the van," Marshal Sugar told him.

The Baron glared at him.

"They'll get cold, but they won't freeze."

The Baron was escorted to the bench, where the deputy marshals ran heavy chains through his ankle shackles and waist chain. They ran these chains through rings welded to the bench, pulling them tight and forcing the Baron to sit hunched over.

"Okay," said Marshal Sugar, "let's get the other one." Five deputy marshals remained with the Baron, while the others moved down the hallway to another cell.

This cell was the home of Tyler Bingham, who was also known as the Hulk and Super Honkey. Both nicknames referred to his physique; he was almost as wide as he was tall, and he could bench press over 500 pounds.

The Hulk was waiting for them. He had heard voices, voices he didn't recognize, coming from the vicinity of the Baron's cell. Dressed in his yellow jumpsuit, which indicated his Hole-status, he stood against the back wall of his seven by ten foot cell.

Marshal Sugar nodded for the CO to open the cell door. Rolling his eyeballs, the CO did as instructed. As the CO pulled the cell door open, the Hulk launched himself at the marshals. Growling deep in his chest, he shot out the door as if out of a cannon. Grabbing one of the deputy marshals around the waist, the Hulk pulled the man to the ground. As the two men crashed to the floor, the Hulk tried to grab the marshal's pistol from its holster. He had his fingers on the butt of the 9mm Glock when five marshals grabbed him, with another trying to batter his head off with a flashlight.

Although partially stunned by the rapid blows to his head, the Hulk roared and fought like a man possessed. But only for about five seconds. Then the probes from two Tasers caught him, sending an arcing current of hot lightning through his massive body. Screaming, the Hulk wriggled, arched and bounced like he was having an epileptic fit.

After thirty seconds, Marshal Sugar raised his hand and the Tasers were switched off.

The Hulk was quickly stripped naked and his body cavities were examined with flashlights. Coating the index finger of his latex-covered hand with KY Jelly, one of the marshals did a quick rectal exam of the Hulk.

Marshal Sugar noted the Hulk's luxuriant gray walrus mustache, his shaved head, and the tattoos on his arms. On one arm was a tattoo of the Star of David, on the other arm a black swastika. Marshal Sugar wondered about that for a moment. Was it sarcasm, mockery, or some odd hodgepodge of white supremacist thinking?

Marshal Sugar shrugged. "Get him dressed and shackled," he said as he walked away. "Put a restraint on his elbows. This guy is strong and his attitude sucks."

The deputy marshals smiled. That was an understatement.

When the Hulk finally regained consciousness, he found himself hog-tied: leg shackles, waist chain, his hands cuffed behind his back and, like a ribbon on a Christmas present, his elbows pulled close together behind his back by a plastic tie.

"Get him up," said Marshal Sugar.

Four marshals lifted the prisoner to his feet and steadied him. The Taser was hard on the body's nervous system and short-circuited the brain.

"Okay," said Marshal Sugar, "let's go."

The parade of marshals moved back to the Baron's cell, two of the marshals almost dragging the Hulk along.

The Baron was quickly released from his bench and, like a black phalanx with two yellow figures in the middle, the procession walked back the way it had come.

The convicts were placed in separate vans, where they were chained to ring bolts, which sprouted from the floor. The Hulk's elbow restraints were removed and his hands were double-cuffed in front. The Baron received the same treatment. Marshal Sugar was not a malicious man. He didn't pull the wings off flies, and he didn't torture criminals. Anyone who did that was lost already.

The cavalcade roared to life and drove out through the main gate. Marshal Sugar pulled a cell phone from his pocket. "We're on our way," he said into it. "ETA ten minutes."

Five miles away, at the Crescent City airport, which was nothing more than a landing strip with a few small offices and a couple of old hangars, the pilots of an unmarked Boeing 727 began their final take-off check.

The Boeing 727 was a JPATS aircraft. JPATS stood for Justice Prisoner and Alien Transportation System. One of eight full-sized aircraft operated by JPATS, this plane was engaged in a high-priority transport flight for the Department of Justice. Its location was known only by a select few individuals, so that anyone who had an interest in sabotaging the flight could not do so. And since its convict-passengers would all be taken by surprise, none of them could plan their own escape or make arrangements for outside help in escaping.

Most JPATS employees, including the US marshals, called it Con Air.

Nine minutes later, the convoy arrived at the landing strip. The Baron and the Hulk were escorted onto the plane and seated. The Baron was seated six rows directly behind the Hulk, so that he could not communicate by means of hand signals. Both criminals received triple locked waist chains.

While the triple locking was taking place, Marshal Sugar told the two prisoners how it was going to be. "As long as you behave, you'll only be restrained by handcuffs, waist chains and shackles. If you decide to act like buttholes, then we will treat you like buttholes. You'll wear reinforced mittens"—he held up a pair of what appeared to be cyborg-like, mechanical mittens, which most of the marshals called "Dr. No hands" after the bad guy in the first James Bond movie—"and if you spit, bite or use abusive language, we will strap your head in this." He held up what looked like a baseball catcher's mask, one that had been specially modified to isolate and disable the wearer's mouth.

"And if we have to," continued the marshal, "I will shove a gag in your mouth and then duct tape your mouth closed." He squinted at the two criminals. "So. The choice is yours." He looked around at his deputy marshals. "We're big believers in free will around here. You do as you choose. In response to your choice, we do as we choose."

The deputy marshals nodded in agreement. They were highly-trained professionals, most of whom had served in the military before joining the US marshals service. The most important part of their marshal training was psychological. They were taught how to remain detached, cool and professional under the most provocative conditions. They didn't lose their tempers and react violently, nor did they allow their personal prejudices to influence their treatment of prisoners. In other words, no petty abuses took place, as was often the case at correctional institutes.

Marshal Sugar said, "Okay. Let's get this show on the road. We got places to go, people to see, things to do."

The deputy marshals who worked with Sugar had heard that line a thousand times. It always made them smile. It meant they had more prisoners to pick up. In this particular case, eighteen more. All of them extremely violent. One of the men they would pick up was known as "the most dangerous man in prison."

It should be an exciting day.

IT WAS CALLED OPERATION ARROW. Phase One was underway and involved the surprise collection and transportation of twenty brutal criminals, who were being held in maximum-security prisons all over the United States. After collection, the plane would fly back to Los Angeles international airport, where the prisoners would be escorted to various holding facilities until it was their turn for trial.

Twenty-three of the forty prisoners faced the possibility of the death penalty, if convicted. They were on trial for thirty-two murders and over 100 attempted murders, including stabbings, strangulations, poisonings, contract hits, and conspiracy to commit murder, most of which occurred inside prisons in the United States. But some of the murders had been committed outside prisons, in the real world.

Along with murder, other charges that faced the forty criminals included extortion, robbery, and narcotics trafficking.

The indictment had been filed by Assistant US Attorney Gregory Jessner. At 110 pages, the indictment was long and the result of many years of investigation.

Forty-two years old, Gregory Jessner was a slender man. He wore his brown hair short and appeared mild-mannered and soft-spoken.

But Jessner was as smart as God, with a magnetic energy that pulsed inside him to power the heart of a lion and the tenacity of a bulldog.

Jessner had filed his lengthy indictment against these forty savage criminals for one simple reason: the death penalty appeared to be the only answer. Isolating these criminals in solitary confinement was ineffective, because they always found ways to communicate with each other. They bribed guards, used hand signals, or wrote in coded messages. In one instance, acting as their own defense attorneys, they had subpoenaed one another in order to appear at court hearings together. Such men, already destined to spend the rest of their lives in small, concrete boxes, merely laughed when the authorities added more time to their sentences. Who cared? It was like beating a dead horse.

Jessner decided the time had come to use his last resort—execute these super-criminals. "Capital punishment is the one arrow left in our quiver," said Jessner. "I think even a lot of people who are against the death penalty in general would recognize that in this particular instance, where people are committing murder repeatedly from behind bars, there is little other option."

Prosecutor Jessner was used to handling murder cases. It was part of his job. Yet he was struck by dismay when he considered the total indifference with which these men killed again and again. The slaughter of other human beings meant so little to them that they called it "taking care of business." They thought of murder the way most people think about buying a pack of gum at the local 7-Eleven or a coffee-of-the-day at Starbuck's. Murder was nothing but a regular activity of everyday life.

The Racketeer Influenced and Corrupt Organizations Act (RICO) would be the arrow Jessner drew from his quiver, a federal law used to pursue criminal organizations. Authored by G. Robert Blakely, the RICO Act came into being in 1970, its name deriving from the character that Blakey's favorite actor, Edward G. Robinson, played in the movie *Little Caeser*.

Under the RICO Act anyone guilty of two or more of thirty-five stipulated crimes could be tried as a racketeer. The penalties imposed by the RICO Act were severe. Thus between the death penalty on the one hand, and the RICO Act on the other, Prosecutor Jessner hoped to conclude the murderous activities of these forty super-criminals.

"I suspect they kill more than the Mafia," said Prosecutor Jessner. "They kill more than any single drug trafficker. There are a lot of gang-related deaths on the streets, but they are usually more disorganized and random." He considered for a moment, and added, "I think they may be the most murderous criminal organization in the United States."

WHEN PROSECUTOR JESSNER used the word "they" he meant the Aryan Brotherhood. The most violently ruthless gang in the world, the Aryan Brotherhood came to bloody birth in San Quentin prison in 1964. The prison population of San Quentin—called the 'Q'—began choosing sides based on skin color. Blacks only socialized with other blacks. Hispanics refused to speak with anyone who wasn't Hispanic. To protect themselves against the blacks and Hispanics, a few outlaw bikers—who were white—formed their own clique. Back then the cliques weren't called gangs, they were called "tips."

The black tip was the Black Guerilla Family, and had ties to the Black Panthers and the Nation of Islam. Mexican Mafia or La Eme was the name the Hispanics chose. The white boys called their tip the Diamond Tooth Gang, which referred to their teeth. To add an aura of fear and terror to their persona, the white guys glued bits of broken glass to their teeth. When they smiled, the sunlight glittered off the glass in their teeth as if they were diamonds.*

---

* A number of gangsta rappers later adopted this jailhouse dental fashion. The rappers put real diamonds in their teeth. And the current trend of wearing baggy pants real-low on the buttocks—called 'sagging'—also began in prison and carried over into popular culture.

After a while they changed the name from the Diamond Tooth Gang to the Blue Bird Gang. No one seems to know why exactly. Whatever the origin of the name, the Blue Bird Gang began to attract other white members at the 'Q'. Soon this gang of "white warriors," as they called themselves, dropped the Blue Bird name and designated themselves the Aryan Brotherhood—a direct reference to their skin color.

The Aryan Brotherhood recruited only the biggest, the baddest and the toughest white inmates. It was an exclusive order of white warriors. Their motto was "blood in, blood out." This meant that each potential member had to "make his bones" before he became a full-fledged member. "Making one's bones" meant spilling blood in hand-to-hand combat. Either the blood of another prisoner from a rival gang, or the blood of one of the guards. It didn't matter which, but blood had to be spilled.

Once accepted, the member was branded with a tattoo. This idea was taken from the title of a very popular novel among white inmates—a Louis L'Amour western, *The Brand*.

Usually the actual Brand or tattoo was that of a green shamrock, the letters AB, or 666—the mark of the beast in the last book of the Bible. The Brand meant that the person was owned by the Aryan Brotherhood, and all its members were branded. The term "the rock" is specific to the shamrock brand* that many members wore.

Each new member of the Aryan Brotherhood had to take the pledge:

---

* This shamrock brand was taken from the Arabian 'shamrakh', which symbolized the Persian Triad. Triads, unlike 'trinities' which are three-in-one, have three distinct members. In this case, Heaven-Man-Earth, that is the divine, the human and the natural, with man the mediator between the celestial and the terrestrial. The human mediators are 'white-warriors.' The shamrock is the mark of the white warrior and symbolizes the sunwheel or the black sun. According to Michael Thompson, an AB member who defected, the shamrock brand refers to the AB's antipathy toward the Christian concept of the Trinity as presented by St. Patrick in Ireland.

An Aryan brother is without a care,
He walks where the weak and heartless won't dare,
And if by chance he should stumble and lose control,
His brothers will be there, to help reach his goal,
For a worthy brother, no need is too great,
He need not but ask, fulfillment's in his fate.
For an Aryan brother, death holds no fear,
Vengeance will be his, through his brothers still here.

This pledge had certain similarities to the religious vows taken by Japan's kamikaze pilots in WWII, and the Thugs of India, who murdered and robbed in the name of Kali, goddess of destruction.

In the beginning, each member of the Aryan Brotherhood had a vote in all things, in every decision. So if some snitch was to be murdered, or a defector was to be killed as an example to what happened to such traitors, everyone voted and the majority ruled. But the democracy didn't last long, because the Aryan Brotherhood was growing like a cancer. Within a few years, it had members in all of California's prisons and many of the federal prisons in the United States. Older members realized that it was time for a change.

A three man commission was set up, which functioned as a blasphemous Father, Son and Holy Spirit of violence, murder and death. Commissioners made the big, strategic decisions for the Brotherhood. Under them were councils, which had five to seven members. The councils ran the day-to-day operations of the gang. They could order hits and contract murders, if necessary. Each prison system had its own council. For example, all the prisons in the state of California were governed by one five-man council. Texas had a council; Arizona had a council, and so on.

TYLER BINGHAM AND BARRY MILLS, aka the Baron, sat on the Commission of the Aryan Brotherhood. The third Commissioner was Thomas Silverstein, who was sometimes called Terrible Tom. More about him later.

These three men were the shotcallers, the terrible triumvirate of the Aryan Brotherhood. They decided who would live and who would die. Who would run drugs, who would rob banks, who would extort money, who would do their evil bidding. Their power was absolute. Anyone who stood in the way was killed. The long arm of the Aryan Brotherhood reached anywhere and everyone.

1967

ACCORDING TO THE demographic studies, Windsor, California, a small town just north of San Francisco, had approximately 5,000 households, of which 8.4 percent were single mothers living with their children, and 23.9 percent were classified as non-families. In other words, a bunch of unaffiliated people who lived in the same house. Barry read these numbers in the local newspaper and memorized them. He figured he belonged to both groups: he lived with his single mother, but they weren't a family, because neither of them gave a shit about each other.

In fact, Barry Mills didn't give a shit about much, except for that one special feeling. The one where adrenaline surged through his body, making him feel invincible, as if he was the fucking Prince of Darkness seated on his throne in Hell, gazing out over his legions of fallen angels. Powerful and invincible!

That's what Barry cared about—the rush. It was a call to action. That's why he was leaving. He stood at the bus station with his ticket in hand. South. He was going to SoCal, where it was warm and the girls were pretty. Maybe he'd find the ultimate rush there.

Nineteen and bored. That pretty much summed up Barry Mills. It was time to ramble on, he figured. Do something. Chase that rush. Just thinking about it made him feel edgy and exhilarated.

When the bus arrived, he boarded, handing his ticket to a fat guy with white hair and red cheeks. Like Santa Claus almost. Christmas in August. Barry laughed at the thought. With a belch of smoke, the bus departed. Barry never looked back. After a while, the stream-of-consciousness quality of the landscape put him to sleep. He snoozed for the next eight hours, until the bus slowed and some internal gyroscope told him he had arrived. The Greyhound terminal didn't look like much, dirty old cement with graffiti scrawled here and there. But it was Ventura, California! Sun and beach and surfing.

The bus lurched to a stop and he waited for the losers to gather their things and get off before making his own way to the exit. Finally—fun in the sun! He glanced around, trying to figure the way to the beach when someone called his name.

"Barry Mills?"

Barry turned and saw two black uniforms. Ventura cops. He ignored them, as if he was just taking in the scenery. The two cops moved in close.

"Can I see some ID ?" asked one of the cops.

"You talking to me, officer?" asked Barry. He patted his pockets. "Gee, I musta gone and lost my wallet."

"Happens all the time," said one of the cops, grinning at his partner.

"I guess you need to come with us," said the partner. He hooked his thumb toward a patrol car parked at the corner.

"What for?" asked Barry, pressurizing his voice.

"For grand theft auto."

"I just got here on the bus. If I had a car, stolen or not, do you think I'd be riding some stinking bus?"

"Not here," said one of the cops. "Sonoma County issued the warrant. Seems you borrowed a car that didn't belong to you up in Windsor."

"No way, man. I never been to Windsor. I don't even know where it is."

"You can argue it with the court," said the cop. "We just arrest 'em. Somebody else sorts 'em out. Let's go."

"Fuck!" said Barry. "See if I ever come to Ventura again. You guys keep hassling the tourists and shit and pretty soon no one'll come here."

"I know just how you feel," said the cop. "But if you feel bad now, just wait till you see our jail. You'll wish you'd gone to Hell instead."

The cops cuffed Barry and put him in the patrol car. Then they drove him to the jail. Barry took one look and did indeed feel worse for having seen it.

He sat in a filthy holding tank with a bunch of brokedick bums for three days. He was fed on coffee and a plain cake donut for breakfast, and late in the afternoon a peanut butter and jelly sandwich and one of those little cartons of milk that had a picture of some smiling cow on the side. Bessie was her name.

On the fourth day, they cuffed him and walked him across the street to the court house, where he was told to sit and wait his turn. When finally he went before the judge, some pencil-necked prosecutor with glasses was explaining that Sonoma County had issued a warrant for one Barry Mills for grand theft auto.

"He boosted the car from the parking lot of the local country club," said the prosecutor, then gave Barry a *what a dumb shit* look.

The judge asked Barry whether he had counsel.

"What?" Barry didn't understand the question.

"Do you have a lawyer?" rephrased the judge.

"How the fuck would I have a lawyer?" protested Barry. "I just got here three days ago and before I took three steps off the bus they arrested me."

The prosecutor looked at the judge. *I told you so.*

"Send him back to Sonoma," said the judge, already thinking about the next case.

Barry Mills was in the holding tank another three days, before moving to a box van with two other guys, who looked pretty tough, and being taken north on I-5.

The Sonoma County Jail was nicer than the one in Ventura. In the Sonoma Jail they fed you three times a day, and put you in your own cell. The court assigned Barry a public defender, who advised him to plead guilty and ask for probation.

"Since it's your first offense, the court'll go easy on you," said the public defender.

Barry thought that sounded good and so pleaded guilty. The judge denied probation and sentenced him to one year in the Sonoma County Jail. It was the last time Barry would ever listen to an asshole public defender. Since his offense was non-violent—all he'd done was boost a car—they put him on the Sonoma County Honor Farm, which is where he met Buddy Coleman, a petty thief. Three weeks later, Barry and Buddy escaped. It was easy. All they did was walk away while on work detail.

After one week, they were arrested and charged with escape without force. The judge sentenced Barry Mills to one year and one day in prison.

ONE YEAR and eighteen days later, Barry Mills walked into a 7-Eleven convenience store in nearby Stewarts Point, a quaint little town overlooking the Pacific Ocean. He was accompanied by a man called William Hackworth. Each of them carried a gun that had yet to be paid for, on loan from a friend who was expecting $100 apiece by the end of the week.

The friend had said, "No sale. Come back when you got cash."

"Shit, man," whined Hackworth. "How can we get the cash if we don't have any guns?"

The salesman thought about it. "Okay," he said. "You got a point."

He gave them the guns, warning, "If you don't pay me, I'll hunt you down."

"Don't worry," said Hackworth, "you'll have your money in a week."

Two nights later, Mills and Hackworth walked into the convenience store, picked up two cans of soda pop and went to the counter. "Give us all the money in the register," ordered Hackworth, waving his gun in the clerk's face.

The clerk, Raymond Berleyoung, shrugged and gave them the money.

"Down on the floor," commanded Hackworth.

Berleyoung prostrated himself on the floor. Hackworth took the wallet and checkbook from Berleyoung's back pocket, and then whacked the clerk in the head with the gun.

When they counted it later, they couldn't believe it: $775! More than the money, Mills enjoyed the rush he got from the armed robbery. He felt as if somebody had plugged him in and turned him on. Waves of energy flowed through him, giving him clarity. Being a criminal was supercool.

Three hours later, Mills and Hackworth were arrested and charged with armed robbery. The robbers pled not guilty. William Hackworth testified for the prosecution and, in exchange for his testimony, received probation. Consequently, Barry Mills was convicted of first-degree armed robbery and sentenced to five years to life in prison. He was transported to San Quentin State penitentiary, which was where California kept its rarest specimens.

Prison was supposed to be a place of punishment, but Barry Mills loved it. Prison was a whole different world, where everything was deviant and primordial. Power was the only rule. Outside prison he had felt like a leper, unclean and shunned, but inside prison Barry Mills was on top.

Mills began working out with weights to bulk up and get strong. At the 'Q,' Mills met members of the Aryan Brotherhood. Fascinated by their warrior philosophy and their sense of belonging, he became a prospect—which meant he was allowed to hang around and run errands. It also meant he came under the protective umbrella of the Aryan Brotherhood, so nobody fucked with him. Mills listened attentively to what was going on around him. At the right time, he asked questions and got answers. Uneducated but highly intelligent, he soaked up knowledge and soon achieved an advanced degree in crime. He majored in drug-running, money laundering, extortion, armed robbery, weapons manufacturing, assault and battery, manipulation, terror and murder.

Barry Mills earned "his bones." He became a full-fledged member of the Aryan Brotherhood and was branded. In his pursuit of the rush, coupled with his superior intelligence, he rapidly rose to the position of trusted lieutenant.

On December 29, 1977, San Quentin released Barry Mills. Merry-fucking-Christmas!

Mills migrated south, ending up in San Diego, California, where crime was rampant, life was cheap and Mills could cater to his rush addiction. For a while he ran drugs, mostly heroin and cocaine, up from Mexico. But that got boring. Before he could do something with a little pizzazz, however, he was arrested in connection with a robbery. While in San Quentin, Mills had helped plot a raid on a bank in Fresno, California, for a couple of Brothers. Upon their release, the Brothers gathered an experienced crew. The robbery was brutal and fast; the crew was in and out within three minutes. They hoped to get $2 to $3 million cash, but only got away with $21,000.

The role Barry Mills played in the robbery came out when the gang was caught and tried. Somebody made a deal with the prosecutor and snitched.

Barry Mills was sentenced to twenty years in federal prison. Transported to the United States penitentiary in Atlanta, Georgia, Mills began doing his time. Only to Mills it wasn't doing time, it was living. Inside, he met another Aryan Brother—Tyler 'the Hulk' Bingham. Bingham had been one of the crew members in the Fresno bank robbery. The two men became good friends. After all, they had a lot in common. Both believed they were special: they had warrior spirit, superior intellect and superior physique. And they both loved the rush they got from spilling another man's blood.

As the Hulk put it so eloquently, "The smell of fresh human blood can be overpowering but killing is like having sex. The first time is not so rewarding, but it gets better and better with practice, especially when one remembers that it's a holy cause."

The Hulk had a sensitive, religious side. He didn't kill just to kill. He killed with reverence and for a belief. The Hulk was an ardent, fanatical Darwinian and believed in natural selection and survival of the fittest. Dominance was his religion.

IN 1965, Tyler Bingham was a frustrated man. He was managing a gym in Sacramento, California. Iron World Gym was the name of the place. Engaged to be married, earning $12,000 a year, with a degree in fine arts that had been a waste of time, it all changed for the Hulk when one day he picked up a copy of *Esquire* and began reading an exposé on the Mafia entitled 'The High Life of Crime.' The investigative report, by Gene Ferris, told the story of Mafia underbosses, who smuggled drugs into the country and extorted money from all kinds of businesses, from mom and pop grocery stores to the Teamsters Union. It also described the lifestyles of these criminals, which included huge mansions, expensive cars, and $1,000 restaurant tabs.

The Hulk turned the page. A photograph showed a sleek, well-built man dressed in a cashmere overcoat. He had a retinue of well-dressed, muscular men following in his wake, his bodyguards. The caption under the photo read: Gaspipe Casso, reputed Mafia underboss accompanied by his 'torpedoes.'

The Hulk was mesmerized.

According to the text on the next page, 'Casso reportedly made more than $5 million last year from the sale of illegal drugs. How much more did he make from all his other nefarious enterprises?'

The Hulk couldn't believe the man in the photo made that kind of money from smuggling drugs. And he walked around like he hadn't a care in the world. The guy was untouchable. Hell! I could do that, thought the Hulk.

The Hulk was strong as an ox, and spoke with a hillbilly twang. That and his drooping walrus mustache made people think he was stupid. In reality, his IQ approached genius level. As he gazed at the photograph in the magazine he just knew that this guy Gaspipe was living the kind of life that he, Tyler Bingham, should be living. Right there, right then, the Hulk made his decision. In the days to come, that was all he thought about. His soul had been moved. He read the article over and over again.

The Hulk didn't know anything about drugs, except anabolic steroids. Those were cheap and legal in 1965 and no one was going to pay big money for those. The Hulk started looking around, following the money. The money was in the banks, so he decided he had to go to the banks and take it and to that end started researching famous bank robbers and daring bank heists in books at the library. There was a problem, however, in that the books didn't explain the mechanics of robbing banks; they simply related an exciting story.

The best way to learn, thought the Hulk, was with on-the-job-training. He bought a gun and a ski mask, drove his pick-up truck to Stockton one Saturday morning, and pulled into the parking lot of a downtown bank. At the front door he made a note that the bank closed at noon on Saturdays. He looked at his watch. It was 11:30 a.m. He returned to his truck and waited until 11:55, before strolling into the bank, his gun tucked into the back of his waistband.

The Hulk glanced around. He was the only person in the bank other than the tellers. Donning his black ski mask, he pulled his gun out and walked up to the nearest teller, a young blonde woman, very pretty, counting out her drawer.

"Put all the money in a bag and give it to me," said the Hulk, pointing the gun at her chest.

The teller looked up thinking it was some kind of joke. The gun and the mask convinced her it was not. Stifling a scream, she started to raise her hands.

"Don't put 'em up," said the Hulk. "Use them to put the money in a bag and hand it to me."

The teller obeyed, cramming the money from her drawer into a cloth bag. The Hulk noticed the two other tellers looking over, wondering just what the Hell was going on. Without hesitation, the Hulk stepped back. "You two," he said, pointed the gun in their direction. "Empty your drawers into bags and hand the bags to me." His voice was loud but not threatening, he didn't want them to start screaming.

Sixty seconds later, the Hulk walked out of the bank. He removed his ski mask with his gun hand and carried three cloth bags of cash in the other. Slowly and with great care, he backed up his truck and drove out of the parking lot as if it was any other day; as if he had just finished his banking and was on his way to the supermarket to spend his money.

Back in Sacramento, the Hulk counted the loot. $9,000—almost one year's salary in less than five minutes! He laughed and threw himself on the bed.

What a rush!

The Hulk was addicted and he kept robbing banks, learning as he went. He definitely had a knack for it. Instead of driving his pick-up truck, he rented nondescript cars that were difficult for witnesses to identify. Buicks and Plymouths were his favorites. He bought a shoulder holster for his gun and wore a sport jacket over it. In fact, he dressed totally out of character. When he strolled into the banks, he looked like some accountant on his lunch break: glasses, briefcase, wingtips. His cardinal rule was Never Hurt Anyone. Armed robbery was a serious offense, and robbing banks was a federal offense, which meant the FBI got in on it. But armed robbery with assault was something else—if they caught you, they tossed you in prison and threw away the key.

His other rule was that if the situation didn't look good, or if things started to unravel in the middle of the robbery, he walked away. Hysteria was not healthy. That's when things went sour. Somebody would do something unexpected. If that happened, there was too much risk of shooting someone. So he simply turned and walked out, got in his tan Buick and drove away.

After a while he lost track of how many banks he robbed. A lot, that much he knew. He had so much money he decided one day that instead of robbing a bank, he would walk in, open a savings account and make a large cash deposit. He had trouble keeping a straight face as he sat in front of the new accounts manager and filled out forms. He laughed all the way home.

The rush was still motivating him. The sheer joy of adrenaline humming inside his body was like a vibrating guitar string connected to his heart.

THE STRING BROKE in 1973. The Hulk walked out of one bank to find a squad of cops waiting and he was arrested. Turned out they had been waiting for some other guys following an anonymous tip that a gang was planning to hit that bank. The cops had staked the place out, including two undercover officers in the lobby.

The Hulk hired a kick-ass defense attorney. Knowing the odds were against him, he had done his homework and knew whom to call. Since the cops charged him with one armed robbery, he only got sentenced to five years in prison. If the prosecutor had known about the others, it would easily have been twenty years.

The Hulk took up residence in the United States prison in Marion, Illinois. In 1973, USP Marion was the maximum of the maximum-security prisons in the US. It was the zoo where they caged the wolves that ate men. But the Hulk thought it was great, kind of like a Club Med on the dark side of the moon. There were tons of weights on the yard, so he pumped a lot of iron. If you had the money, you could have a black and white television in your cell. The food was good and there was lots of it. He was bulking up and getting ripped. Because of his strength and size, nobody fucked with him. And he made some new friends, guys who belonged to a white prison gang that called themselves the Aryan Brotherhood.

He was pumping iron in the yard one day when this 'dog' with a shaved head walked over. The Hulk was doing sets of curls with 100 pound dumbbells.

"Yo, dog," said the dog. "Pretty heavy metal ya'll got going there."

The Hulk nodded.

"Ya'll take care of yourself, huh?"

The Hulk nodded.

"Any of these black cats be bothering ya'll?" asked the convict, gesturing at a group across the way.

"No."

The dog flashed a snaggletoothed grin. "I be guessing not." He glanced around. "My name be being Bob. But most call me Bully Boy cuz my size."

Originally from Mississippi, Bully Boy Bob was in prison because he was a failure in life. First he failed school. Then he failed at drug smuggling. He'd been driving an elderly, wheezing Cadillac loaded to the gills with cocaine when the cops stopped him. While they were putting the cuffs on him, one of the cops gave him a look of pity. "I ain't never seen no white man drive a car like that," the cop had said, shaking his head.

The Hulk looked at the guy. Bully Boy was tall and thick, but kind of fat. Shrugging, he continued with his curls.

"Me and my white boys kinda hang together, ya know? That way we don't be having any trouble with any of the cats." Bully Boy stared at the Hulk to see if he was making an impression. "We be having drugs and stuff, too."

The Hulk set down his dumbbell. Bully Boy had his attention. "Go on," said the Hulk.

That was that. The next thing the Hulk knew he was being sponsored as a prospect. Two weeks later, he waded into a brawl on the yard, where some white dogs and black cats were mixing it up, trying to gut each other. Some big, black cat came at him with a shank. The Hulk broke the cat's jaw with a single punch. Then he proceeded to pulverize five more black cats. It was easier than bench pressing 500 pounds. Nothing to it.

The Aryan Brotherhood was electrified. They voted him in that same day. They branded him, which was kind of cool. A tattoo of a green shamrock sat on the top of his hand. The Hulk shaved his head the next day. Examining himself in a mirror, he liked it. It gave him a menacing look of impending doom.

After serving two of the five years he owed the US government, the party ended. The Feds paroled the Hulk and he went back to Sacramento, back to his old life of robbing banks. Except now he was a little more brazen, even a little careless. He missed his white brothers back at USP Marion, so he didn't really care if he got caught or not. Secretly, he was looking forward to another vacation.

But it took three years before he got the opportunity. One day in May of 1976, he got word that some Aryan Brothers were recruiting a crew to hit a bank in Fresno. The Hulk jumped at the chance. All he had to do was go along, carry a shotgun and look mean. The job had already been planned out by some shotcallers in San Quentin, so there really wasn't anything to do, except show up rough and ready.

As they came out of the bank, the FBI was waiting for them. A couple of the Brothers wanted to shoot it out and go out in a blaze of glory. Fuck that shit! The Hulk dropped his shotgun and put up his hands.

The trial didn't go well. One of the Brothers, to save his own bacon, became an informant. Singing like a canary, he named everybody he could think of, or had ever heard of. The Feds lapped it all up and issued warrants for half the state of California. All the way through the trial the Hulk just glared at the snitch, gave him the evil eye. The Hulk knew the Brotherhood would take care of business. They always did. The snitch's name would be "put in the hat."

The Feds transported the Hulk to USP Atlanta, Georgia. He had gotten a twenty year sentence, which he didn't mind much. He just hoped USP Atlanta had lots of weights in the yard. Lo and behold, it did. The place was newer, cleaner and the weather was better. Lots of sunshine. The Hulk could work on his tan. He would feel healthier, be happier, have a positive outlook.

There was an added bonus. The Aryan Brotherhood had a strong presence at USP Atlanta. They ran the prison. Drugs, booze, anything, everything. It was the Hulk's kind of place.

The "hog with the biggest balls" at USP Atlanta was Barry Mills. The Hulk liked him the moment they met. The guy was a warrior. He gave the Hulk two of his books and said, "Read these. They're seminal works. Then we'll talk."

The two books were *How to Make Friends and Influence People* and *The Prince*. One by Dale Carnegie, the other by some guy called Machiavelli. The Hulk took from the first book the idea that to really influence people you had to mess with their heads. *The Prince* told him how to do that: Terror.

Barry Mills nodded and smiled when the Hulk told him what he had learned. "It's not about white power and white supremacy," said Mills. "That's too limiting. It's about supremacy, pure and simple."

The Hulk nodded. "I getcha. The dead guy," he said, tapping the cover of *The Prince*, "says we have to be willing to do whatever is necessary to get power and maintain it."

Barry Mills looked the Hulk in the eyes and smiled. "Then let's do it."

The Hulk clenched his fists. A jolt of power surged through him, like a blue shiver. "Yeah."

TOGETHER, THE BARON and the Hulk began a reign of terror. They opened the door of the abyss and unleashed Hell.

TWO

Con Air

THE 'CON AIR' BOEING 727 took off from the landing strip near Crescent City, California, and headed east. Two hours later, the plane touched down at Florence, Colorado, which was the home of United States penitentiary Administrative Maximum Facility. Also known as ADX Florence, Florence ADMAX, Supermax, and the Alcatraz of the Rockies, it was an incredible super-prison run by the federal government. It was where the Feds stashed some of the most deadly criminals in the world. ADX Florence was designed to "inflict misery and pain."

By comparison, one of Stalin's Gulags was like a picnic in the park. The Gulags worked you to death, starved you to death and froze you to death. But at least there were other people around to talk to. The goal at ADX Florence was to bore you to death, isolate you and drive you insane. In ADX there was "no human contact."

As he entered ADX Florence, US Marshal Clarence Sugar felt a tingle up his spine. An exquisite and eerie quiet invaded his ears. For a moment he felt like he was totally alone, the last living man in a world made entirely of poured concrete. A wave of paranoid claustrophobia curled around him, sucking at him. The feeling passed when he turned to his deputies walking behind in formation. They looked a little green around the edges.

Up ahead a federal correction officer appeared as if out of nowhere. The CO was tall and burly with short-cropped hair and carried a clipboard.

"Marshal Sugar?" asked the CO, extending his hand.

Sugar shook the hand. "Yes. We're here to—"

"Pick up and transport four AB members," interrupted the CO. "I know. We're glad to get rid of them, especially under the circumstances."

"Whattaya mean?" asked Marshal Sugar.

"The indictment for murder," smiled the CO. "They're all guilty as Hell. Most of them should have been executed a long time ago."

Marshal Sugar nodded. The man was right. If it wasn't for smart attorneys and appeals and delaying motions and a court system that moved at a geologic pace, most of the inmates here would be dead and buried. But Marshal Sugar didn't like the CO's tone of voice, which implied prejudice and judgment. Which was not professional. The guy's job was to follow the rules, obey the laws of the land, respect the rights of the inmates as defined by the courts, and keep peace in prison. Just like Marshal Sugar's job was to transport criminals and make sure it was done in a safe manner.

"None of them are aware that they're being moved," said the CO. "They've all eaten so you don't need to worry about feeding them for a while."

"Okay," replied Marshal Sugar. He turned to face his deputies. "We'll use five man teams. One team per prisoner. Everybody be alert."

"These guys are maximum hazard," added the CO. "Every one of them has killed and they like it. So watch your asses."

Marshal Sugar rolled his eyes to the ceiling, but said nothing. It would have been unprofessional.

Four teams of five marshals moved off down the gray hall.

JOHN 'YOUNGSTER' STINSON, Richard 'Bart Simpson' Terflinger, Bob 'Blinky' Griffin and Ronald 'McKool' Slocum weren't used to guests much less US marshals strapped for action.

The four Aryan Brotherhood members stayed in their cells twenty-three hours a day. Their only human contact occurred when the CO delivered food trays through a slot in their doors. The CO was under orders to speak only when necessary, which was rarely. Once a day—never at the same time—each of the electronic cell doors would open, allowing the occupant one hour of exercise in a recreation cage.

But today something was up. John Stinson figured it was a cell-shakedown and strip search, until he noticed the black fatigues with US marshal patches on the shoulders and the unfamiliar faces. He smiled to himself. Things were looking up. His routine was so bland you couldn't even call it a routine, so any change in it was welcome.

Once Stinson realized he was being transferred, he didn't mind the goon squad. He didn't complain, didn't struggle, didn't spit, didn't call anybody "nigger cocksucking faggot punk." He was cooperation itself, because the view was about to change.

They escorted him to a van with four marshals and one driver. He had seen McKool, surrounded by black-clad marshals, standing beside another van. Stinson gazed out the windows, smiling hugely. He felt like he was off for a barbecue at the beach.

Instead they drove him to an airport and escorted him onto a waiting jet. As he shuffled his shackled legs along the plane's center aisle, he saw two men: Barry Mills and Hulk Bingham. He never thought he'd see them again as long as he lived.

"Baron," he shouted, expecting the marshals to punch him for calling out.

The Baron turned in his seat and smiled. "Yo, Youngster. How's it hanging?"

"Things are looking up," answered Stinson, laughing. He looked back, surprised that one of the marshals hadn't hit him.

One of the marshals put a finger to his lips. "Shhh," he said. "This is a no talking flight."

Stinson nodded, "That's cool, man. That's cool."

They put him in a seat and triple cuffed his hands. Stinson heard shackles clanking and more shuffling behind him. Looking over the back of his seat, he saw Terflinger, Griffin and McKool being escorted on the plane.

Most members of the Aryan Brotherhood had nicknames, usually assigned by other members because of some personality quirk or a resemblance to a movie or cartoon character. Nicknames provided a sense of belonging to the group, since only the 'in' people knew the nicknames. Members used the nicknames almost as a term of endearment. It was a way for men, who claimed they had no need for love or affection, to camouflage their feelings.

Of the four men, Stinson and McKool were the most dangerous. But all four believed that murder was a viable and effective problem-solving device. All four had killed since entering prison years ago. Originally, Stinson and McKool were bank robbers; Terflinger and Griffin smuggled drugs and ran guns, along with occasional extortion just for fun. At one point, from his cell in the LA County Jail, Stinson controlled a huge drug consortium on the outside.

One of the marshals, a big guy, who looked like he could take care of himself, stood up front and said, "Okay. As I'm sure you've figured out by now, you guys are being transferred. I can't tell you where you're going because I have orders not to. So please don't ask." He looked around the plane. "If you're good boys, you'll be treated with respect. You respect us, we respect you. That's the way it works here on Con Air." He smiled a little.

"But if you fuck up, then there are consequences. We will gag you and immobilize your hands." Marshal Sugar glanced around. "We have more passengers who will be joining us. So sit back and enjoy the flight."

CON AIR TOOK OFF and turned south. A few hours later it landed just outside Beaumont, Texas, and was met by twelve deputy marshals from Houston, 100 miles to the east. The extra marshals would baby-sit the criminals already onboard, while Marshal Sugar and his deputies drove to the maximum-security penitentiary and picked up more bad guys.

Of the forty Aryan Brotherhood members named in the federal indictment, a baker's dozen of them were warehoused at USP Beaumont, which, besides being home away from home for ten different prison gangs, had the added attraction of its location right in the middle of one the flattest, hottest and most humid places on earth.

Rafael Gonzalez-Munoz was one of the thirteen gang members that Marshal Sugar would collect from USP Beaumont. A vicious killer, Munoz originally ruled over a vast drug kingdom in Mexico. He was one of the leaders of La Eme, the Mexican Mafia. Always seeking to expand his empire, Munoz had moved his operation into Southern California, Arizona and Texas.

One of Munoz's talents was prophecy—he could see trends. Like the CEO of a Fortune 500 company, he knew when it was time to restructure his business. While others reacted, he acted. He made the switch from marijuana to cocaine at just the right time. Then he got out of cocaine and focused on methamphetamine before anyone else even thought about it. Because he gave his customers what they wanted, before they even knew they wanted it, the money rolled in.

His hero was Al Pacino in the movie *Scarface*. Munoz wanted to be like him. When rival gangs tried to move in on his territory, Munoz didn't hesitate, but responded with raw violence. He had thousands of Mexican Mafia soldiers who obeyed his orders. No one and nothing stood in his way.

The DEA tripped him up, surrounding one of his warehouses in Corpus Christi. Munoz and his homies decided to shoot it out with the Feds. Amped on crystal meth, holding an AK-47 assault rifle, Munoz rained lead. Unfortunately for Munoz, the Feds were a better shot and he was hit in the shoulder and thigh.

Rafael Gonzalez-Munoz was found guilty by jury of seven RICO violations, including second-degree murder and attempted murder. The judge gave him thirty years to life and threw him into USP Beaumont to think about the error of his ways.

Repentance was "for pussies" and Munoz didn't think about it. Instead, he negotiated an alliance with the Aryan Brotherhood. Seeing a trend, he figured it was easier to join them than fight them. According to Munoz, "these white dudes knew how to take care of business. They had connections, muscle, labs... everything, man."

Munoz was unsure the Brotherhood would ally with him. He was Mexican Mafia, which meant he was Mexican. Definitely not white like the Aryan Brotherhood, who were supposed to be white supremacists. But something funny happened. It turned out the Aryan Brotherhood used to be about white power and all that shit. They weren't anymore. Now they were about supremacy, pure and simple. They would do whatever it took to keep them on top. Even hitch their honkey horse to a Mexican gang.

The Mexican Mafia and the Aryan Brotherhood hooked up, doing favors for each other. A favor was a hit—contract murder. Munoz had some enemies and some defectors in California prisons he wanted to bleed. The Brotherhood was pleased to oblige. In return, Munoz provided drugs and tax money to the Brotherhood. And if the Brotherhood needed a favor, Munoz's homies took care of it.

The Aryan Brotherhood took to calling Munoz 'Cisco,' because they thought of him as a sidekick, like Cisco was to Pancho in the old Mexican western on television.

US MARSHAL Clarence J. Sugar stood at ease, watching as his deputy marshals loaded the thirteen bad guys from USP Beaumont on the bus. Specially fitted with individual reinforced cages for the confinement of its passengers, it was jail on wheels. The property of the US marshals service, and delivered to the airport by the Houston deputy marshals (who were baby-sitting the plane and its high-profile passengers), the bus was heavily armored with black bullet-proof glass windows. The vehicle could sustain anything short of a light anti-armor rocket. Each prisoner was escorted onto it by four deputy marshals. Once the prisoner was seated and locked in his cage, the next prisoner was led out.

Marshal Sugar glanced at the bus and smiled. He said to one of his deputies, "It's the only way to go RVing."

"Yes, sir," replied the deputy. "Why stay home when you can vacation in style."

Marshal Sugar laughed and nodded. Across the way, he saw the last prisoner being escorted. "That's number thirteen, right?" he asked the deputy.

"Yes, sir." The deputy glanced at his clipboard. "Rafael Gonzalez-Munoz."

The man doing the shackle shuffle toward the bus was small and lean. He didn't look much like an international drug lord, thought Marshal Sugar. He looked more like a nerdy college student, who couldn't get a date and had low self-esteem.

Marshal Sugar shrugged. "Okay. Once he's secured, double-check the count and let's get out of here. We still have one stop left. Then a long flight back to LA."

"Yes, sir."

CON AIR flew north. It carried nineteen brutal passengers, who sat with triple handcuffs and shackled legs, and twenty marshals, who appeared relaxed, but who noticed everything.

Marshal Sugar stood in front of the convicts. "Meals will be served soon. Your hands will be single cuffed so you can eat, but only for a few minutes. And only three at a time. Because of your improvisational skills and your zeal, the meal is sandwiches and chips. No utensils. And only paper cups."

All the paper cups and napkins would be accounted for. If anyone's cup went missing, that man would be strip-searched, gagged and immobilized. Marshal Sugar didn't believe threats worked with these men. So he didn't waste his breath threatening them. How do you threaten a man who's been in solitary confinement for years?

"Quiet conversation with your neighbors will be allowed from this point on," added Marshal Sugar. "We'll be picking up one more guest, then we'll be on our way."

"Where we going?" asked Hulk Bingham.

Marshal Sugar shook his head, indicating he couldn't say.

"Who's the last guest?"

Marshal Sugar looked at the Hulk. Before he could say he couldn't say, Barry Mills—the Baron—cut in. "Wrong question, Hulk. What you should ask yourself is this: Who's missing?"

Mills continued: "The only one missing who's not already in Southern California is Tom. Which means we're on our way to Kansas. Then to Los Angeles or San Diego, probably LA."

Marshal Sugar gave Mills his best deadpan look.

A smile touched Mills' lips, but not his eyes. His eyes remained flat and hard, like black holes that had collapsed in on themselves. "Yeah, it's gotta be Tommy," he drawled, then closed his eyes and leaned his shaved head back.

THOMAS SILVERSTEIN was America's most dangerous prisoner. His nickname was Terrible Tom.

When asked for his professional opinion about Terrible Tom, one prison psychiatrist laughed and shook his head. "There is no applicable term for him. He's way beyond any textbook definition." The doctor thought for a moment, then said, "I'd call him a psychosocial killer. Murder is the way he makes love to other human beings. It's like sex for him."

Silverstein wasn't Tom's real name. His real name was Thomas Conway, Jr. He grew up in Long Beach, California. His parents divorced when he was four years old, and his mother married a guy named Sid Silverstein. Sid legally adopted the boy. But Tom hated the name Silverstein because it was so Jewish. And he hated coming home from school every day, because his mom and his 'dad' fought like two cats in a bag. His parents considered screaming and slapping, punching and kicking, throwing dishes and demolishing doors normal behavior.

Socially, Tom was a catastrophe that kept on happening. Timid Tom would have been an appropriate nickname for the young Tommy. He was shy and withdrawn. He didn't fit in at school and he had no friends, only enemies who were bullies and saw easy pickings in Tom. To cap it all, everyone thought he was Jewish, which made him more of a pariah than he already was. Everyday he came home from school either frightened or beat up, some days both.

His Mom called him "Tragic Tom," because, she said, "your life reminds me of one of those Greek tragedies, where everybody walks around wretched, saying woe is me."

One day he arrived home, crying.

"What's the matter?" asked his mother, setting down her cigarette to take a sip of her gin and tonic. She had intended to do some cleaning that day, but fixed herself a drink instead. One drink led to another and pretty soon she didn't feel like cleaning. She switched on the television and lit a Chesterfield.

With blood oozing from the corner of his lip and a bruise on his cheek, Tom just looked at the floor and sniffled.

"You pathetic little crybaby!" yelled his mother. "Tell me what happened or I'll give you something to really cry about."

"I—I got hit," said Tommy, starting to whimper.

"Did you fight back?"

"No," whispered Tommy.

"What did you do, you little wimp?"

He had run, but Tommy couldn't answer because his mother would hate him.

"You ran! Didn't you, you little piece of shit?" screamed his mother.

Tommy began bawling. He tried not to, but he couldn't stop it.

His mother leaned forward, taking a huge puff of her cigarette. "Look at me, crybaby," she commanded, smoke curling out from her nose and mouth. "Look at me!"

Tommy looked up. His mother's face was sharp. "The next time you come home crying because some boy beat you up..." She paused for another drag on her cigarette. "I will whip you myself. Two beatings instead of one," she snarled.

Tommy wiped his nose on his sleeve. "I'm sorry, mother. I'm so sorry."

"Get out of my sight, you sissy," she hissed. "You make me sick."

Tommy ran to his room, where he collapsed on his bed, curling up like a fetus. He sucked his thumb and cried himself to sleep. No one came to check on him. No one called him for dinner.

Tommy was eleven years old.

Years later, Terrible Tom Silverstein recalled, "That's how my mom was. She stood her mud. If someone came at you with a bat, you got your bat and you both went at it."

Tom's sister, Sydney, said, "We were taught never to throw the first punch, but never to walk away from a fight. My brother started getting into trouble because he was running away from a violent environment at home. Then he got into drugs, and he became a brother I never knew."

Three years later, age fourteen, Tom Silverstein was sent to a California reform school. In 1966, reform school was a nice-nellyism for gladiator school, because the only subject it taught was violence. And the learning process was unsentimental and hands-on. Tom came away with a nuts-and-bolts approach to brutality. Like a wolf in the coldest of winters, kill or be killed became Tom's slogan, his religious song.

But a wisp of humanity remained. Starved for affection and approval, Tom wanted to feel plugged-in. He wanted to connect with other human beings. So he started hanging out with his real father, Tom Conway Sr., who used people until they were of no more use. Then he brushed them off, and moved on. Tom Sr. robbed banks. At least that's what he told people. In truth, Tom Sr. was a petty thief, and not a very good one. He was a wannabe.

When the two Conways hooked up, they spurred each other on. Tom Sr. told bigger lies about himself and his accomplishments. He even gave advice to his son on how to be a bank robber. Tom Jr. listened carefully and then applied what he learned from his old man. Dropping out of school, Tom made a choice. He became a professional criminal. He started out small, hitting convenience stores, and corner gas stations. Sometimes he got away with only a few bucks, other times he made hundreds of dollars. Whatever the amount, he split it down the middle with his old man. Although Tom Jr. was doing all the work, taking all the risks, they were a team and Tom felt a loyalty to his blood-father. Things were looking up.

It went to Hell in 1971, when Tom Jr. was nineteen years old. Walking into a 7-Eleven store late on a Friday night—when there would be lots of cash in the till—Tom stuck his gun in the cashier's face. "Take all the money from your drawer and put it in a paper bag," he ordered.

"Sure, man," said the cashier. "Just don't shoot me, man. Okay?" The cashier groped at the money, jamming it in a bag. Then he handed it to the robber.

Tom pointed his gun at the guy's nose. "Say anything to the cops and I'll make it my business to come back and kill you," he stated and then left.

The cashier didn't say anything. He didn't have to. Surveillance cameras caught the incident on tape and Tom was quickly identified by the cops. A warrant was issued and the hunt was on.

Tom Conway Jr. was arrested the next afternoon as he left a hamburger joint. Tom had a thing for chocolate, and a cheeseburger and chocolate malt helped soothe the beast within him. The cops cuffed him and carted him off to jail.

Tom's public defender advised him to cop a plea. "If you take this to trial, you'll need to find a new lawyer," the public defender told him, "because I won't be part of any legal suicide." Because of the surveillance tape from the 7-Eleven, he reminded Tom, "they got you dead to rights."

"Fuck you," replied Tom. But he knew the lawyer was right and so copped a plea bargain. He pled guilty and in return was promised a reduced sentence, which meant three to ten years, instead of ten to fifteen. They shipped him off to San Quentin prison.

Being a new fish at San Quentin was like dying and going to Hell, only this particular Hell wasn't divided into levels based on sin. The Hell that was the 'Q' divided itself on skin color. Blacks over there, whites over here, and Hispanics over yonder. It was not surprising, and Tom had experienced racial bigotry while in grade school, where everyone thought he was a Jew—which meant he was a "kike," which meant he was less.

One good thing about the 'Q' though, nobody cared if he was Jewish or not. They just cared if he was white or black or brown. And Tom figured out real fast that if he wanted to survive, he needed to hook up with a gang. If he didn't marry into a white gang, he'd be nothing but a "bitch." And bitches didn't last long.

On the yard one day, Tom met a big white guy with a shaved head and muscles on his muscles. Tom was on the bench press, struggling to get one final rep, when two hands the size of hams helped him get the bar up and racked. Tom sat up, wiping his forehead with the tail of his T-shirt. "Thanks, man," he said. "I was about to drop that fucker on my chest. Would not have been pretty." Tom stood up.

The big guy laughed. "Leave a big dent in your chest," he boomed. "Mind if I work in?" he asked. Without waiting for an answer, he grabbed two forty-five-pound plates from a nearby stack. Sleeving them on the bar, he reached for two more and put them on. Then he slid onto the bench and gripped the bar.

"That's more 'n 400 pounds, man," said Tom.

"Yup." The guy racked the bar off and did ten reps, easy.

"Jesus, Mary and Joseph," exclaimed Tom. "You're strong as an ox."

"Moose," said the guy.

"Well, I guess, if you say so," agreed Tom. "Moose are pretty strong, too."

The guy gave Tom a funny look. "Moose is my name. Moose Forbes."

"Oh, right."

Moose got up and added two more plates to the bar. "New fish, huh?" he asked Tom.

Tom nodded. "Got three to ten for armed robbery."

Moose wasn't impressed. "You hooked up?"

"No," said Tom. "I want to, but I don't know what the protocol is."

Moose squinted at him. "The what?"

"You know, the protocol. The correct way of going about it," explained Tom.

Moose laughed, shaking his head. "You talk like a college boy. Where you from?"

"Long Beach. An' I ain't no college boy."

"That a fact?" said Moose, baring his teeth. "This ain't Long Beach, it's the 'Q.' And there ain't no protycol, cuz there ain't no applications to fill out. It ain't a fucking country club, college boy."

Tom took a step back. He gazed at Moose and waited.

Moose couldn't believe it. Didn't this little fuck know who he was? If he wanted a dogfight, he'd come to the right dog. Moose loved the shit. Moose took a step forward.

As if by magic, a shiv gleamed in Tom's hand. Tom stood waiting.

Moose charged, his arms reaching out.

Tom slipped to the side. As Moose passed by, the shiv licked out and kissed his ribs.

Moose pulled up and turned to look at Tom, and then lifted his shirt to look at his ribs. Blood welled from a six-inch gash in his side. Pulling his shirt down, Moose glanced around. The other inmates were going about their business, talking, pumping iron, laughing, smoking. It happened so fast, no one had noticed.

Moose stared at Tom for a moment, then turned and walked away.

Tom shrugged and went back to lifting weights.

The next day a guy who called himself Spots waved Tom over. Because of his many tattoos, Spots looked like a leopard. Spots told him that the Aryan Brotherhood had accepted him as a prospect.

"The who?" asked Tom. He'd only been there a week. He didn't know the names of all the gangs.

Spots did a double-take. "Shit, man," he said. "You know, the Brand."

Tom shrugged. "Never heard of 'em."

Spots rolled his eyes. "Fuck me, man. The Brand runs this place. Drugs, guns, pruno, all of it."

"If you say so. What do they want with me?"

"They reaching out, man," explained Spots. "You know, you can hook up. Be part of the Brotherhood. No one fuck with you. An' if they do, the Brotherhood got your back."

Tom thought about that. "Sure. What do I have to do?"

Spots smiled. "Nothin'. Everythin'. Whatever they tell you. After you earn your bones, then you in." Spots clenched his fist in front of his chest.

"Okay," said Tom.

Spots nodded in approval. "You be sponsored by Moose. He be telling you what's what."

"Okay."

Spots walked off.

Tom learned that Moose, rather than being pissed off, was impressed with Tom's fury and willingness to jump in the shit. Blood in, blood out. Tom had already spilled Moose's blood, so Moose had sponsored him, telling the Aryan Brotherhood that "the little fucker's faster 'n greased lightning."

Within a year Tom had taken the pledge and was branded. Being branded was okay with Tom, because he knew it was a rite of passage. It was expected. He'd read about it. Ancient warriors, like the Babylonians and Sumerians, would mark themselves with the blood of their enemies. Tom enjoyed the camaraderie he found in the Aryan Brotherhood, and he appreciated the protection it provided, but he never got the rush from it the others did. Most of them were adrenaline junkies, who loved the idea of terror and power. Their drug of choice was violence. Being in the "toughest prison gang" gave them an emotional high, a kind of exalted state, where they believed they were invincible mystical warriors of some pagan religion.

In Tom's opinion, the mystical warrior stuff was bullshit. Tom simply wanted respect. He didn't hate violence. He didn't love violence. He found it inevitable. To get respect, sometimes he had to become violent. That's just the way it was.

TOM SPENT four years at the 'Q.' Then the powers-that-be paroled him, and he once more hooked up with Tom Sr., who had hooked up with Tom's uncle, Arthur. Nervous and skinny, with lank hair and bad personal hygiene, Arthur was into nose-candy—cocaine—and needed lots of cash to pay for his habit. Arthur thought of himself as a badass and loved playing the part. He had a regular arsenal of guns in his trashy apartment on the third floor of a rent-subsidized complex, along with a freaky girlfriend who mainlined heroin and a Siamese cat that Arthur always forgot to feed.

Tom didn't think much of the whole arrangement. In his opinion, uncle Arthur was a goof. But he went along with it because it was family. Dad said they had to stick together, so they did. They hit three convenience stores over the course of three weeks. Tom insisted on masks because of the surveillance cameras that had tripped him up once before.

Only Arthur didn't want to wear a mask. Arthur used his nose to suck up copious amounts of coke rather than for breathing, and consequently he spent a lot of his time writhing in twitchy paranoia. Wearing a mask gave him extreme claustrophobia, which gave him the heebie-jeebies and left him gasping for air.

So the two Toms wore masks, while Arthur went without. It didn't work out well at all. The cops identified Arthur and then followed him around for a few days, making up a list of his known associates. These included Tom Jr., Tom Sr. and a young female who "looked like death warmed over," according to one of the cops.

After the third robbery, the cops moved in and arrested everybody, recovering most of the stolen cash. The trial was a fiasco. Twitchy Arthur couldn't keep his mouth shut. He was going through withdrawal and was more paranoid than ever. Pale and sweating, he rolled over on his nephew and brother without really meaning to.

"Tommy was the leader. We just did as he told us," chirped Arthur. "Me and his dad was just taking orders. Tommy's a smart boy. He was the brains."

Arthur got five years in prison. Tom Sr. got five to seven years in prison. And Tom Jr. got fifteen years. He was twenty-three years old. The Feds shipped Tommy off to Leavenworth, which was a maximum security prison in Kansas. Because of its heat and humidity, Leavenworth was called the Hothouse. Murder occurred regularly; drugs were everywhere. To control the lucrative drug trade, gangs fought in an ongoing, vicious war. The place was awash with blood.

The Aryan Brotherhood ran horse, and controlled the supply in and out of Leavenworth. Horse was prisoner slang for heroin, which was number one on the narcotic hit parade of the late seventies. Since Tom was already branded, he immediately hooked up with the Brotherhood members in Leavenworth. It was business as usual: get the drugs in, via mules or corrupt guards, distribute it, collect money owed and, above all, keep an eye on the competition. Other gangs tried to move in all the time. When they did, the Brotherhood took care of business.

The horse business depended upon mules. Mules were convicts who transported drugs in condoms, balloons, small tubes, or sometimes even in plastic wrap, which they inserted into their rectum or swallowed and later retrieved from the toilet bowl. Horse was smuggled in by girlfriends, wives and visitors, who transferred the drugs to the inmate, who either swallowed it, if it was in a balloon, or excused himself to the bathroom, where he quickly keistered it. After the visit, the mules would deliver the drugs to the Aryan Brotherhood. For their effort, the mules received a cut, which was a fee for their services. Usually the fee was a portion of the horse.

Danny Atwell was not branded. Nor was he a prospect. He didn't want anything to do with that shit. He just wanted to do his time and get out. But he got regular visits from his wife and family members. And the Aryan Brotherhood wanted Danny to go mule. Even though he was scared to death, Danny refused. He didn't want his family members dragged in the sewer.

Danny died.

His name had gone into the hat. Thomas Silverstein and two other Aryan Brotherhood members were assigned to take care of business. They caught Danny coming out of the shower and stabbed him to death. It took about five minutes.

Tom and the other two Brothers were charged with murder. They all pled not guilty, because what happened in prison stayed in prison. No one saw anything, so no one would say anything. But somebody forgot to tell the snitches, who came out of the woodwork to tell their lurid tales of drugs, mules and contract murder. Singing like rock stars, the snitches played their usual game. They said what they knew the prosecutor and the jury wanted to hear. In the end, Tom was convicted and sentenced to life in prison.

The names of all the snitches went into the hat. The Aryan Brotherhood had long memories and would not forget.

To this day, Tom Silverstein says he didn't kill Danny Atwell. He admits to two other murders, but not that one.

The Feds moved Tommy to the United States penitentiary in Marion, Illinois, which, at the time, was the latest supermax prison and had the dubious distinction of being the most violent in America. It was the ultimate in waste management, the place where they dumped the gang leaders and the nutcases who killed because they liked it.

In short, Marion was the supermax supermarket of psychopaths.

They put Tommy in a control unit, which was a newfangled term for the Hole. He got out one hour a day and ate in his cell. Isolation made Tommy creative. He had to do something or go bonkers from boredom, and so started reading and drawing. As Silverstein put it, "I could hardly read, write or draw when I first fell. But most of us lifers are down for so long and have so much time to kill that we actually fool around and discover our niche in life, often in ways we never even dreamt possible on the streets. We not only find our niche, we excel."

Redemption wasn't part of Tommy's niche. There was a DC Blacks member in the control unit, called Robert Chapelle. The only thing

Chapelle hated more than whites was whites who were Jewish. To him, Silverstein was "a kike. One of them what four-pointed Jesus on the cross."

Tommy felt Chapelle didn't respect him, and that, in Tommy's world, was more than flesh and blood can bear. One day, during his one hour of exercise, Tommy passed by the cell of another Aryan Brotherhood member, Clayton Fountain. Fountain reached into his crotch and pulled out a thin length of wire, which he slipped into Tommy's hands. Continuing his exercise walk around the tier, Tommy passed the cell in which Chapelle lay asleep, his head close to the bars. Tommy poised the wire above Chapelle's throat—it looked chrome against Chapelle's black skin—and, eyes narrowed with malice and delight, looped the wire around Chapelle's neck and strangled him. Tommy found ease in that moment. Chapelle's struggles diminished into shadow until there was nothing at all in the world, but death.

Tommy left the wire wrapped around Chapelle's dead throat, and went on walking. The next time he passed Fountain's cell, he smiled and gave Fountain a thumbs up.

"Vengeance is mine, saith the Lord," said Fountain, grinning. "I will repay."

Tommy nodded and kept walking.

As with most criminals, Silverstein and Fountain overcompensated for their lack of self-esteem. In other words, they couldn't keep their mouth shut. They had to brag about their crimes because that was the only thing they had to brag about. Soon the two Aryan Brotherhood members boasted to any inmate who would listen about how they had snuffed Robert Chapelle. Murder gave them status and elevated their reputation.

Prison officials charged Silverstein and Fountain with Chapelle's murder. In the trial of the two men, the inmates to whom Silverstein and Fountain had boasted played the snitch game, telling the jury of the grotesque deed. The jurors cringed in horror and found both men guilty of first-degree murder. The judge sentenced each to life in prison, which meant Silverstein now had to serve two consecutive life terms. His life was over.

Tom Silverstein could not be executed because at that time, in 1981, a federal death penalty for one inmate murdering another inmate did not exist. Silverstein maintained his innocence and declared federal officials had framed him for the murder of Robert Chapelle, because they hated him. In the next breath, he blamed the DC Blacks.

When the Bureau of Prisons moved DC Blacks leader Raymond 'Cadillac' Smith to USP Marion, they put him in a cell near Tommy.

Cadillac Smith was a drug pusher and cop killer from Washington DC. He hated "honkey red-neck motherfuckers." Robert Chapelle had been his friend and, being a religious man, Smith believed in tit for tat. His motto was "dirty deed for dirty deed." Tommy Silverstein had done a dirty deed and, therefore, Tommy had to die.

From his cell, Cadillac Smith could see Tommy's cell. "Goin' kill your white ass, Jew-boy," announced Cadillac.

Tommy pressed his face close to the bars of his cell, looking down the way toward Cadillac. "Look, Cadillac," said Tommy. "I didn't kill Chapelle. I mean it, man. I did not do it."

Cadillac gave an untamed laugh. He stuck his arm out between the bars of his cell, holding his fingers in a V-shape. "White boy speak'n' with forked tongue," he said. "I'ze gonna kill you, Jew-boy. Real soon."

Cadillac attempted to make good on his promise. First he tried to stab Tommy, but Tommy was too quick—"faster 'n greased lightning"— and got away. Then Cadillac got his hands on a zip-gun smuggled in by another DC Black. Zip-guns were beautiful in their simplicity: a telescoping car aerial with a .22 caliber bullet clamped into its fat end. Collapsing the aerial acted as a firing pin and discharged the bullet. Neat and effective. The only problem was accuracy.

One day Tommy was on his exercise walk and passed Cadillac's cell. Cadillac took aim and slammed the aerial shut. Bang! The bullet missed Tommy by a foot or more, ricocheting off the opposite wall. Tommy stopped and stared at Cadillac.

"Motherfuck!" shouted Cadillac. He tried to reload but couldn't. The fat end of the zip-gun had mushroomed and wouldn't hold the bullet in place. A pair of pliers would remedy that, but of course he didn't have any pliers.

"Strike two, you stupid shithead," snarled Tommy. He took a step closer. "Game over cuz there won't be a third time." Tommy walked away.

Three days later, Tommy and Clayton Fountain were in an exercise cage, where they did push-ups and ran in place. While the two white Brothers did calisthenics, Cadillac Smith was escorted to the showers by a guard. "You got one hour to get beautiful," the guard told Cadillac, then the guard left to get some coffee.

In the cage, Fountain pulled his pants down, bent over and pulled a hacksaw blade and a shiv from his rectum. Tommy carried a shiv in his rectum, too. He eased it out with care, because he didn't want to slice his sphincter. Using the hacksaw blade, the two inmates cut their way out of the exercise cage and scurried toward the showers.

Cadillac Smith had just finished lathering himself up, when Fountain and Tommy jumped him. "Bye-bye, Cadillac," hissed Tommy as he plunged his shiv into the man's flesh.

"Yeah," chimed Fountain, goring his shiv into Cadillac's stomach. "Say hello to Chapelle for us." With diabolical energy he thrust again and again.

Cadillac Smith was stabbed sixty-seven times. The medical examiner said, "The man was probably dead after the first dozen wounds, many of which were fatal."

The other white inmates at USP Marion started calling Silverstein Terrible Tom. They whispered his name in awe. In the subculture of prison, Terrible Tom became a demigod whose notorious reputation preceded him.

Already serving two life sentences in the Hole and with no death penalty for the murder of a fellow inmate, it seemed Terrible Tom would get away with murder yet again. Prison officials couldn't execute Tom, but they could sure make him wish he were dead. They withheld his mail and shook down his cell every time he turned around. Three guards escorted him everywhere.

Officer Merle Clutts was one of the guards who didn't like Terrible Tom. Clutts thought Tom was "the spawn of Satan," but he remained professional and did not torment the man—simply followed the rules and enforced them by the book.

During a shakedown of Tom's cell, Clutts discovered contraband material and so confiscated Tom's art supplies. "You'll get them back when you earn them," Clutts said. "By following the rules like everybody else."

Flaming with righteous energy, Terrible Tom wanted to rip off Clutt's ears and piss in the wounds. He made a promise to himself that he would. And soon.

Terrible Tom plotted his revenge. He communicated with Aryan Brotherhood members in USP Marion, arranging for weapons and help. On October 22, 1983, having just finished his shower, Terrible Tom was shackled, handcuffed and escorted back to his cell. One of his three escorts was Merle Clutts.

As the group passed an exercise cage, the inmate inside it said, "CO Clutts, need a hand here." Clutts strolled over to see what the inmate needed, while the other two officers walked on with Terrible Tom.

"Permission to speak with a friend, sir?" asked Tom, pausing in front of a cell. The cell belonged to Randy Gometz, who was an Aryan Brotherhood member.

"Sure. Go ahead," replied one of the two guards. Guards often allowed prisoners to chat on their way to and from the showers.

Terrible Tom grasped the bars of the cell and began talking. Gometz pulled a stolen key from inside his mouth and unlocked Tom's handcuffs. Tom reached through the bars and pulled a shank from Gometz's waistband, and then ran as fast as his shackled legs would allow toward Clutts.

Dumbfounded, the two guards momentarily hesitated before pursuing the convict.

"This is between me and Clutts!" Tom shouted, before slamming into Clutts and stabbing him with extreme ferocity. The shank plunged in, blood flowed out.

As he perforated Clutts, Tommy "felt wickedly angelic, like the Angel of Death descending on Egypt."

By the time the two guards were able to pull Clutts away, he was senseless in puddles of his own blood and drool. Clutts died within minutes.

Three hours later, Clayton Fountain pulled the same stunt. Another inmate with a stolen key and a shank, unlocked Fountain's handcuffs. Fountain turned and attacked all three of his escorts like a rabid dog, fatally wounding Officer Robert Hoffman.

When asked why he did it, Fountain shrugged. "I didn't want Tommy to have a higher body count than me," he replied with a smile. Hoffman's blood was still caked on his hands.

In 1984, Terrible Tom was moved to another prison because he was growing too famous at Marion. Fellow inmates regarded him as something special, like a saint. His exploits were incredible, the stuff of legend. Inmates worshipped him. He was shipped to USP Atlanta, where he was placed in a maximum security isolation cell.

The shit jumped off in 1987. Hundreds of pissed off Cubans, detained at USP Atlanta while the Feds decided what to do with them, started to riot. These were brash, dangerous criminals, with nothing to lose—the Feds, more than likely, would end up sending them all back to Cuba, where they would be lined against a wall and shot as traitors. The Cubans took over the penitentiary, capturing and holding hostage 100 members of the prison staff.

The Cubans unlocked every cell door at the prison, including Tommy's. All the animals in the zoo were free of their cells, but still trapped in the prison, which was surrounded by the FBI and elite soldiers from Delta Force. Tommy didn't care. He was just happy to be out of the Hole. Terrible Tom roamed the prison walls, wearing a shower thong and carrying a bottle of Tequila, taking it all in like a tourist on a cruise ship.

The Tequila came courtesy of one of the Cubans, a big, black guy with a shaved head and a Fu Manchu mustache who everybody called Blind Boy because of a cast in one eye. His real name was Roberto Messia.

When the rioters had opened Tom's cell door, they grabbed him and led him out into the yard. He squinted at the brightness. When his eyes adjusted, it looked to him as if World War Three had taken place: part of the prison had burnt to the ground, leaving a blackened, smoldering skeleton.

The rioters led him over to Blind Boy Messia, who carried a shotgun taken from one of the guards in one hand and a bottle in the other.

"So. Terrible Tom," said Blind Boy. "What should we do with you?" He waggled the shotgun casually.

Terrible Tom did a double take. Blind Boy did not sound Cuban. He had a high British accent. "You don't sound Cuban," said Tom.

Blind Boy laughed. "You don't look so terrible."

Terrible Tom smiled and stood waiting, as Blind Boy gazed at him. He tossed the bottle to Tom, who caught it. Glancing at the label on the bottle, Tom raised his eyebrows. "Now we're living," he enthused.

"We don't have time or patience for any inconveniences," Blind Boy advised. "So stay out of the way." From the look on his face, he expected a reply.

"You won't even know I'm here," said Terrible Tom.

Blind Boy gave a little nod, then said, "Enjoy yourself."

And that was that.

Negotiations between the Cubans and the Feds lasted for seven days.

"As a gesture of good faith, you need to give us Thomas Silverstein," the Feds told the Cubans. Soon afterward, a bunch of Cubans jumped Terrible Tom in the prison yard, pinned him down, handcuffed him and shackled his legs. Then they turned him over to the Feds, who turned him over to US marshals, who pushed him into a transport vehicle and whisked him off to a nearby airport. The marshals loaded him onto a plane that flew him to Leavenworth, Kansas. Terrible Tom was the only convict on the flight.

At USP Leavenworth, the Feds had a special room waiting. Resembling a large zoo-like cage, the room sat in an isolated wing of the prison—range thirteen. 'Range' was in reference to the wing being out in the middle of nowhere, and the number thirteen referred to the floor numbers used in skyscrapers—specifically the fact there was never a thirteenth floor, because it was considered bad luck. It may have been there, but it wasn't acknowledged.

Prison officials jokingly nicknamed the special room "the Hannibal Room," because it resembled the cage in the movie *The Silence of the Lambs*. But the joke contained more than a little truth. Whoever lived in the Hannibal Room endured constant surveillance, had no human contact, and the lights were never shut off. There was no day or night in this Hell—only the steady, sickly emanations of florescent bulbs. There was no one to talk to, no one to hear, no one to touch, no one to hate, no one to love. Mechanical eyes stared from every corner—all the time.

They put Terrible Tom in the Hannibal Room in 1987.

2002

FIFTEEN YEARS LATER, the goon squad showed up at the Hannibal Room.

US Marshal Clarence J. Sugar led the way. Behind him tramped fifteen deputy marshals. Next to him walked five officers of USP Leavenworth, who wore helmets with full-face masks, not unlike motorcycle helmets, and carried Tasers as part of a whole spectrum of weapons, including Mace, pistols, and billy clubs.

"Technically, it's range thirteen," one of the officers told Marshal Sugar. "But most call it the Hannibal Room or the Silverstein Suite."

Marshal Sugar nodded.

"He watches a lot of TV and draws," continued the officer.

"Who?"

"Terrible Tom," said the officer. "Likes reality shows. *Survivor, American Gladiator*—that kinda shit."

Marshal Sugar gave the man a skeptical glance, as the platoon moved relentlessly toward its goal.

"Spends a lot of time drawing," reiterated the officer. "Really talented. I can't believe some of the shit he does. Like he's professional or something, ya know? The way he shades stuff with just a pencil is hard to wrap your head around it's so good."

Marshal Sugar thought the officer sounded like a tour guide. A guide captivated by his subject, which seemed to be the myth, legend and living habits of Terrible Tom.

The officer continued, "There's all sorts of weirdo collectors who would pay top dollar for any of his drawings. But he won't sell 'em." He looked over at the marshal. "Even if he did, the money wouldn't do him any good." He paused. "Too bad though. Cuz they sure are good. Wait'll you see 'em."

The marshal didn't say anything.

"Wait'll you see *him*," added the officer, raising his eyebrows.

"What do you mean?" rumbled Marshal Sugar.

"Long, wild-man hair, white beard down to here." The officer touched the edge of his hand to his chest. "Looks like that movie actor guy—Donald Sutherland—dressed up like some weird Santa Claus. 'Course, Terrible Tom's Jewish, but you know what I mean."

Marshal Sugar frowned.

"The reason his hair is so long," clarified the officer, "is cuz he's not allowed scissors or a razor. Too risky." The officer chuckled to himself. "They're afraid he'll do a Clutts. You know, kill another guard."

Like everyone else associated with the federal prison system, Marshal Sugar was familiar with Thomas Silverstein, aka Terrible Tom. It sounded like the guy was a regular Chinese puzzle. Or plain insane. A talented artist on one hand, a crackerjack killer on the other—who happened to look like Donald Sutherland in a ZZ Top beard.

The author Pete Earley wrote a book called *The Hot House*, which was based on unprecedented access to the inmates and guards at USP Leavenworth. Marshal Sugar had read it. He considered it a good book, but one with an agenda—to diss the penal system. It almost lionized the inmates, especially Terrible Tom, who was the star of the show. Earley portrayed Tom as intelligent, rational and downright normal. And the fact that 'they' kept him locked up—like an animal—in the Hannibal Room made 'them'—the prison officials—look like the monsters. Like 'they' were kids, pulling the wings off flies and bees, then roasting the insects under a magnifying glass.

Upon finishing *The Hothouse*, Marshal Sugar, half-convinced that Earley was right, did a little research. Earley had a website, on which it was possible to listen to some of the prison interviews with Terrible Tom. Marshal Sugar listened to Silverstein babble on and on about his demons, who, at a guess, were the guards and how they delighted in tormenting him. Then he ventured into a stream-of-consciousness description of his hellacious killing of Merle Clutts, which included mimicking the dying man's screams and Tom's grunts as he plunged the shank into the guard's flesh. Silverstein even described how it feels to stab a man, relating the squishy sound flesh makes as it takes the knife.

The guy was a wacko. His insanity stood out like a cow flop in a backyard swimming pool.

THE MARSHALS CAME TO A HALT. On this side of the massive steel door that faced them was USP Leavenworth; on the other side was range thirteen. Once unlocked, the guards walked through to another world. The air was different, heavier, and without any odor, as if it came from a bottle. Overhead lights burned brightly, making everything clearer, like in high-definition.

In the middle of the room was a giant rat cage. Inside the cage, the figure that had been seated in a chair stood up as the marshals entered the room. Shoulder-length gray hair and a white waterfall of a beard made him look like some crackpot Biblical prophet back from forty years in the desert.

A real ding-a-ling, thought Marshal Sugar. Then he noticed the eyes, which burned acetylene torch blue. A very dangerous ding-a-ling.

Terrible Tom smiled. "Good afternoon, gentlemen," he said. "What an unexpected visit. In fact," he laughed, "it's the first one I've had in fifteen years. Come in, come in."

"Okay," said Marshal Sugar, turning to his deputies. "Secure the prisoner. Gather up his personal belongings and bag 'em. We got a plane to catch."

Terrible Tom popped a Hershey's Kiss in his mouth. "Anybody want a kiss? Unfortunately, they come to me without foil wrappers or little flags. I miss that part." He shook his head sadly. "Kind of ruins the experience."

The marshals moved forward in a standard formation. The Leavenworth officer unlocked the door of the cage, and said, "Tom, these are US marshals. They're here to transfer you. No one wants a fuss, so your cooperation would be helpful."

Terrible Tom gave a harsh laugh, one that he had cultivated over the years. "Your wish is my command. Complaints? No complaints from me. I wouldn't miss it for the world. I'm looking forward to it."

Marshal Sugar stepped forward. "I'm glad to hear that. Now, if you would please turn around, lie down on the floor and place your hands on the top of your head."

Terrible Tom did as instructed. Marshals swarmed over him, cuffing him and shackling his legs. Then they stood him up and patted him down. One of the marshals carefully passed a metal detector over his body. Stepping back, the deputy said, "Please do three deep-knee bends."

With four Tasers directed at him, Terrible Tom squatted all the way down and all the way up, three times.

"Okay," said Marshal Sugar. "Let's go."

The Leavenworth officers led the way, followed by three marshals. Then came Terrible Tom, a marshal on each side and one right behind him, like three three-dimensional shadows.

Terrible Tom was loaded into a van, where he was chained to steel rings that reached up from the floor. Six marshals took their seats in the van. As the parade of vehicles drove off, Terrible Tom gazed out the window. He hadn't seen the world in fifteen years and was enjoying the view. Hard across the way he saw storm clouds in the distance fast approaching. He'd almost forgotten about weather... and the billboards and signs.

It was like going to Disneyland.

At the airport, the marshals escorted him onto the plane. As he clinked and clanked down the aisle, he looked around. The inmates on the plane stared back at him. Not a sound.

Once seated and triple cuffed, with another set of shackles to his legs, Terrible Tom looked to his left and saw a familiar face.

"Tom," said the Baron, smiling.

"Hey, Baron."

"Tell me about it," urged the Baron.

The two killers talked quietly, then the plane started to roll. It accelerated, pushing Tom back in his seat, and the wheels left the ground.

He daydreamed for an instant that maybe he really would be going to Disneyland.

THREE

Ringleaders and Rats

DISNEYLAND WAS CLOSE to Hollywood, but Terrible Tom wouldn't see either place.

Con Air landed at Los Angeles international airport. The plane bypassed the main terminal and taxied toward a remote hangar. Nearby, a forklift loaded heavy crates onto a flatbed truck trailer.

A parade of US marshal vehicles sat parked and waiting as Con Air came to a halt. Its engines wound down and the forward hatch opened to greet a gantry. Security was tight. Heavily armed marshals were everywhere. All wore body armor and most carried automatic assault rifles. A few with high-powered sniper-rifles were camped out on rooftops with spotters.

One at a time, the twenty passengers of Con Air descended the stairs to the tarmac to be escorted to their assigned vehicles. When loaded, each vehicle departed in the company of two escort cars. This threesome was designated a group. As one group left the airport, it was joined by three LA police cars, designated Chase 1, Chase 2 and Chase 3. In each of these rode four police officers, wearing body armor.

The prisoner of each group was destined for isolated maximum-security cells across southern California. The Hulk and Barry 'the Baron' Mills went directly to the West Valley Detention Center in Rancho Cucamonga, which is in San Bernadino. Here, cells were waiting in a special wing of the jail, recently evacuated of all other prisoners. Terrible Tom was at West Valley Detention Center too, but he had his own private wing, which was nowhere near the other two members of the Aryan Brotherhood.

They were in Los Angeles for the trial of forty members of the Aryan Brotherhood, including the shotcallers—the so-called National Commission: Barry Mills, Tyler Bingham and Thomas Silverstein. They would be tried for thirty-two murders and approximately 100 attempted murders. Of the forty Aryan Brothers, sixteen could face the death penalty. None of the forty would be tried at the same time and same location, but instead there would be five different trials spread out over seven southern California counties. The Big Daddy of these was in Santa Ana, because it touched the Baron, the Hulk and Terrible Tom—the Commissioners.

For almost four years the passengers of Con Air languished in their cells while the preliminary legal proceedings took place: motions were filed, counter-motions were filed, statements were taken, and hundreds of preliminary hearings were held. And plea bargains were offered.

In March 2006, in Santa Ana, California, the trial began. The venue was the Ronald Reagan Federal Building and US Courthouse in what was called the "Nuremberg Room," drawing parallels with the courtroom in Nuremberg, Germany, where twenty-two leaders of the Third Reich were tried. Real Nazis were tried at Nuremberg in 1945 and 1946 for "crimes against humanity." Recycled Nazis were on trial in Santa Ana. Members of both groups were glorified evildoers who showed their devotion by adopting malevolent, mystical symbols: swastikas, shamrocks and lightning bolts. The real Nazis plastered the symbols on weapons, walls, flags, helmets, and uniforms, while the recycled Nazis took it a step further. They tattooed the symbols all over their bodies. All were criminals. All coveted power. All were greedy. Each group sought to establish an empire built on violence, terror and blood.

BARRY MILLS' attorneys, Mark Montgomery and Frank Sansoni, decided early on not to call either Barry Mills or Tyler 'the Hulk' Bingham as witnesses. Both criminals were too volatile, too angry, too spastic. But the attorneys would call Thomas Silverstein, aka Terrible Tom.

US District Judge David Baxter had already authorized it, stipulating that "the witness will be shackled in court like Hannibal Lecter. He will come out here in chains and sit here in chains."

Sherry Sikes was the lead prosecutor. She had been selected because she was smart, never gave up and loved verbal sparring. If the defense got her on the ropes in a corner, she came out pounding.

Sikes was young and blond, and pretty enough to have been a movie star. She had been assisting Gregory Jessner, the US Attorney who had originally filed the indictment against the Aryan Brotherhood. Before the case came to trial, Jessner resigned and went into private practice. Some people thought Jessner left because his name had been "put in the hat." When asked about it, Jessner had said, "I don't know. It's a pretty big hat. I worry. You can't help but worry."

"The people call Kevin Roach," said Sherry Sikes.

Two bailiffs escorted a figure that conjured an image of the mythological Paul Bunyan to the witness stand. Along with a huge, fluffy beard and shaved head he was hard and massive. A distinct AB tattoo was visible on his right forearm. This was Kevin Roach.

The Baron sat on the second tier of the docket, wearing cheap, heavily tinted sunglasses. His attorneys had advised against the sunglasses, telling him "they make you look sinister. The prosecutor's going to paint you black enough. You don't need to go along with it, help her out."

That was the point as far as the Baron was concerned. He wanted to appear sinister. He wanted to emanate terror. Maybe the fucking snitches and the jurors would get the message. Don't fuck with me!

So the Baron wore the sunglasses.

Now he took them off, so he could get a better look at Roach. And so Roach could see his eyes.

Roach noticed and glared back.

Judge Baxter noticed too. "Mr. Mills," he said. "You have been warned against trying to intimidate witnesses with 'the evil stare.' "

The Bailiffs close to the Baron turned toward him, waiting to see how he would respond to the judge's words.

The Baron held Roach's eyes a moment longer then put his sunglasses back on.

Roach had been a member of the Aryan Brotherhood. In fact, he was a high-ranking councilman, one of the elite shotcallers. He took his orders directly from the Commissioners: Mills, Bingham and Silverstein.

Now Roach was a rat, a snitch, a squealer, a defector.

Acutely violent and convicted of two murders, Roach had been transferred to the supermax in Florence, because of his attitude. Roach's attitude was demonic. He attacked guards and other inmates just "for fun." At ADX Florence, boredom and inactivity soon got to him and he told the Feds—agents of the ATF—that he might be interested in "rolling over."

The Feds were ecstatic. Roach was a big fish ready to swim upstream. They had to keep him safe, because his fellow inmates had a zero-tolerance threshold for snitches. Roach was moved to H Unit, an isolated area next door to the control room of the supermax. For a while, Roach had the run of the place, like his own suite in a hotel. Naturally, the guards called it the Roach Motel.

Pretty soon, the Feds moved another Aryan Brotherhood defector into H Unit. Brian Healy came from the SHU at Pelican Bay in California, and had been singing the snitch's song for the last two years. He had a sweet deal. If he cooperated and testified, his sentence would be reduced. Eventually, he would get back to the real world.

The two snitches told the Feds everything they knew: about invisible ink made from urine that magically re-appeared when heated; about writing in code; about a number of Aryan Brotherhood murder plots; about Aryan Brotherhood connections with drug cartels in Latin America; and how the Brotherhood moved huge shipments of marijuana, cocaine, heroin and crystal meth around the country.

In return, Roach and Healy got VCRs and televisions, access to laptop computers and the internet, Pizza Hut pizza and Carl's Jr. hamburgers, even porn videos. And they got to walk freely in H Unit.

Today was the day. Roach was here to testify, to settle his bill. Sitting on the witness stand, Roach felt relaxed and ready to talk.

THE CLERK: "Stand and raise your right hand. Do you swear to tell the truth, the whole truth, and nothing but the truth under penalty of perjury?"

The witness: "I do."

The clerk: "Your full name, sir."

The witness: "Kevin Roach."

Sherry Sikes stood ten feet in front of Roach. "Mr. Roach, are you currently incarcerated?"

"Yes."

"If you please, Mr. Roach, I would like to ask you to look over at the docket area. Look at the men seated there and tell the jury if you recognize any of them."

"Yes."

"Would you tell the jury who you recognize."

"The Baron, the Hulk and Terrible Tom," said Roach.

"Are those their real names?"

"No. Their real names are Barry Mills, Tyler Bingham and Thomas Silverstein."

"Do all three of these men belong to a gang known as the Aryan Brotherhood?"

"Yes."

"Are they just members or do they hold other positions?"

"They're the Commission," shrugged Roach.

"Could you please tell the jury what the Commission is?"

"The Commission is a group of three men who run the Aryan Brotherhood. They call the shots," explained Roach.

"Could you be more specific about what shotcallers do?"

"Sure," said Roach, looking at the Baron. "Around 1995 or 1996, the AB decided to become the king of the hill. They wanted to be the most powerful criminal organization in the world."

"And how would they accomplish that?" asked Prosecutor Sikes.

Roach shrugged as if it was obvious. "By protection," he said. "The leaders of all the crime organizations come to prison. On the streets they're comfortable but in prison their safety nets are gone. We control what happens in prison."

"And by 'we' you mean the Aryan Brotherhood, correct?"

"Yes."

"Go on, please."

"Well," said Roach, "the Hell's Angels, the Italian Mafia, the Mexican and Colombian drug cartels—the Baron offered all of them the AB's protection while in prison. If they don't have our protection their organizations will crumble because nobody will survive in prison without it." There was pride in his voice. "No criminal empire can stand against the Aryan Brotherhood."

"Let me see if I understand you," said Sikes. She looked at the jury, making sure they were getting this. "The leaders of these criminal organizations come into prison and pay the Aryan Brotherhood for protection? Is that correct?"

"Yes."

"How do they pay, Mr. Roach? With money? Or by some other means?"

"Some pay money. The money changes hands on the outside. Their people pay our people," said Roach.

"You said some pay. What do the others do?"

"They pay," explained Roach, turning his palms up. "But sometimes it's doing a favor rather than money."

"Can you give the jury an example of a payment by favor, Mr. Roach?"

"Sure," nodded Roach. "Little Nicky paid by training AB warriors in tactics on the outside."

Sherry Sikes held up her hand. "Who is Little Nicky?"

"Nicodemo Scarfo," smiled Roach. "Most call him Little Nicky. Me and him did time together."

"And what was Mr. Scarfo's job? Which organization was he with?"

"Mafia," said Roach. "Head of the Mafia in Philadelphia and Atlantic City."

"I see," nodded Sherry Sikes, giving the jury a level stare. "And Mr. Scarfo did not pay money for protection?"

"No."

"Then how did he pay?"

"Like I told you," stated Roach, "by training AB members in tactics."

"And what are tactics?"

"You know, things like moving drugs. How to get 'em from one place to another, like from one country to another. In boats, or on planes, or in cars that are being shipped in containers."

"So, Mr. Scarfo gave the Aryan Brotherhood tips, as it were, on how to smuggle illicit drugs?"

"Yes."

"And these tips were the way Mr. Scarfo paid the Aryan Brotherhood for protection?"

"Yes."

Prosecutor Sikes walked over to where her co-prosecutor, Rodney Pierce, sat at a table. They whispered to each other briefly. Then Sikes returned and got back to her questions. "Now, Mr. Roach, could you give the jury an example of someone who paid money to the Aryan Brotherhood for protection?"

"That's easy," declared Roach. "John Gotti."

Sherry Sikes stopped and stared at Roach. "You mean the notorious Mafia leader from New York?" she asked.

"Sure," replied Roach. "The Teflon Don himself."

Sikes glanced at the jury, checking to see if they were listening. Their attention levels were dialed to maximum, their eyes fixed on Roach.

"Please tell the jury," encouraged Sikes.

"Sure. After he took his fall, Gotti came into prison. Only he wasn't as tough as his rep. Outside he had lots of guys who took care of him. Inside it was different. He either had to 'check in' or get some protection or die," said Roach.

"What do you mean by 'check in'?" asked the prosecutor.

"Protective custody. If a prisoner checks in, he's going to protective custody. It's a safe place for snitches, cowards and such in prison. The guards make sure you stay healthy."

"Thank you. Please go on about Mr. Gotti."

"Gotti didn't want to check in and he didn't want to die," explained Roach, holding his hands out as if to say *what else*. "Instead he made a deal with the Baron."

"The Baron is Barry Mills, correct?"

"Yes."

"And what was the deal that Mr. Gotti and Mr. Mills made?"

"Gotti would get the Baron an attorney—a good one—to appeal one of his murder raps. But he didn't come through," said Roach.

"Who didn't come through? Mr. Gotti or Mr. Mills?"

"Gotti. He didn't get an attorney for the Baron," replied Roach.

"What did Mr. Mills do when Mr. Gotti failed to fulfill his part of the bargain?"

"The Baron put the word out. The AB stopped providing protection for Gotti," stated Roach.

Sherry Sikes furrowed her brows. "Excuse me, Mr. Roach. Perhaps I'm misunderstanding. I understood you to say Mr. Gotti paid money to the Aryan Brotherhood for protection."

"He did. That was when Gotti first came in. Later, after the Baron pulled the protection of the AB, a guy named Walter Johnson—a black inmate—hit Gotti. Punched him right in the eye," explained Roach, laughing as he recalled Walter Johnson getting shitty with John Gotti.

"How did Mr. Gotti react to being physically assaulted by Mr. Johnson?" asked Sikes.

"Pissed off! Gotti went ballistic. He wanted Johnson dead. And I mean right away," answered Roach.

Rodney Pierce, the co-prosecutor, interrupted. "Excuse me, your Honor. Could I have a moment to confer with my colleague?"

Judge Baxter nodded. "Make it quick."

"Thank you," said Pierce. Sherry Sikes moved to the table, where Pierce whispered something to her. Sikes nodded and walked back to where she had been standing.

"Mr. Roach, your knowledge of Mr. Gotti's reaction seems quite distinct. For the sake of clarification, is your knowledge hearsay or did you actually see Mr. Gotti become upset?" asked Sherry Sikes.

"Me and Gotti were in the pen together, in Marion," said Roach. "I was there. I saw him. I talked to him."

Sherry Sikes nodded slowly. "Thank you. Now you stated that Mr. Gotti wished Mr. Johnson harm. Please tell the jury about that."

Roach laughed. "Not harm. Gotti wanted the guy dead. So he sent word to the Baron. He told the Baron he'd pay $500,000 to have Johnson killed."

"And what was Mr. Mills' response to such an offer?"

"He took it. The Baron told us to accept the contract and he wanted me to get word to all the brothers because John Gotti was willing to pay a good sum. He wanted to show that the Aryan Brotherhood could get anyone, anywhere."

"What happened then, Mr. Roach? Did the Aryan Brotherhood carry out the contract?"

"No. We couldn't get to Johnson. He heard about it and checked himself into protective custody," said Roach. "If we could've gotten to him, we could have hit him. I had two .22s and a zip-gun."

"By two .22s, do you mean bullets?"

"Sure," shrugged Roach. "Somebody smuggled them in and they were passed to me in the library."

"So, you're telling the jury that someone brought .22 caliber bullets—two of them—into prison? And gave them to you to carry out a murder contract?"

"Yes."

"And all these events—the contract to commit murder, the command to carry out the contract and the bullets to commit the murder—occurred because Mr. Mills gave the order?"

"Yes."

Sherry Sikes gazed at Roach. "Where was Mr. Mills when he gave the order to kill a man in prison in Marion, Illinois?"

"In Colorado. The supermax prison in Florence," said Roach.

Sikes shook her head in disbelief. "So you're telling the jury that a criminal in a supermax prison in Colorado gave the order to murder another prisoner in another prison in another state? A state halfway across the country?"

"Yes."

"How is that possible?"

Roach shrugged. "Power."

Silence draped the courtroom as all eyes gazed at the Baron.

Judge Baxter pushed the hush aside. "We'll take a short recess," he announced.

Twenty minutes later with everyone back in their places, Prosecutor Sikes continued. "Mr. Roach, when you were an active member of the Aryan Brotherhood, did you hear of a 'race war' against a rival gang?"

"Yes. But I didn't take part in it," replied Roach.

"What was the name of the rival gang?"

"The DC Blacks."

"Would you please tell the jury what occurred in this 'race war'?"

"Sure. DC Blacks put a hit on two of the Brothers in the pen in Lewisburg. Lewisburg is in Pennsylvania," said Roach.

"What do you mean by 'hit'? In other words, did the rival gang members actually attack two members of the Aryan Brotherhood in Lewisburg prison?"

"Sure. Attacked 'em and killed 'em."

"And what was the Aryan Brotherhood's response to the killing of two of its members?"

"The Baron and Hulk sent a message to Lewisburg. To Skinny Benton," replied Roach.

"Is that Mr. Benton's real name? Or a nickname?"

"Skinny's real name is Albert," smiled Roach. "But everybody calls him Skinny."

"Is Mr. Benton a member of the Aryan Brotherhood?"

"Sure. At the time, he was the shotcaller at Lewisburg."

"And shotcaller is synonymous with leader, correct?"

"Sure. I mean, yes."

"What message did Mr. Mills and Mr. Bingham send to Mr. Benton at Lewisburg prison?"

"They told Skinny to wage war on the DC Blacks."

"Could you clarify what you mean by 'wage war'?"

"To kill 'em," said Roach. "To kill as many DC Blacks as they could."

"Did Mr. Benton carry out those instructions, do you know?" asked Prosecutor Sikes.

"Sure. Skinny and his warriors didn't waste any time. They killed two of 'em."

The prosecutor cocked her head and said, "Excuse me for repeating myself, but just for clarification, the murder of the two DC Blacks at Lewisburg occurred because of the direct order of Mr. Mills and Mr. Bingham?"

"Yes."

"Mr. Roach, are you aware of any other murders that either Barry Mills or Tyler Bingham ordered?"

"Yes."

"Would you please tell the jury about it?"

"Sure. The Baron—Barry Mills—got a message to John Greshner and told him to hit Rhino Andreasen," said Roach.

"Is John Greshner a member of the Aryan Brotherhood?"

"Yes."

"And Mr. Greshner was ordered to murder Rhino Andreasen, you said?"

"Yes. Rhino told the Feds about a bank robbery. So the Baron put his name in the hat. You don't do that and live."

"What don't you do and live?"

Roach shrugged. "Snitch. Roll over on the Brotherhood and what they done."

"So, because Mr. Andreasen cooperated with the authorities, Barry Mills ordered Mr. Greshner to kill him?"

"Yes."

"And did Mr. Greshner carry out the order?"

"Oh, sure," nodded Roach.

"Mr. Greshner murdered Rhino—Mr. Andreasen?"

"Yes. As soon as he got the message, he hit him."

"And where did this murder take place?"

"In prison. At Leavenworth."

Sherry Sikes turned to the jury. "They thought about it, they plotted and they sent a message. This was not a spur-of-the-moment event," she said in a fat voice, as her eyes scanned the jurors. Then she walked to the prosecutor's table and sat down.

"Mr. Montgomery," said Judge Baxter. "Any cross-examination?"

Mark Montgomery stood. His job as lead counsel, for Barry 'the Baron' Mills, was to discredit the testimony of Kevin Roach. Confident he could do this with just a few questions, he moved in.

"Mr. Roach," began Montgomery, "I was fascinated by your testimony, especially by your quick responses. It's almost as if you didn't have to think about your answers. As if you'd heard the questions before." Montgomery put his fingers together. "Let me inquire, Mr. Roach. "Were you coached in any way before coming here today?"

"No."

"No one said to you, they might ask you this question and this question and this question?"

"No."

"I see," smirked Montgomery. "Is it not true, Mr. Roach, that you were paid for your testimony?"

Roach glanced around. "Sure. I guess so."

Montgomery nodded grandly. "And you were promised a reduced sentence, were you not?"

"No," said Roach, shaking his head.

Montgomery looked shocked. "And why is that? I mean if I agreed to testify against others I would certainly want something in return."

"I don't want my freedom to be based on doing ill to them," said Roach, tipping his head in the direction of the Baron and the Hulk, who sat like statues.

"How noble," declared the attorney. Montgomery pursed his lips and glanced at the ceiling. "Just one more question, if you don't mind." He looked back at Roach. "Why would a member of the Aryan Brotherhood drop out, turn traitor on his fellows, and agree to become an informant?"

Roach thought for a moment. "I was too old to believe all the hype anymore and to believe that it meant anything more than murder, mayhem and robbery," he replied. "I was on the fast track. I had power and prestige. But who do I have power over? A six-by-eight foot cell and a range of twenty guys. It was like being king of the dead, all smoke and mirrors. I was tired of it and I wanted to get out."

Montgomery looked at the jury and shook his head. Then he sat down.

Court recessed for lunch.

IN THE AFTERNOON SESSION, the Baron's attorneys called Michael Hixson to the stand. Hixson was a federal agent with the US Bureau of Alcohol, Tobacco, Firearms and Explosives.

The Baron's attorneys, Mark Montgomery and Frank Sansoni, had subpoenaed Hixson as a hostile witness. By questioning Hixson on the witness stand, the two attorneys intended to prove that all testimony given by the government's informants was manufactured, bought and paid for.

Hixson, a tall, handsome man, was an experienced agent. He didn't fluster easily.

"Mr. Hixson, you were one of the primary agents in the case on trial here today, is that correct?" asked Montgomery.

"Yes."

"In fact, you managed the government's informants, did you not?"

"Yes."

"You were responsible for debriefing the informants?"

"Yes."

"And that included ensuring their safety and comfort and other requirements?"

"Yes."

Montgomery interlaced his fingers near his chin. "I'd like to focus on the comforts you provided for a moment." Dropping his hands, Montgomery continued. "It's true, is it not, that the government provided certain amenities or privileges to convicted inmates who agreed to cooperate?"

"Yes."

"Could you enlighten the jury as to the types of amenities you provided?"

Agent Hixson nodded. "Sometimes I paid for shoes, sometimes for new eyeglasses."

"I see," said Montgomery. "And did you ever make cash payments to these informants?"

"Yes."

"How much did you pay them for their information?"

"I didn't pay them per se," said Hixson. "I gave them money so they could purchase personal items they needed."

"I don't see the difference," declared Montgomery. "Whether you paid them directly for information or gave them money for personal items, isn't that merely a question of semantics?"

"No. That's not the way it worked." Hixson shook his head.

"Well, why don't you tell the jury how it worked?"

Hixson looked at the jury. "The inmates approached us, we did not solicit them. That's important to understand. Once an inmate agreed to turn informant, they usually submitted a list of demands starting with requests for money and for the filing of a motion that would seek a reduction of their prison sentences."

"Were their sentences reduced?"

"In some cases," answered Hixson. "Actually in a few cases—a very few—the inmates received early release."

"They received early release?" asked Montgomery in a tight voice.

"Yes."

"When that occurred—the early release—what occurred precisely?"

"In one case, the witness was released and placed into a witness-protection program," stated the ATF agent. "We also provided him with an amount of money for living expenses."

"How much money?"

"In this particular case, $150,000."

Montgomery let his mouth drop open. "$150,000! Well, isn't that payment for information?" demanded Montgomery. Before the agent could answer, Montgomery went on. "Oh, excuse me! I forgot. It was for living expenses." Montgomery snorted.

Hixson grinned in appreciation of fine acting. Then he continued answering the attorney's original question. "The second thing the inmates wanted, when they agreed to testify, was, where are you going to house us so we don't get killed? And third was, are you going to prosecute us?" He held out his hands. "They all wanted immunity from prosecution."

"In case they were just as guilty of murder as the men they were testifying against?" asked Montgomery.

"Yes."

"Did they receive immunity?"

"In some cases. But not all. I can't give you an exact number because I don't recall," said the agent. "Those who didn't receive immunity were placed in protective custody."

"Do you recall by any chance the name Clifford Smith?" asked Montgomery, peering closely at Hixson.

"Yes."

"Do you recall this? That he was a member of the Aryan Brotherhood?"

"Yes."

"And did you pay him?"

"Yes."

"Why?" asked Montgomery, holding his hands out in wonder.

"I paid for time and information, not for convictions," explained the agent.

Montgomery looked incredulous. "You actually paid murderers, professional criminals, who, by the way, are usually pretty good liars, for time and information?"

"Yes. The payments were similar to the way you"—he gestured at the attorney—"charge for billable hours. Although they are in prison, it's their time."

"Clifford Smith is already serving a sentence of sixty-five years to life," said Montgomery in a sarcastic tone. "And you wanted to compensate him for the time he spent with you?"

"Yes."

"I don't suppose you recall how much you paid Mr. Smith, do you?"

"$1,400 over the time I worked with him," replied Hixson matter-of-factly.

Montgomery walked away as if distraught, then walked back and faced the jury. "Ladies and gentlemen of the jury," he said. "I don't know about you, but I cannot believe what I just heard." He threw his arms wide. "Testimony that was bought and paid for!"

Judge Baxter said, "This is a good place to stop. We will reconvene court tomorrow morning at 9:00 a.m."

THE NEXT MORNING, the bailiffs ushered Barry 'the Baron' Mills and Tyler 'the Hulk' Bingham to their seats. Rattling and clanking, the two super-villains nodded and waved to Judge Baxter and the jury. The Baron and the Hulk were enjoying the show. They *were* the show.

Attorney Mark Montgomery entered. Dressed in a dark suit, white shirt and dark tie, he had spent the previous night preparing for today's performance. A superb criminal defense attorney, Montgomery's greatest talent lay in his showmanship. In Montgomery's opinion, the winning attorney wasn't the one who knew more about the law. The winner was the one who gave the best performance. And Montgomery had no doubt he was the best actor.

This morning's performance would be the *coup de grace* to the testimony given yesterday by Kevin Roach. Montgomery called Danny Weeks to the witness stand. Most members of the Aryan Brotherhood were thick, massive men, similar to the imposing beasts at a bullfight. In comparison, Danny Weeks looked like a gazelle, built for speed. For one thing, his head wasn't shaved; he wore his hair like a cap, short and smooth. For another thing, he wasn't covered in tattoos, although he did carry the Brand. Like most of the Brotherhood, he favored a mustache.

Once upon a time, Danny Weeks had been a shotcaller. Now he was worse than a snitch. He was a snitch who snitched on the snitches. Nothing was worse. According to prison rules, snitches deserved to die. A double-snitch deserved to be boiled in oil, then crucified upside down.

Initially, Danny Weeks had rolled over because he wanted a reduced sentence. He wanted to see daylight again, drink beer, eat a chili-dog with onions, and ride his Harley. So he had agreed to cooperate with the Feds, who moved him into the H Unit with Kevin Roach. Like most paranoid schizophrenics with anger problems and bad attitudes, the two gangsters couldn't get along.

According to Danny Weeks, "Roach was full of shit. Thought he was hot, blue and righteous, ya know?" Weeks made a scoffing noise. "Really he's just a punk."

Naturally, Roach disagreed. "Danny's a pussy. He couldn't take the heat. Wanted to snitch so he could get out, but still wanted to be a shotcaller."

When the two gangsters came to blows, the Feds moved Danny Weeks out of H Unit. That was when Danny started snitching on the snitches. He wrote letters to newspapers, telling them about H Unit. The media loved it. When his reports appeared in print, people began wondering what was going on in the H Unit of ADX Florence. Who was running the place? The jailers or the inmates?

THE CLERK: "Stand and raise your right hand. Do you swear to tell the truth, the whole truth, and nothing but the truth under penalty of perjury?"

The witness: "I do."

The clerk: "Your full name, sir."

The witness: "Daniel Weeks."

Mark Montgomery smiled. "Mr. Weeks, for a short period of time you were incarcerated with Kevin Roach, were you not?"

"Yes, sir."

"Where was that? In which facility were you incarcerated?"

"At the supermax prison in Florence."

"Did you have your own cell? Or were you in some special section of the prison?"

"We was in H Unit," replied Weeks.

"And what was H Unit?"

"Where they kept the guys who was rolling over—guys who was giving the lowdown on the Brothers." Weeks rubbed his nose.

"Can you please tell the jury what the nature of that 'lowdown' was?"

"The Feds wanted to know what we know about the Aryan Brotherhood. You know, drugs, how messages was sent, who to hit, who needed what."

"I see," nodded Montgomery. "And did you cooperate with the authorities? Provide them with any and all information you had at your disposal?"

Weeks frowned at the attorney. "Yeah, for a while I did."

"Does that mean that you stopped cooperating with the authorities?"

"Yeah."

"And why did you stop cooperating?"

"Cuz it was bogus, ya know?"

"Would you please tell the jury what you mean by 'bogus'?"

"Well," Weeks said slowly, "the guys in there was making stuff up. They was making the Feds think they was shotcallers and all."

Montgomery nodded in sympathy. "So you disagreed with the information they were providing to the authorities? You felt the information was not accurate?"

"You got that right," chimed Weeks.

"Mr. Weeks," interrupted Judge Baxter. "Please answer yes or no to the questions."

"Sorry," said Danny Weeks, looking at the judge. Then he looked at Mark Montgomery. "Yes."

"Could you please explain to the jury why the information was inaccurate?" asked Montgomery.

"Yes," said Weeks, peeking at the judge. "The Feds gave 'em files to read. After they read 'em, they talked it over and decided on what to tell the Feds."

Montgomery acted shocked. "Let me get this straight," he asked in a sincere voice. "You're telling the jury that the informants were given confidential files?"

"Yes."

"Which the informants read?"

"Yes."

"And that the informants then compared notes and concocted a plausible story?" Montgomery's voice got louder and bristled with disbelief.

"Yes."

"Then they told that story to the authorities?" Montgomery's voice bulged out like that of a hellfire and damnation preacher at a tent revival.

"Yes."

Wagging his head sadly, Montgomery asked, "Why would the informants do such a thing?"

"To make themselves look good," answered Weeks. "Kevin told me that he was playing the biggest game of his life, and that if he made a wrong move he was through."

Montgomery walked away as if he couldn't stand to hear anymore, then came back. "And you wrote letters to newspaper editors and warned them of this conspiracy, didn't you?"

"Yes," agreed Weeks.

"And after you sent your letters off—letters telling the truth—what happened?" asked Montgomery in a righteous tone.

"Once they was published, they said I was a liar."

"Who? Who had the audacity to say you lied?" growled Montgomery.

"The Warden," replied Weeks.

"You mean he simply called you a liar?"

"No, sir," said Weeks. "He put out a memo to all the guards at the prison that I had taken a lie detector test and that I failed it."

Montgomery shuddered in disbelief. "Why on earth would the Warden—a trusted federal official—do such a thing?"

"Cuz I knew what he was doing," said Danny Weeks, giving his shoulders a *what else* shrug.

"What do you mean 'what he was doing'? Please explain that to the jury."

"The Warden was showing pictures of his guards to the guys, asking them which ones was dirty. They looked at 'em and said this one's dirty, this one's not."

"So the Warden was seeking information about corrupt members of his staff?"

"Yes."

"And the informants would indicate which staff members were corrupt?"

"Yes."

Montgomery cocked his head as if conceding a point. "Well, I mean if they're corrupt..."

"They wasn't," insisted Weeks. "The snitches said they were dirty just to jam them up. Cuz they didn't like 'em."

"You're quite sure of this?" asked Montgomery.

"Sure I'm sure. I knew that one of 'em—Officer Principe—was placed on home leave cuz Roach said the guy was dirty. And I asked Roach about it. He told me Principe had been down there working the bubble when he first rolled over. Principe treated Roach so bad that he told the Feds the guy was hooked up with us. Roach wanted him to get indicted for helping us do our business at ADX." Weeks paused, and looked at the jury. "I told Roach that's kinda hard on the guy. He said, 'Fuck the puke. He's lucky I can't kill him.'"

Montgomery looked as if he'd just been slapped. Then he turned to the jury. "I'm at a loss for words," he said, and walked back to his chair, smiling on the inside.

AMONG THE NAMES and nicknames—like the Baron, the Hulk, Blinky, McKool, Tank, Skinny, Turtle, Cisco, and Lucifer—Joseph Principe's name was the last name listed in the federal government's 110-page indictment against the Aryan Brotherhood. The heaviest, go-for-broke bad guy case ever brought to court by the Department of Justice.

Most of the names on the indictment made up the high-ranking honchos of the Aryan Brotherhood. The rest of the names were 'associates,' wannabes and flunkeys.

Who was Joseph Principe?

Principe was from the Bronx, which meant he was streetwise before he reached puberty. After graduating from a mediocre high school where he got mediocre grades, Principe decided he didn't want to be mediocre his whole life. So he joined the US Army, which was pretty much the definition of mediocrity. Principe bailed out and signed up for classes at Manhattan College, a pretty mediocre school. Except Principe majored in philosophy. He put his degree in philosophy to good use and bought into the fundamental principle of greed. Except Principe excelled at it. He got a job at the American

Stock Exchange and made a lot of money, which he mostly spent on big boy toys and fancy clothes and women. He was so busy living the good life he forgot about what paid for it—his job. When his numbers dropped off, he was let go.

Principe found a job working as a private investigator, tracking down insurance scams and getting the goods on unfaithful spouses. It was lousy, sleazy work that made mediocrity look like the good life.

He got engaged to a woman who encouraged him to "get a better job, make some money, get some status." Principe looked around, surveying his options. The Bureau of Prisons was hiring people to be prison guards, who were technically known as federal correctional officers.

Principe signed on. "I never thought of it as a fighting-crime thing," he said. "It was a job I could handle, I guess, that I didn't think would bother me too much."

His first stint was at USP Lewisburg in Pennsylvania. The place was full of bad-ass convicts and louder than Hell. Principe became an adrenaline addict and liked it. He got along with his peers, who, for the most part, were guys just like him. They wanted a steady paycheck, a mortgage, a good retirement plan, and a little action to keep things interesting.

In 1994, ADX Florence opened their supermax, an elite prison for the worst criminals. Elite guards would be needed. The idea appealed to Principe, so he put in for a transfer.

ADX Florence was a high-tech fortress, like a futuristic citadel in a sci-fi novel. Big Brother was definitely watching—and not just the inmates, but the guards too. Principe began to feel like he was RoboCop, what with all the rules and everything. Programming took the place of choice. The guards had no discretion, they were just machines who followed orders and the rules. Lots of rules. Sometimes Principe did little favors for the inmates, such as allowing them to talk to each other, or pass items from one cell to another cell. No big deal, really.

Being one of the elite made Principe miserable. Then the powers-that-be cracked down and life got hellish. Any guard who didn't follow the rules left himself open to being branded "dirty."

On August 16, 1999, Principe was placed on home duty, which meant he was under investigation. They didn't want him to show up for work. He would be paid, but he had to stay at home. Principe said no one told him what he'd done wrong. No charges were mentioned. Principe told himself things couldn't get much worse, but they did. His father died, and his wife decided she'd be happier as his ex-wife. The divorce got messy, what with the custody battle over the kids.

Principe's attitude decayed. Dark thoughts invaded his head, which he started writing down as poems. He bought a Harley Davidson and some biker duds, let his hair grow and cultivated a goatee. A semi-automatic pistol kept him company as he roared around on his bike. He got a couple of tattoos, and made the type of friends one might refer to as marginalized or peripheral personalities. Which was a fancy way of saying scumbags.

Gino, who worked in a bar that Principe frequented, came to Principe with a sob-story one day. Gino wore his long, greasy hair in a ponytail.

"I owe some money to dangerous people," said Gino, looking over his shoulder.

"What kind of dangerous people?" asked Principe.

"You know, underworld people. People who are part of the organization."

"You mean mobsters? Like the Mafia?"

Gino shrugged. "I need a loan," he whispered.

"How much?"

"$1,500," replied Gino, twisting his hands nervously.

Principe thought about it. "Okay," he said. "But you gotta pay me back as fast as you can."

"Of course," nodded Gino. "Can I borrow your car? Just for an hour or so, so I can go pay the money."

Principe went to the bank, got the cash and returned. He gave the money and his car keys to Gino.

Five days later, Gino returned from Vegas, parked the borrowed car in Principe's driveway and knocked on Principe's front door. Principe felt like he'd been played for a sucker and was pissed off. He slapped Gino around, handcuffed him and knocked him around some more. Principe walked into another room, got a pair of his ex-wife's sewing scissors and hacked off Gino's long hair.

Principe took the cuffs off Gino and dragged him outside, where he punched him again. "Go get my money, asshole," he instructed. And then walked back into the house.

Gino went to the cops and Principe was tossed in the county jail. Charged with kidnapping and assault, Principe's predicament got worse when an ex-girlfriend came forward to accuse him of stalking and sexual assault. The girl's charges escalated to include kidnapping and menacing. At Principe's arraignment hearing in court, the judge set bail at $1 million. Any bail bondsman would require surety for the whole million, which meant Principe was stuck in jail because he didn't have that kind of cash.

Principe's attorney thought they could win if they took the case to trial. Principe claimed Gino and the ex-girlfriend lied. He admitted he had slapped Gino around a little, but that was all. He had no clue what the ex-girlfriend's agenda was.

During the trial, one of Principe's pals, another guard at ADX Florence, took the witness stand. "Joe bragged about what he had done," said the pal. "He told me how he slapped Gino around. The guy was cuffed and helpless, and Joe really kicked the bejesus out of him."

Stunned by the testimony, Principe's attorney took him aside and said, "Look, Joe. That witness just sank us. You're looking at thirty-two years unless you cut a deal."

"I don't understand," whined Principe. "I don't know why he did that."

"Neither do I," said the attorney. "But he did. So, it is what it is." He paused. "So, what do you want to do?"

Principe sighed. "Make the deal."

Principe pled guilty to kidnapping and two counts of menacing. In return, he got eight years.

Principe was shipped to the Arkansas Valley Correctional Facility, and had paid one year of his debt to society when the Feds showed up. Michael Hixson, the ATF agent, and Robert Smith showed him a copy of the 110-page indictment against the Aryan Brotherhood. Principe's name was on it. He was charged with aiding and abetting Aryan Brotherhood business, by deliberately allowing AB members at ADX Florence to talk with each other on two occasions, and with falsifying an incident report. The incident involved a fight between Tyler 'the Hulk' Bingham and another ADX inmate named Leroy Elmore. Elmore was black. Principe lied about the fight, reporting that Elmore had a shank and attacked the Hulk, who was only defending himself.

If convicted of the charges, Principe faced twenty years to life in prison.

When originally presented with the indictment, Principe claims to have told Hixson: "This is bullshit." He says Hixson didn't argue the point, but said: "This is easy. You're either with the government, or you're with the Aryan Brotherhood. What's it going to be?"

"You're out of your mind," Principe responded. "I got nothing to say to you."

"This is a life sentence," said Smith. "The Aryan Brotherhood or the Dirty White Boys are going to get you. We're trying to help you save yourself."

Principe almost laughed. "I already tried the government. You let me drown. I'm a convict now."

Thirty days later, US marshals loaded Principe onto a plane and flew him to California. The marshals drove him to Terminal Island and threw him in the Hole, where he waited two years for the trial now taking place in Santa Ana. The walls closed in.

SHERRY SIKES, Assistant Attorney for the US Department of Justice, stood up. "The people call Thomas Silverstein."

A cold tension filled the courtroom. Five marshals escorted into the courtroom what sounded and looked like the Ghost of Christmas Past. A pale, bearded figure rattled to the witness stand. His hands were cuffed and attached to a waist-chain. Leg shackles hindered his leg movements. Once he was seated, three of the marshals moved away. The other two remained next to the witness stand.

The clerk: "Raise your right hand."

One of the marshals stepped forward and whispered something to the clerk: The witness couldn't raise his hands. The clerk recovered nicely.

The clerk: "Do you swear or affirm to tell the truth, the whole truth, and nothing but the truth under the penalty of perjury?"

The witness: "I do."

The clerk: "Please state your full name."

The witness: "Thomas Silverstein."

"Mr. Silverstein, are you presently incarcerated?" asked Sherry Sikes.

Terrible Tom, who sat very still, said "yes."

"How long have you been incarcerated?"

"For most of my life," replied Terrible Tom.

"And how much longer do you expect to be incarcerated?"

"For the rest of my life," said Terrible Tom, with just the shadow of a smile on his lips.

"Mr. Silverstein," inquired the prosecutor, "are you a member of the prison gang commonly referred to as the Aryan Brotherhood?"

"Yes."

Sikes nodded. "And as a member of the Aryan Brotherhood, do you hold any title or position?"

"Yes."

"Would you please tell the jury what your title or position is?"

"Commissioner," said Terrible Tom.

"And if you don't mind, would you please tell the jury what, specifically, a Commissioner is, and what a Commissioner does? In other words, what is the function of a Commissioner in the Aryan Brotherhood?"

Terrible Tom's eyes sparkled. This was the longest conversation he'd had in fifteen years. "There are three Commissioners. They function as shotcallers, which is a vulgar term for decision-makers."

"And what kind of decisions do you make as a Commissioner?"

"Policy decisions, such as which gangs the Brotherhood will affiliate with, which contracts to accept or reject. And who will carry out the contracts."

"What kind of contracts are you referring to?"

"Murder contracts. We call them hits," said Terrible Tom.

Sherry Sikes opened her eyes wide. She wasn't expecting honest answers. "Please excuse my surprise, Mr. Silverstein. But I was led to understand that the Aryan Brotherhood has a strict code of silence. A code of secrecy. Is that true?"

"Yes. Yes, it is," smiled Terrible Tom. "It's called 'lie or die.'"

"Then why are you breaking the code of silence?"

Terrible Tom shrugged. "Why not? I have nothing to hide. I have the perfect alibi. For the past fifteen years I've lived in a cage surrounded by guards."

"So, what you're saying is that you have no knowledge of any contract murders committed by the Aryan Brotherhood? Murders that took place by order of the Commission?"

"No. I heard of some things going down. You know, through the wire," said Terrible Tom.

"The wire?"

"The rumor mill. Gossip. The news system in prison," explained Terrible Tom.

"Could you please tell the jury if you heard of the murders of two DC Blacks gang members, in the Lewisburg penitentiary, in 1997?" asked Sikes.

"Yes, I heard that two died," said Terrible Tom. Then he smiled and added, "But I heard that both cases were NHI."

"Please define NHI for the jury," said the prosecutor.

"No humans involved," stated Terrible Tom, looking right at the jury.

"By that phrase—no humans involved—you mean that the two victims were black, don't you Mr. Silverstein?"

Terrible Tom nodded, grinning wickedly. "Yes."

Some members of the jury looked away, other jurors exchanged glances with each other.

Sherry Sikes asked, "Did the Commissioners, either as individuals or together, order the deaths of the two black inmates at Lewisburg?"

"Not to my knowledge," said Terrible Tom. "And I would have known."

"How would you have known?"

"Someone would have sent a message, letting me know what was going down."

"So, in effect," asked the prosecutor, "you were kept in the loop? You always knew what was taking place, even in other prisons?"

"Yes."

"Mr. Silverstein," inquired Sikes. "Have you ever heard the name John Marzloff?"

"Yes," said Terrible Tom, leaning back a little in his chair.

"Is Mr. Marzloff a member of the Aryan Brotherhood?"

"No, he is not."

"Do you happen to know where Mr. Marzloff is?"

"I don't know. Since he is not a Brother, I wouldn't follow his movements," replied Terrible Tom.

"You didn't know he died—was murdered—in 1979, in prison?"

Terrible Tom slowly raised his eyes, looked directly into the eyes of the prosecutor. "No."

"Then I guess you have no knowledge of the fact that Barry Mills— another member of the Commission—murdered Mr. Marzloff?"

"No. I did not know that."

"And would you please tell the jury, did you order the murder of Mr. Marzloff?"

Terrible Tom smiled. "No. I hardly knew him."

Sherry Sikes looked at the jury. "Please remember that answer," she told them. Then she turned to Judge Baxter. "Nothing further."

"Mr. Montgomery?" asked Judge Baxter, looking at the defense table.

Montgomery half-rose from his chair. "Nothing, your Honor. It's obvious the witness has no knowledge of the events in question."

At her table, Prosecutor Sikes smirked and shook her head.

Montgomery smiled over at her as the marshals escorted Terrible Tom back to his holding cell.

GLEN WEST was called to the witness stand. West was a former member of the Aryan Brotherhood who had rolled over and made a deal with the Feds. In exchange for his testimony against the Aryan Brotherhood, the Feds would drop the charge facing him of conspiracy to commit murder, and they would place him in the witness protection program.

Heavily muscled, with a shaved head, West was a walking talking billboard of tattoos. A Nazi lightning bolt graced the back of his head.

Sherry Sikes began. "Would you please tell the jury, are you a member of the Aryan Brotherhood?"

"Yes," replied West. "Anyway, I was."

"How long were you a member of the prison gang known as the Aryan Brotherhood?"

"For twenty-one years. From 1981, that's when I was branded. Until 2003."

"Mr. West," asked the prosecutor, "do you know Barry Mills?"

"Yes."

"Is Barry Mills one of the leaders—shotcallers, I believe is the term—of the Aryan Brotherhood?"

"Yes."

"Would you please tell the jury when and where you met Barry Mills?"

"In Marion. The pen in Marion," said West. "Back in about 1983."

"So you were in the same prison as Mr. Mills at that time? 1983?"

"Yes. My cell was next to his," said West.

Prosecutor Sikes looked at the jury. Then she looked at West and asked in an even voice, "Mr. West, did Barry Mills order the murder of Gregory Keefer?"

West fidgeted a little, glanced around. "Yes," he replied.

"And could you please tell the jury *why* Barry Mills ordered the murder of Gregory Keefer?"

"For a couple of reasons," West told the jury. "Keefer owed Barry money for drug sales. Taxes. He owed the Baron taxes. And cuz he gave a couple of shanks—knives you'd call 'em—to the Mexican Mafia."

"You are quite certain that Barry Mills gave such an order—to have Gregory Keefer killed?"

"Yeah, I'm dead certain," replied West. When he realized what he'd just said, he smiled and looked around to see if anyone else thought it was funny.

No one else thought it was humorous.

"Why are you so certain that Barry Mills gave the order to have a man murdered?"

"Cuz he told me," insisted West.

"Would you please tell the jury what Barry Mills told you?"

"The Baron told me that I should 'prepare for a lockdown because he was going to have Puppet kill Keefer,'" stated West.

"For clarification, who is Puppet?"

"Puppet was Bill McKinney. But everybody called him Puppet," explained West.

"So Barry Mills told you that Mr. McKinney—who was called Puppet—was going to murder Gregory Keefer?"

"Yes."

"And you are certain that Barry Mills ordered him to kill Gregory Keefer?"

"Yes."

Sherry Sikes nodded. "And did Puppet carry out the order of Barry Mills?"

"Yes."

"What did Puppet do?"

"He stabbed Keefer," said West, lifting his eyebrows as if to say *what else?*

Sherry Sikes looked at the jury. "Mr. West, could you please tell the jury if you recall Barry Mills ever mentioning the name John Marzloff?"

"Yeah, he told me about the guy."

"What did Barry Mills tell you about John Marzloff?"

"He told me that he killed Marzloff cuz he got the order to do it. Cuz Marzloff was gonna roll over on a guy."

"Let me see if I'm clear on this, Mr. West," said the prosecutor. "Barry Mills murdered John Marzloff?"

"Yes."

"And the reason he murdered Mr. Marzloff was because Mr. Marzloff was going to testify against another member of the Aryan Brotherhood?"

"Yes."

"And the person Mr. Marzloff was going to testify against gave the order for Barry Mills to murder Marzloff?"

"Yes, that's right."

The prosecutor paused. Then asked slowly, "And who was the person who gave the order to Barry Mills to murder John Marzloff?"

West squirmed, shifting in his chair. "Terrible Tom."

"You are referring to Thomas Silverstein, correct?"

"Yes."

MICHAEL PARKER, who was one of Tyler 'the Hulk' Bingham's attorneys, took over. His job was to cross-examine the witness and demonstrate that Glen West was a liar.

Parker got right to the point. "Mr. West, did you recently provide testimony in two federal cases in Oregon?"

"Yeah, that's right," replied West, moving restlessly.

"And what was the outcome in those cases, do you recall?"

"I really don't remember," muttered West.

"Well, let me remind you," twinkled the attorney's voice. "In both those cases, is it not true, Mr. West, that you were found guilty of perjuring yourself?"

Glen West shifted in his chair, but did not reply.

"You lied under oath, did you not?" repeated the attorney.

"Yeah, I guess so," answered West, looking at the floor.

Up in the docket, chains rattled as Barry 'the Baron' Mills turned his dark sunglasses in the direction of the Hulk, who sat a few feet away. Returning the stare, the Hulk gave Mills a tight little nod. Then both men stared straight ahead, sitting stone-still, as they waited for the marshals to escort them out of the courtroom.

FOUR

The Boys Are Back In Town

THE PROSECUTORS did not feel good about the condition of the case so far. US Assistant Attorneys Sherry Sikes, Rodney Pierce and Paul Vaughn realized that the testimonies of the government's informants—the snitches—sounded less than credible. "Like a bunch of trained seals," said one of the prosecutors, shaking his head. "Lying whenever we toss 'em a fish. Liars lying on command."

Believable witnesses were needed to control the damage being done by the unbelievable witnesses. Reliable witnesses who weren't convicted killers, robbers, drug lords, extortionists, or racketeers. In other words, people who weren't habitual liars. So they called Patrick Coombs to the stand.

Patrick Coombs was a former federal warden who had spent his entire working life with the Bureau of Prisons. A compassionate person, he had gotten his undergraduate degree in Criminal Justice, because he "wanted to make a difference." He enjoyed college life so much that he hung around for an extra three years. At the end of which he was awarded his masters degree in criminal justice.

Recruited by the Bureau of Prisons, which was always on the lookout for smart people who could be slotted into administrative positions, Coombs quickly discovered that "making a difference" was but a pipe dream. And the reality of prison was "paying the piper," which meant prison was about retribution, not about rehabilitation. That's the way the inmates wanted it. Very few criminals wanted to be rehabilitated—in fact, they laughed at the goody-two-shoes types who tried to help them.

At first, Coombs felt as if he had been betrayed, then realized he had betrayed himself. He had assumed that most criminals were the products of their environment: bad homes, lousy parents, poverty, poor education. In other words, he fell for the claptrap the sociologists were selling—people weren't bad, just their environment.

Boy was that wrong!

The Bureau of Prisons made him an assistant warden and the training was on-the-job. The very first thing Coombs learned was this: There are bad people who make bad decisions. And the bad people make bad choices because they want to. They like being bad. Lesson number two: Inmates create their own environment. They are mean, violent, angry people who enjoy being mean, violent and angry. They treat other people like shit because life is shit—cheap shit. To most inmates, life was to be abused, thrown away and murdered. They lived in a brutal setting in which they only really felt alive when they were taking the life of another person. Murder was a rush. Murder got them high like crystal meth. It made them feel good. They liked it that way, so they made it that way.

Coombs learned there were a lot of things wrong with the penal system, but the real problem was the inmates—the wild beasts—within it. Sartre was right. Hell was other people.

And prison was Hell full of hellish people.

From that point on, Coombs never again thought of himself as "making a difference." Instead, he was a lion tamer in a circus. His job was to snap the whip and poke the chair at the lions, making them perform tricks that were unnatural to them. Tricks such as acting like human beings and not brutalizing one another. The trick of being housebroken.

COOMBS TOOK the witness stand. He raised his right hand and took the oath. A gray-haired, wrinkled man in a dark gray suit and white shirt, he sat and waited patiently for the questions. Beneath barbed-wire eyebrows his eyes blinked a lot.

"Mr. Coombs, you were the warden of the United States Federal penitentiary in Leavenworth, Kansas, is that correct?" asked Sherry Sikes.

"Yes."

"And you are now retired, correct?"

"Yes."

"Were you the warden at Leavenworth penitentiary in 1983?"

"Yes, I was."

"During your tenure at Leavenworth, did you come into contact with members of the prison gang known as the Aryan Brotherhood?"

"Quite often, yes."

"Why did you use the words 'quite often'?"

"The Aryan Brotherhood were a constant problem at the prison, as they were and continue to be at most federal facilities."

"Could you please tell the jury why the Aryan Brotherhood were a problem?"

"Because of their proclivity for violence," said Coombs. "The Aryan Brotherhood's goal was to control the inmate population. To do that, they employed terrorist tactics. They were the most violent monsters I had ever seen."

The prosecutor nodded. "In 1983, at Leavenworth, do you recall the murder of Richard Andreasen, whose nickname was Rhino?"

"Yes, distinctly. I witnessed it," replied Coombs.

"Would you please tell the jury what you witnessed?"

"I saw two inmates with twelve-inch knives attack and repeatedly stab Mr. Andreasen. They would thrust these knives not only into his body, but all the way through his body. They were hitting the concrete underneath his body with the knives. I tried to intervene and stop it. One of the murderers attacked me and tried to stab me."

"Can you identify the two inmates with the knives?"

"Greshner and Criswell," said Coombs emphatically. "John Greshner and Ronnie Joe Criswell. Both of whom were members of the Aryan Brotherhood."

"What happened then?" asked Sherry Sikes.

"A response team of prison guards arrived and subdued the two inmates with the knives." Coombs paused, then looked at the jury. "After being subdued, Greshner was licking the blood off his hands and laughing about it."

The jurors stared at Coombs, and then their eyes glanced across the courtroom to where Barry 'the Baron' Mills and Tyler 'the Hulk' Bingham sat like two stones in a garden.

"No further questions," the prosecutor told Judge Baxter.

The defense attorneys were whispering to one another. "Any cross-examination?" asked the judge.

"Not at this time," replied Montgomery.

THE PEOPLE called Al Benton, who was the government's star witness.

Albert 'Skinny' Benton was anything but skinny. Large and meaty, Skinny stood three inches over six feet. His skin had a moist sheen to it, as if he was too warm all the time. A long-time, zealous member of the Aryan Brotherhood—and the Brand to prove it—Skinny had decided to roll over on his fellow warriors. His reason was simple. He wanted out of prison. He was sick and tired of being locked in a forty-eight-square-foot cement box day after day. And snitching was the only way it would ever happen.

Convicted of a double murder, Skinny was down for sixty-three years. Which meant the rest of his life. He'd never get out alive. But if he testified, things would change. In exchange for his testimony, Skinny would be allowed to plead guilty to assault instead of getting hit with a third murder charge. Additionally, Skinny's sentence of sixty-three years would be reduced to nine years. He'd be out in no time at all.

When Skinny had first heard the terms of the deal, he thought about it for about three seconds, then said, "Okay. Ya'll wrap it up, I'll take it."

Albert 'Skinny' Benton came from Arkansas, which some people thought explained everything. Many imagined Arkansas was populated with nothing but inbred, no-account white trash who lived in trailer parks. Albert wasn't inbred, but he fitted the bill on the other two items.

Albert's father, George, was a violent alcoholic. The more George drank the meaner he got. And because he drank, George couldn't hold a job, which made him drink even more. His wife, Henny, hated George with a passion that burned white hot. A holy hatred. But she was a strict Lutheran and wouldn't divorce him.

Henny owned a small, corner grocery store that sold cheap, fattening food, beer, cigarettes, and dirty magazines. The way Henny saw it was that most people were destined for Hell anyway, so she sold them what they longed for and eventually purchased a mobile home on two acres just outside of town. She wanted to protect her small boys—Albert and George Jr.—from the influence of sin and ungodliness. Albert only left the trailer to attend school, then he had to come right home. He wasn't allowed any friends over, and was warned against "riffraff and scum." He spent most of his time in his small room, reading or carrying on imaginary conversations with imaginary friends.

Henny demanded perfection from her two boys. She preached daily sermons to them about the depravity of the world and the evil of the devil's brew, alcohol. All women, according to Henny, were prostitutes sent by the devil to tempt men into sin. Henny excluded herself, of course. To counteract these evils, Henny read the Bible to her sons for two hours every afternoon. She chose explicit passages from the Old Testament to drive her point home. Passages that spoke of the evil in men's hearts, murder, divine punishment and the final judgment of the Great White Throne.

Albert was a "late bloomer" and didn't start to grow until he was a teenager. Which meant that as a child Albert was small and prissy, and bullies picked on him, calling him "Nancy boy" and "Sweet stuff." Albert tried to defend himself, but he was a lousy fighter and got beat up on a regular basis. Arriving home bloody and bruised, Henny warned him of the result of his sinful ways. "The sign of Cain is upon you," she told Albert. "You're destined for Hell and the wrath of God, just like your father."

Albert believed her.

George Benton died of a heart attack when Albert was a senior in high school. That's what the doctor said it was, a massive heart attack. But Albert knew it was the alcohol and divine justice from God.

By that time, Albert and his brother, George, Jr., were powerful young men. They had part-time jobs and Albert pumped iron every afternoon at a local gym. His body bulged with muscles and energy flowed through him like electricity through a wire.

George Jr. rebelled against his mother. He thought she was crazy, telling Albert she "was a Jesus freak. Always thumping her Bible and screaming about backsliding and going to Hell."

Albert couldn't believe it. "Hey, ya'll don't be talking about your own mother like that," he told his brother.

George scowled. "The fuck ya say? Don't be telling me what to do, Mama's Boy. I'll kick your sorry ass for ya."

The two brothers glared at each other.

A few weeks later, Albert came home from the gym. He asked his mother where George was. Henny didn't know. "He'll be home soon, I'm sure," she said.

The next morning, Albert informed the police his brother was missing. George was discovered dead in a ditch. There were no signs of a struggle and no marks on the body, but the autopsy revealed he had died of a broken neck.

There was a police investigation, but no arrests were made. George was buried at the local cemetery, the Lutheran priest presiding, and life went on. Albert lived with Henny, until she died of cancer, and then alone in the mobile home, working part-time in construction. He began reading goth and extreme metal zines and also white supremacist literature, which warned against "the rising tide of color in the white world. An ocean of color that will one day wash away our white way of life."

Albert Benton became a suspect in the murder of Jackson Johns, an African-American who worked at a local factory. The police found the decapitated body of Johns buried behind Benton's mobile home. The dead man's ribcage had been split and the heart cut out. The cause of death was two .45 caliber bullets to the back of the head.

Armed with a search warrant, the police entered Albert's trailer to find one ten-inch bowie knife, which was bloody, a .45 semi-automatic pistol and five boxes of ammunition for the pistol.

Albert was arrested and tossed into jail. The pistol was discovered to have been stolen from a gun shop in Florida, which resulted in the FBI taking an interest. Albert escaped while being transported from jail to the courthouse, overpowering two FBI agents and taking one of their guns with him. He needed money to get out of town and out of Arkansas, and used the gun—a 9mm Glock—to rob the Bank of America. A loan officer tried to intervene and Albert broke the man's neck, killing him.

The police showed up and were forced to wound Albert before they could arrest him.

At his trial, Albert was convicted on two counts of first-degree murder. Albert's attorney, who was a smooth-talker, persuaded the jury of "mitigating circumstances. And that Albert Benton does not deserve the death penalty."

Mitigating circumstances was a euphemism for the fact Albert's mother had been a nutcase and had pretty much raised her sons to be nutcases, too. Two psychiatrists testified that it wasn't really Albert's fault, but rather Henny's fault he had killed two men and robbed a bank. The jury couldn't agree whose fault it was. They found Albert guilty, but not guilty enough to condemn him to death.

The judge sentenced Albert to sixty-three years in federal prison. He was taken to USP Lewisburg, where he was welcomed by the Aryan Brotherhood with open arms. Within a few months, Albert was branded: a green shamrock on his hand and 666 on his shoulder. The mark of the Beast—666—the enemy of God in the Bible.

Albert's fellow warriors christened him 'Skinny.' Being part of the Aryan Brotherhood was almost like being a Lutheran. Failure to adhere to its strict commandments resulted in quick punishment, which was usually death.

Albert felt at home. He loved prison.

AS AL 'SKINNY' BENTON was escorted to the witness stand, the defense attorneys for Barry 'the Baron' Mills and Tyler 'the Hulk' Bingham believed the courtroom battle was going their way. They had discussed it the night before. Mark Montgomery summed it up when he told Frank Sansoni, "In order for the government to prevail, the Bureau of Prisons is going to have to concede that they were incompetent and screwed up. That's an enormous problem in the prosecution's camp right now. They don't want to admit that they couldn't control the people they were supposed to be controlling."

Sansoni nodded his agreement. "You're right," he said. "And don't forget that we've been able to discredit almost every single one of their witnesses."

"Yeah," smiled Montgomery. "We'll keep the pressure on. Sooner or later it will implode."

ACROSS THE WAY, at the prosecutor's table, the US Assistant Attorneys were feeling equally confident. Warden Coombs' testimony had been especially gratifying. Another nail pounded into the coffin. That the witness for the government was about to question Al 'Skinny' Benton should hammer in a few more nails, making it pretty much airtight.

There was one other big gun in the government's arsenal of weapons: the language of the RICO statute. RICO was written in such a way that the beauty of its subtlety almost blinded anyone who read it. The subtlety was this: once a plot was proven, conspiracy law required that the conspirators show there was no crime. In other words, the prosecutors only had to prove that the Baron and the Hulk had plotted to have inmates murdered—they did not have to prove who the murderers were. Just proof of the plot would do the trick, and the trick was the death penalty for Barry Mills and Tyler Bingham.

The burden was now on the defense attorneys, Sansoni and Montgomery, who had to prove there was no plot and no murders. If they couldn't show that, the Baron and the Hulk were peering down the long, dark tunnel of death.

SHERRY SIKES stood and walked toward the witness. In the docket, under the shadow of black-clad marshals, sat Barry 'the Baron' Mills and Tyler 'the Hulk' Bingham. The Baron wore his cheap, black sunglasses, which gave him the appearance of a venomous spider.

Taking a last glance at her notes, the prosecutor began.

"Mr. Benton, are you currently incarcerated?"

"Yes."

"And for the purpose of clarification, are you a member of the Aryan Brotherhood?"

"Not no more," replied Al 'Skinny' Benton.

"But you were a member of the Aryan Brotherhood, were you not?"

"Yes."

"Were you a member of the Aryan Brotherhood in 1997?"

"Yes."

"And at that time—1997—you were incarcerated in the federal penitentiary in Lewisburg, Pennsylvania?"

"Yes."

"Mr. Benton, please think back. In 1997, at Lewisburg prison, did a conflict occur between members of the Aryan Brotherhood and the DC Blacks?"

"Yes."

"And did you participate in the 1997 conflict?"

"Yes."

"Could you please tell the jury about your part in the 1997 conflict?"

"It was a race war," drawled Skinny, looking at the jury. "The Baron and the Hulk sent me a message. The message told me to go to war on the DC Blacks."

THE MESSAGE was a letter from Barry Mills, deep in the bowels of ADX Florence, to Al Benton, who was at USP Lewisburg. Barry Mills wrote the letter after he had conferred with the Hulk and the two men agreed something needed to be done. "The Rock needed to be polished"—which meant that the green shamrock brand of the Aryan Brotherhood was to make itself known and in a very striking way.

The DC Blacks had already made a move at USP Marion, where they had brutally attacked members of the Aryan Brotherhood. A bold challenge to the supremacy of the AB in the federal prison system. If the challenge were not immediately squashed, the Aryan Brotherhood's lofty position in the prison ranks would be at risk. The DC Blacks would take over, and that meant a massive loss of revenue for the Aryan Brotherhood, along with disrespect, which was even worse. Drugs, prostitution, alcohol, gambling, protection and contract murder, were controlled throughout the federal prison system by the Aryan Brotherhood and that was a revenue of millions of dollars. No one could put a dollar figure on how much the loss of respect was worth. In prison, respect was the Holy Grail.

So, Barry Mills wrote a letter to Skinny Benton. Part of it was written in pencil to avoid any suspicion among the Feds, who read and copied every letter that every inmate mailed and received at ADX Florence. Mills wrote about family news, what he was reading, and talked about his new hobby—crochet—which was a good way to ease his boredom. He suggested that Skinny give it a try. In other words, the letter was full of junk. If the Feds knew that a hit had been ordered on the DC Blacks, by law the Feds were obliged to warn the DC Blacks. On top of which they would cut off the Baron's mail privileges and file attempted murder charges against him.

The other part of the letter was the important part, and related to "taking care of business." Mills wrote this part in his urine, making it invisible to the naked eye. The Feds wouldn't know it was there, but should they discover the ruse, they wouldn't be able to make head or tail of it because Mills wrote in code. The code Mills used was a bilateral cipher that used two different alphabets, a code within a code that couldn't be deciphered without the key.

Barry Mills had read about the code in a biography he'd gotten in the prison library of Sir Francis Bacon, the seventeenth-century father of empiricism. Mills had insisted that all the shotcallers in the Aryan Brotherhood memorize the key to the code. That way, all they had to do when they received his letters was apply heat, using a small flame from a match, and read the letter. Then, of course, carry out his instructions.

Mills' letter to Skinny Benton ordered Skinny and his warriors to "wage all out war" on the DC Blacks at Lewisburg. Skinny smiled as he read the letter. This would be fun. The DC Blacks were about to meet the Grim Reaper.

Skinny gathered the Brotherhood in the main yard at Lewisburg. The other inmates knew something was up when they saw the Brand congregating. It looked like a church service for white monsters with tattoos and shaved heads.

"I need some warriors ta be steppin' up and take care a business," announced Skinny in his deep-fried drawl.

The congregation nodded as if in Amen.

"Two days from now"—Skinny held up two fingers—"we hit DC hard." He smacked his fist into his other palm. "At the same perzact time in what ya'll call your organynized attack. The time'll be two o'clock. Most'll be on the yard catching some rays, some'll be in their cells, some'll be in the showers. Ya'll pick where ya'll want to hit 'em. The when is two o'clock." Skinny looked around. "Ya'll got it?"

The congregation nodded. Wicked grins appeared beneath lush mustaches. In two days there would be a blood sacrifice.

On August 28, 1997, at two o'clock in the afternoon, Lewisburg prison was awash with blood. It happened like this:

Four DC Blacks laughed and lathered themselves in the showers. Except for shower thongs, they were naked and unarmed. Their shanks were with their clothes about twenty feet away, which wasn't real smart, but who was gonna jump four bad-ass DC Blacks? No one in their right mind would do that, unless they wanted to commit suicide.

Eight ghosts with shaved heads filtered into the shower, each armed with a knife. Without pause or hesitation, the ghosts attacked. Tattooed arms flicked in and out like bullwhips, stabbing, cutting, slicing. Blood flowed into the water. Heaving grunts and muffled curses filled the steamy air, as ferocious animals, some white, some black, struggled to butcher each other.

Three minutes later, it was over. Four DC Blacks sprawled on the shower floor, their blood gurgling down the drain. Eight ghosts, panting from their exertions, glanced at each other. The lust for more blood, more action, was upon them.

"Okay," said one of the ghosts. "Let's go. An' when you hit the yard, remember, spread out an' act normal."

The ghosts filtered out. The four DC Blacks, under the steady stream of the showers, didn't die, but they spent a long time in the prison hospital. When they finally got out of the hospital, scars decorated their bodies like lights on a Christmas tree.

Over in the northwest corner of the yard, Skinny Benton was carving up Abdul Salaam. A shotcaller for the DC Blacks, Salaam was a stone-cold killer. Only this time he wasn't doing the killing, he was being killed. Skinny counted as he sledge-hammered his knife into the black man's body. *Thirty-three, thirty-four, thirty-five.* Skinny stopped and looked at Salaam, who appeared dead. Covered in blood, Skinny turned and walked away as if he'd just finished a game of cards.

Inside the prison, on the second-tier of A-wing, DC Black Frank Joyner lay on his bunk in his cell. He was awash in his own blood. Two Aryan Brotherhood members stood gazing down at what—five minutes ago—had been a man. Now it was a bloody piece of meat.

One of the two white inmates pulled a blanket over Joyner, which made it look as if he was taking a nap.

As they walked away, the two men discussed the Phillies. They were both baseball fans and were worried about the Phillies' chances of making the playoffs.

The Medical Examiner determined that Frank Joyner had died of thirty-four stab wounds. Salaam Abdul had died of thirty-five stab wounds.

The Aryan Brotherhood had taken care of business. Blood in, blood out.

SHERRY SIKES looked at the jury, checking their reaction to Al 'Skinny' Benton's testimony. Some of the jurors looked pale, others looked half-dazed, as if they couldn't believe what they'd just heard.

"So, Mr. Benton," asked the prosecutor. "You admit that you stabbed Salaam Abdul to death?"

"Yes," answered Skinny Benton. It was part of his deal. He had to tell the truth.

"And you killed Mr. Abdul at the direct and express order of Barry Mills and Tyler Bingham?"

Skinny sniffed and looked right at the woman. "Yes."

The prosecutor glanced at her notes. "Mr. Benton, have you ever heard of John Marzloff?"

Skinny glanced over to where Barry Mills and Tyler Bingham sat. "Yes."

Sherry Sikes looked down at the floor, then raised her eyes slowly to Skinny. "In 1979, did Barry Mills murder John Marzloff?" She waited patiently for Skinny's answer and the inevitable explosive cry.

The explosion took place first. "I object!" erupted Mark Montgomery, jumping to his feet. "The question is irrelevant and prejudicial."

"How's that?" asked Judge Baxter.

"Mr. Mills is not on trial for the murder of John Marzloff—that's the irrelevancy. And the question is prejudicial because it implies that Mr. Mills is capable of murder," explained Montgomery.

Judge Baxter looked at Sherry Sikes.

"Your Honor," said Sikes, "I am in no way *implying* Mr. Mills is a murderer. He is a murderer. He has already been tried for the murder of John Marzloff. Of which he was convicted and for which he is serving a life sentence."

Mark Montgomery's face was black with anger. "Your Honor, that is irrelevant to the present indictment. And is prejudicial!" protested Montgomery.

Judge Baxter nodded. "I believe Mr. Montgomery is right." He looked at the prosecutor. "Where are you going with this?"

"I'm trying to demonstrate the chain-of-command in the Aryan Brotherhood. Murder occurs on command, which means the person giving the command is ultimately responsible."

Judge Baxter blinked. "Interesting," he said. "And I see your intent, but it's prejudicial. So I'm going to sustain." He looked at the jury. "Ladies and gentlemen, you will disregard the question about John Marzloff's murder."

Sherry Sikes knew the jury would not disregard the question. That was why she asked it. She wanted to plant the seed in the juror's mind. Montgomery knew it too. That's why he was so angry. Once the question was asked, there was no way to take it back or ensure the jury disregarded it.

Skinny thought it was all bullshit. All this yammering and hammering over what was fittin' and what wasn't. He'd agreed to tell the truth as part of his deal. So that's what he was doing. But he also knew which side his bread was buttered, and wasn't afraid to fancy it up a little, put bells and whistles and silver-streamers on it.

The prosecutor decided on an indirect approach. Perhaps she could make her point and avoid the prejudicial aspects. "Mr. Benton, I'm not going to ask you who murdered Mr. Marzloff. What I am going to ask you is this: Was an order given to kill Mr. Marzloff?"

"Yes."

"And this order was given in 1979?"

"Yes."

"Did the order come from a member of the Aryan Brotherhood?"

"Yeah, Terrible Tom," replied Skinny.

Sherry Sikes nodded. "Just to be clear—you're saying that Thomas Silverstein gave the order to have John Marzloff murdered."

"Yes."

Peering at Skinny from the corner of her eyes, Sikes asked, "And do you know why Thomas Silverstein gave the order to kill John Marzloff?"

"Yeah. Johnny owed Terrible Tom money. For some drugs. Johnny was tryin' ta rip off Terrible Tom." Skinny shrugged. "Tha' don't happen. So Tom reached out and took care a bidness."

"One more question, Mr. Benton," said Sikes. "At the time he gave the order in 1979, was Thomas Silverstein what is known as a Commissioner in the Aryan Brotherhood?"

"Yes."

Nodding, Sherry Sikes turned to the jury. "It is evident that Commissioners"—she pointed to Barry Mills and Tyler Bingham—"decide who lives and who dies."

As the prosecutor walked back to her chair, Mark Montgomery was already beginning his cross-examination.

"Mr. Benton, you already told the court that you were incarcerated, right?" asked Montgomery.

"Yes."

"Why?"

"Huh?" asked Skinny, leaning forward.

"What crime did you commit that resulted in your imprisonment?"

"Murder," replied Skinny, looking around.

"And how long were you sentenced to prison for the murder you committed?" asked Montgomery.

Skinny licked his lips. "Sixty-three years."

"Yet it's my understanding that you will only serve nine years out of the sixty-three? Is that right?"

"Yes."

"And why is that?"

Skinny squinted at the attorney, who smiled.

"Isn't it because you agreed to testify against Mr. Mills and Mr. Bingham? And if you did testify, then your sentence would be reduced?" asked Mr. Montgomery.

Skinny shrugged. "Yeah."

"Mmmh," nodded Montgomery with pursed lips. "So, in effect, Mr. Benton, you would agree to say anything—anything at all—if it was in your interest?"

"No," protested Skinny, shaking his head. "I said—"

Montgomery cut him off. "Is it not true, then, that your testimony has been bought and paid for? And that you will say what they paid you to say?" asked Montgomery, dipping each of his words in sanctimony.

"No," disagreed Skinny. "Tha's a lie."

Montgomery gave a scoffing laugh. "*Lying* is what you are doing. It's what they paid you to do."

Skinny glared at the attorney. If things was different, Skinny would put some hurt on this guy. And he'd enjoy doing it.

Montgomery walked back to his seat. Up in the docket, the Baron sat hidden behind his sunglasses, remembering John Sherman Marzloff.

1979

TERRIBLE TOM sealed the letter, knowing full well that the Feds in the mailroom would open it, read it and make a copy of it. Then they'd re-seal it and send the letter on its way. Addressed to a female friend of Terrible Tom's, the letter seemed to be harmless enough, speaking of his boredom and depression, which he blamed on his circumstances—incarceration. Terrible Tom maintained that everything he had done in prison was pure self-defense, a Darwinian survival of the fittest. Which meant the Bureau of Prisons was responsible for his crimes, not Terrible Tom.

The letter was meant to be read between the lines. Remarks about family members were instructions to members of the Aryan Brotherhood. And the inquiry about a nephew's health was not a concerned uncle's expression of worry, for there was no nephew named Johnny. It was, in fact, a death sentence, an order to kill. Little Johnny was John Sherman Marzloff, who had screwed Terrible Tom on a drug deal, and Terrible Tom wanted Little Johnny dead and buried.

In other words, the letter was a murder contract, one put out by Terrible Tom on John Marzloff, an associate of the Aryan Brotherhood. Associates were fawning flunkies, sometimes called 'peckerwoods'— they wanted to be members of the Aryan Brotherhood, but hadn't yet made the grade; they hung around doing odd jobs for the shotcallers, hoping some of the prestige would rub off on them. They were the pilot fish that tagged along with sharks, feeding off the table scraps of the big boys.

Marzloff, the bottom-feeder, had started thinking he was a shark. The punk-ass bitch owed Terrible Tom money and he didn't want to pay up. Marzloff had forgotten one thing. "If you want to kick the big fish in his ass, you'd better have a plan for dealing with his teeth."

The instructions in Tom's letter would be made known to Barry Mills, in USP Atlanta, where Marzloff was incarcerated. Mills would get a visit in the near future, probably from the wife or girlfriend of another Aryan Brotherhood member. She would stroll into the visiting room, give Barry a big hug and whisper, "Tom wants Marzloff hit," and then spend the next hour prattling on about domestic nonsense, like the price of groceries, car pools, the latest celebrity gossip, and children. Barry, nodding and smiling, would be planning the hit.

On May 29, 1979, John Sherman Marzloff was in the recreation shack at USP Atlanta. He was playing ping-pong with another inmate and was losing. Muscular from pumping iron every day, Marzloff passed himself off as a member of the Aryan Brotherhood, because he wanted other inmates to think he was bad, that he was someone to fear. He shaved his head, wore a walrus mustache and paraded Nazi tattoos. Of course, he never came right out and said he was an Aryan Brother, and he didn't have a shamrock or AB tattoo. The Aryan Brotherhood would kill him for that. But he never passed up an opportunity to drop some names and hint at dark secrets and fateful deeds.

No one knew much about Marzloff, except that he was a tweeker, using and selling drugs in prison—heroin, cocaine, marijuana and speed. He was in USP Atlanta for a series of small-time bank robberies, none of which garnered any real money. All were unarmed, which meant he was pretty much playing at being a criminal. Real criminals used guns. In prison, Marzloff was a fast-talking white boy, who wasn't part of any gang, who wanted to be part of something big, like the Aryan Brotherhood, but didn't have the necessary fat-headed personality or big enough balls to hack it. In reality, he was a nice guy, who wanted attention, who was easily led and eager to please, who made some stupid mistakes, and got tossed into federal prison, where he acted tough to survive. Prison, and the beasts that lived in it, was a lot more than Marzloff had bargained for.

NOT TOO LONG AGO, an Aryan Brotherhood member named Lucifer approached Marzloff with a business proposition. Terrible Tom, in USP Marion, had a lot of speed he wanted to move. He needed 'cut-outs' to distribute the speed to inmates in the various federal prisons, and to handle the money from the ventures. No selling was involved, because the speed had all been pre-sold. It was an easy deal with guaranteed profit for everybody. Terrible Tom got eighty percent and the cut-outs got twenty percent. Once the cut-outs took their cut of the profits, they were out. They had no other obligations.

Did Marzloff want to be the cut-out at Atlanta prison? That's what Lucifer wanted to know.

Marzloff didn't even have to think about it. It was easy money with little risk. More importantly for him, it was a chance to hang with the Aryan Brotherhood, to be an 'associate.' Once everyone heard who he was working for, Marzloff would be walking on water.

"Sure," replied Marzloff, trying to sound like it was no big deal.

"Okay," said Lucifer, nodding his shaved head. "The first delivery should be tomorrow. I'll get it to you." He turned and walked away.

"Sure," Marzloff called to Lucifer's receding bulk. "Whenever, man."

THE VISITING AREA at USP Atlanta looked like a Wyatt's cafeteria without the buffet line and without the food: Round tables and chairs in the middle of a big concrete building. All visitors were required to walk through metal detectors, but they were spared the indignity and humiliation of body cavity searches. Guards stood inside and outside the room, keeping an eye on things, in particular any undue physical contact, which was anything more than a brief hug and a brief kiss. Long hugs and deep-throat kisses usually meant contraband was being transferred. Inmates with visiting privileges were entitled to one kiss and one hug, both of which needed to be very spiritual in nature.

Lucifer's girlfriend, a biker-mama dressed in black leather pants and a halter top, had driven to USP Atlanta from the Atlanta airport, where she had picked up a package from a Nazi Low Rider member on a Fat Boy Harley. She gave Lucifer a spiritual kiss on the lips. Like a snake, her tongue darted into his mouth and delivered a condom, which was full of speed.

Lucifer swallowed the condom immediately. After an hour visit, the biker babe left and a guard led Lucifer to a holding cell where another guard told him to strip. The guard examined Lucifer's clothes, feeling them carefully. Then he had Lucifer bend over and spread his buttocks. "Cough three times," said the guard. Lucifer coughed.

"Okay," commanded the guard, "now gimme three full squats." Lucifer squatted. The guard tossed him his clothes.

Forty-eight hours later, Lucifer was escorted to the Medical Unit, where a technician collected a urinary sample. If the sample contained any trace of drugs, Lucifer would be charged with a felony. Lucifer didn't use drugs, he was too smart for that. And he had already pooped out the condom, which he had delivered to Marzloff, who processed the speed into ready-made packets called 'dimes,' made from simple writing paper.

Now came the risky part of the operation: The delivery of the goods to the buyers. For a brief period of time—maybe an hour—Marzloff would have the drugs on his person. If searched by a guard, the drugs would be discovered, and he would face felony charges. Of course, the odds were in his favor, because it was highly doubtful that the guards would pick him out of thousands of inmates to hassle, but stranger things had happened.

Marzloff put the dime packets of speed in his pockets and headed out to take care of business. To anyone watching, Marzloff appeared to be doing nothing more than walking around chatting with other inmates. Occasionally he stopped for a longer conversation, which included the ritual inmate handshake called "banging rocks"—knuckled fist against knuckled fist—a lot of trash-talk and a lot of dramatic gestures, because convicts communicated as much by body language as by speech. Marzloff knew a lot of inmates who were happy to see him. In fact, they were so happy to see him they often gave him a brief inmate hug. This routine was repeated over and over as Marzloff, the delivery boy, made his way around the main yard, connecting socially and networking with his friends and acquaintances, all of whom were white.

In prison, nothing is free, especially drugs. A dime packet of speed would go for $200, which was highway robbery. But with only one freeway, in order to travel you had to pay the toll. Once the delivery was made, the recipient had a week to pay. Payment went like this: The inmate-buyer would contact someone on the outside, usually a family member, but it didn't really matter. This outside person would take the required amount—cash only—and deliver it to Marzloff's banker, who was a trusted friend on the outside. The banker would either hold the money for Marzloff or deposit the cash in a local bank, usually a Bank of America. If the banker held the money, he would put it in a shoebox in his closet.

When Terrible Tom wanted his money, he would send his banker to pick it up. More often than not, Terrible Tom's banker was a half-dozen Nazi Low Riders on $50,000 customized motorcycles. Nazi Low Riders, being a very brand-conscious bunch, preferred either Harley Davidson or Arlen Ness for their transportation needs. Style-conscious too, they wore white T-shirts with swastikas and the words White Power silkscreened prominently. They'd arrange to meet Marzloff's banker at McDonald's or Big Boys, where a briefcase full of hundred dollar bills would change hands. The Nazi Low Riders never bothered to count the money. They never even opened the briefcase. One of them would simply strap it to his bike and they'd roar off.

No one was stupid enough to rip off Terrible Tom.

Except John Sherman Marzloff and his banker. They decided that their efforts and their risks were worth a thirty percent cut rather than the usual twenty percent, and so the banker began holding back. When he handed the briefcase to the Nazi Low Riders, it was what swindlers called 'lite.' Marzloff and his banker were cheating a psychosocial killer. No one seemed to notice, much less care, so Marzloff and the banker kept it up. They figured no one knew exactly how much speed was smuggled into the prison, how much was sold, or how much money should be in the briefcase.

Except Terrible Tom. He knew that ten percent of $200,000 a month was a lot of money, and that's how much was missing from USP Atlanta every month.

Terrible Tom didn't get angry. He just shrugged and sent a message by means of his courier to the Baron. When the Baron got the message, he didn't waste any time. He needed a back-up man, because two against one was always better. It prevented nasty accidents from happening, such as Marzloff getting in a lucky punch. Good luck came to those who didn't leave room for bad luck. A back-up man would also provide an alibi, or someone to take the fall, if necessary. The Baron would never snitch on an Aryan Brother, but he could arrange it so someone else did.

The Baron selected Danny Holliday as his back-up. Holliday was a member of the Aryan Brotherhood, who had proven himself in hand-to-hand combat.

"Get a shiv, and meet me tomorrow after noon chow," the Baron told Holliday. "We have some AB business to take care of."

Holliday understood. They were going to hit someone. It didn't matter who or why—it was AB business. That was enough for Holliday.

On May 20, 1979, John Marzloff was playing ping-pong in the recreation shack, and he was losing. He needed a break.

Marzloff raised his hand. "Hold up, dog," he told his opponent. "I gotta take a leak." Placing his paddle down on the table he walked to the men's room. After emptying his bladder, he lathered his hands with blue institutional liquid soap and bent over the sink to rinse them.

He was prevented from turning to see who had walked in the bathroom by a Herculean arm that slithered around his neck, jerking his head back. Agony bloomed in his head and spinal column. His head was slammed forward into the cement wall. Pain was everywhere. Deep, lancing, burning pain.

Marzloff looked down at his hands, which were on the sink, where the blue soap had turned red and oily. "Something smells," he mumbled through the blinding pain.

A deep voice laughed. "It's the smell of death, asshole," said the Baron. The Baron slashed at Marzloff's neck, the shank licking deep into the corded muscles of the neck, slicing through arteries and nerves into the larynx and trachea.

Holliday stabbed his shiv into Marzloff's back and shoulder. Each thrust burped a wet bubble of blood. Marzloff's shirt turned red and stuck to his torso like a second layer of skin. Holliday's hands were so slick with blood he could barely hang on to his shiv.

Raw, thumping energy bloated the room, as if sharks, smelling blood, thrashed and foamed to get at the red nectar of life.

Everything stopped. The Baron released his grip on Marzloff's neck, in which a gash had opened with a sickly grin. Danny Holliday dropped to his knees, panting to catch his breath. Killing someone was exhausting work, like running a mile at an all out sprint.

But death took less time than running a mile and John Marzloff was dead in three minutes.

As Marzloff's body sagged to the floor, the Baron was already moving on to the next step. He tossed his shank into the toilet bowl, and hit the flush button. The toilet flushed and began to re-fill. The shank was still there. It was too big to go down. The Baron shrugged. There was nothing he could do about it, so he moved on to the next step.

"Give me your shiv," said the Baron, looking at Holliday.

"What?" asked Holliday, confused.

"Your shiv," commanded the Baron, holding out his hand.

Holliday handed it to him.

The Baron bent over Marzloff's body and lifted one of the dead arms up. Placing Holliday's shiv under the armpit he dropped the arm. The idea behind the planted shank was to make it look like Marzloff had a weapon and jumped the Baron, who defended himself from the vicious attack. Holliday would back up the story. In other words, the Baron was hoping he could plead self-defense. That was the best he could hope for. Sooner or later, the evil deed would be traced back to him. If it looked like self-defense, things would go a lot easier.

Danny Holliday glanced at Marzloff's body. The sight made him retch. Spitting the bile out of his mouth, Holliday looked again. Fuckin' A, man! The guy's head was almost off. Hanging by a shred of skin. Holliday turned and gazed at the Baron with eerie awe.

"You almost decapitated him," announced Holliday.

The Baron glanced at his handiwork. He felt nothing. He didn't even shrug. It was just taking care of business.

"Let's go," said the Baron. "Get back to your cell, shower and get some clean clothes on. Be sure you get rid of anything with blood on it, including your shoes." He pointed at Holliday's shoes, which were spattered with drying blood.

Holliday nodded and the two men hurried off.

MARZLOFF'S PING-PONG opponent saw the Baron and Holliday leave. He saw their blood-covered clothes. He knew what it meant. He knew what he would see if he looked in the men's room. He didn't want to get involved with the Baron, the Aryan Brotherhood or any murder. He didn't want his name in any hat. So he left and got amnesia.

Within the hour, Marzloff's body was discovered and reported to a passing guard, who called it in. USP Atlanta was locked down while the body was removed and an investigation began. Too many inmates with too much to gain had seen the blood-soaked Barry Mills and Danny Holliday leave the recreation shack and walk across the yard. All the snitches—having received certain assurances from the Feds—like sentence reductions—sang the same melody: "Barry did it."

Barry Mills was charged with first-degree murder. So was Danny Holliday, but Danny Holliday's conscience was bothering him. He couldn't get the picture of Marzloff's hacked-off head out of his head, and was having bad dreams, waking up screaming and covered in sweat. To make the nightmares vanish, Holliday agreed to testify against the Baron, on the condition the Feds would guarantee immunity and protection. This meant a transfer to a minimum-security prison, where no Aryan Brotherhood members or any of their sympathizers, especially no Nazi Low Rider robots or any other peckerwood gangs, could reach him.

As the only eyewitness to the murder of John Marzloff, the Feds gave Holliday the okay.

At the trial, all the snitches testified that they had seen Barry Mills in or near the recreation shack at the time of the murder. It was circumstantial, of course, but what with Mills' blood-drenched clothes it was pretty damning.

"What circumstances caused Barry Mills to be wearing blood-soaked clothing?" asked the prosecutor.

Danny Holliday told the jury that he had gone to the recreation shack with Barry Mills. That he did have a knife, as did Mills. "But I thought we were just going to rob the guy," explained Holliday. "That's what Barry told me. So I was pretty surprised when Barry jumped the guy and jammed him up."

"So you didn't participate in the murder of John Marzloff?" asked the prosecutor.

"No, sir. I had no part in it," replied Holliday.

Barry Mills took the witness stand, which was highly unusual. Most experts agreed that the testimony of accused murderers did more damage than repair. But in this case, it was necessary, because there was nothing else for the defense to play on. Either the Baron took the stand or he got shot down in flames.

Barry Mills told the jury he was innocent. More than that, he was being set up as the fall guy by the real murderer.

"And who might that be?" asked the prosecutor.

"Robert Lee Hogan," declared Mills.

Robert Lee Hogan had, in fact, confessed to the murder of John Marzloff. Over the years, Hogan had confessed to many murders, most of which were unconfirmed. In fact, Hogan would confess to any murder he heard about. The psychiatrists called him "psychopathologic."

Robert Lee Hogan lived in a fantasy world of his own making, a world of sexual oddity in which he copulated with valkyries from Norse legend and fifty-foot tall Amazon women from Mars. In this dream world, Hogan was a blond-haired, blue-eyed, muscular Thor, invincible and "simply irresistible." When members of the Aryan Brotherhood had suggested to Hogan that he had indeed slain John Marzloff, Hogan readily agreed.

Robert Lee Hogan took the witness stand and told the jury he murdered John Marzloff, giving a detailed description of the whole thing.

Hogan's story of the murderous act was right out of his sick fantasy, and the prosecutor pointed out all the lies to the jury, making sure they knew what a nutcase Hogan really was. The jurors didn't believe Hogan, but they found him very entertaining.

The attorney for Barry Mills didn't give up. He told the jury that the Aryan Brotherhood no longer existed as a viable group. At one time they had existed, of course. He didn't deny that. The Aryan Brotherhood had originally formed solely to protect white inmates from attacks by other non-white inmates, who were nothing more than rabid gangs. But over the years, as the need for protection had fallen off, the Aryan Brotherhood had drifted into oblivion. The Aryan Brotherhood was nonexistent, a thing of the past.

It sounded pretty convincing, until the prosecutor got up and presented a letter penned by Barry Mills himself and mailed from USP Atlanta. The letter talked about pending activities of the Aryan Brotherhood, such as the laundering of drug money, the movement of drugs by mules, and new members. It hinted at Barry Mills' planning and participation in these illegal activities, and used Aryan Brotherhood slang to describe them. Lingo such as 'mules,' 'cut-outs,' 'red-hots,' and 'white warriors.'

The prosecutor read parts of the letter out loud to the jury, those sections that proved the Aryan Brotherhood was alive and kicking and that Barry Mills was one of the group's shotcallers. It was damning stuff and the jury ate it up. They found Barry Mills guilty of first-degree murder. The judge sentenced Mills to life in prison without parole.

Mills appealed. His appeal claimed that all the evidence should have been declared inadmissible by the court. It was hearsay and/or circumstantial and inferential. The allegation that the Aryan Brotherhood controlled drug trafficking throughout the prison system was not pertinent to the charge of murder. In fact, it was prejudicial. So, too, the allegation of violence. The allegation—presented as a fact at the trial—that Thomas Silverstein had put out a contract on Marzloff was hearsay. There was no proof of a contract, and if there were, it did not imply that Marzloff's death had occurred as a result of the contract. Finally, the letter presented in court and read aloud as factual evidence only proved the prior existence of the Aryan Brotherhood, at best, but did not pertain to the murder of John Marzloff. The letter had no connection to Marzloff's murder, implied or otherwise. In other words, the evidence was all hearsay, second-hand gossip and unconfirmed.

The appeal did not address the almost headless body and sixteen stab wounds in the head, back, shoulder, and upper arm of John Marzloff. Nor did it mention the eyewitness account of Danny Holliday.

The Appellate Court considered the appeal impartially. It was their job to look through the simple eye of the law. Having considered the appeal, they tossed it out. The Court didn't say so, but the judges were darn sure Barry 'the Baron' Mills had murdered John Marzloff. Not just murdered him, but butchered him as if he were a side of beef.

Barry 'the Baron' Mills was an icy killing machine.

FIVE

The Verdict

July 14, 2006

BARRY MILLS SAT quite still in the docket—stone still—the cold blue orbs of his eyes hidden behind black sunglasses. A few feet away, his lips obscured by the white cascade of his extravagant walrus mustache, hunched the pale bulky body of Tyler Bingham. The two killers watched and listened.

The Assistant US Attorney addressed the jury, summing up the government's case. "You have seen the written messages ordering the deaths of at least five inmates. You have seen graphic, bloody photos of the bodies of the five dead men—men murdered by order of Barry Mills and Tyler Bingham. You have heard the sworn testimony of former members of the Aryan Brotherhood. Every one of whom was an eyewitness to the criminal activities of the gang. Each one of these witnesses provided incontrovertible proof that the defendants— Barry Mills and Tyler Bingham—plotted to kill those who crossed the gang.

"The gang—the Aryan Brotherhood—recruited only the most violent inmates at high-security prisons. Inmates who would protect the Aryan Brotherhood at any cost.

"All together, these two men—the defendants, who are seated right in this room—ordered the executions of seventeen men. And probably many, many more.

"They are guilty of racketeering and murder. In the course of this trial, a definite pattern of racketeering has been demonstrated.

Which is all that is necessary for a verdict of guilt. But the evidence presented to you, ladies and gentlemen of the jury, has gone beyond simply proving a pattern. Dozens of witnesses have corroborated and even cross-corroborated every violent act with which the defendants are accused.

"Barry Mills and Tyler Bingham ordered the death of Arva Lee Ray, who was murdered at the Lompoc penitentiary in 1989. Barry Mills and Tyler Bingham ordered the murder of William McKinney, who was killed in 1993. Barry Mills and Tyler Bingham ordered the race war against the DC Blacks at Lewisburg penitentiary in 1997. It was nothing more or less than a war of hate. This war resulted in the murders of Frank Joyner and Abdul Salaam.

"They were paid $500,000 by John Gotti, the infamous Mafia boss, to kill another black inmate. Fortunately, in this instance, their murderous plan was thwarted. But they did order it. They plotted it—the brutal murder of another man, and would have exterminated him if they could have.

"Barry Mills and Tyler Bingham are cold-blooded killers. Both are serving multiple life sentences for murders that they personally committed." The prosecutor paused. Then in a slow, deep voice she added, "They are guilty of conspiracy. The conspiracy to commit murder and... of actually ordering the murders of five men. Men died as the result of those orders. Five men. Five human beings. Killed without a second thought, without a moment's hesitation.

"Saddest of all is why these murders took place. Some died over drug money. Some died for becoming informers. Some died because their skin color didn't happen to be white. But the real reason for their murders is because Barry Mills and Tyler Bingham believe that they have the right—the sovereign right—to dispense life and death." The prosecutor looked at Mills and Bingham, then back at the jury. "In a sense, they think they are gods, who can do as they please. But they're not. They're not even close." She leaned forward a little, as if sharing a secret. "I'll tell you what they are. They're sick, little monsters."

The prosecutor turned and walked away three paces, then came back and faced the jury. "In good conscience, it is up to you to call them to account for these despicable acts of atrocity. It is up to you to point to them and say, 'Enough!' And the only way to do that, to make that statement, is to find them guilty. The verdict is guilty."

The prosecutor stopped, looked straight into the eyes of the jurors, and nodded at them. "It's up to you," she said quietly. Then she walked over to her chair and sat down.

Defense attorney Mark Montgomery stood up, a thoughtful look on his face, and approached the jury. He stopped in front of them, pressing his palms together as if he was about to pray. He balanced his chin on his fingertips and looked down his nose at the jurors. Rudeness was not his intention. Rather, he wanted the jury to believe that his remarks were unprepared, spontaneous and certainly not rehearsed. Of course, everything he was about to say and every gesture he would make was rehearsed. He lowered his hands, gazed at the jury and nodded a few times. As if deciding at last what he had to say, he finally began.

"Ladies and gentlemen," Montgomery said, "as my esteemed colleague just reminded you, you have seen a regular panorama of photographs, called evidence. You have heard from numerous witnesses, all of whom swore they were telling the truth, the whole truth and nothing but the truth."

He looked down at the floor for a few seconds, apparently troubled, and then continued. "With a few exceptions—a very few, I might add—every one of the government's witnesses is nothing more than today's version of a very old character, one we all know of—Judas. Judas sold out for thirty pieces of silver. Blood money! The kind of money that taints everything it touches. Blood money touched the hands of every one of the so-called witnesses you were forced to sit here and listen to. It touched them and corrupted them. So they did something horrible. They became false witnesses."

He paused, showing his profile to the jury. "We all know what that is," he said. "It's in the Bible. It's one of the Ten Commandments.

Thou shalt not bear false witness." Montgomery made the sign of the cross as if by natural impulse.

"A parade of perjurers! A parade of perjurers who were promised thirty pieces of silver and reduced prison sentences for testimony against the alleged ringleaders of a gang that the government refers to as the Aryan Brotherhood. The existence of which cannot be proven!" Montgomery laughed and shook his head. "If this bogeyman gang does exist, I declare to you that it can't be any tougher or meaner than the Old Ladies Aide Society at my church. I mean look at the age of the defendants. They're almost sixty years old, ready to retire— except they're in prison. Where they are perpetually locked in small cells and have little or no human contact. They get two fifteen minute phone calls per month. And yet you're expected to believe that they control some kind of vast criminal empire, a virtual reign of terror. A kind of Murder Incorporated, where death is a phone call away!" He held his hands up, and then shook his head rapidly. "No! There is no way that is remotely believable—not under the circumstances in which these men live. For God's sake!" Montgomery pointed to where the Baron sat. "Barry Mills crochets! Does that sound like the hobby of a cold-blooded murderer? Of course not!

"I urge you to reject the accusations of this parade of perjurers. That's all they are—accusations. Slurs! There is no logical way these accusations can be true. And more than that, there is no proof that the accusations are true. No proof. None at all."

Montgomery paused to let his words sink in. "The government is asking you to place your trust in these thieves and liars to get a conviction. They aren't worthy of your belief. It's insulting.

"The government's entire case is based on the shaky testimony of snitches who have been paid to lie. This stream of so-called witnesses represents nothing more and nothing less than a form of cross-contamination. One of them lies and that lie infects the others, who tell another lie. That lie engenders more lies. And pretty soon, there's a tottering edifice of lies supporting each other. Even the foundation is built of lies. And what happens? Wham!" Montgomery slapped his hands together. "The whole thing collapses into nothing. Because there was nothing there to begin with. Because that's what lies are—nothing.

"All of the government's informants were housed together in the same unit. The H unit of the federal prison in Colorado. Once they were all there, they were given access to the prison's computer, along with privileged and detailed files on all the cases. They all read the same information. Then they got together for brainstorming sessions, where everyone agreed on what lies they would tell and how they would tell them."

Montgomery jabbed a finger at the floor of the courthouse. "Corroboration between two snitches who have access to the same information is hardly corroboration," he stated in a voice laced with sarcasm. "It's like taking a test in school, where everybody has the answers written on their palms. Answers which the teacher gave them!

"It's called cheating in school. If you're caught you get an F. If you're not caught, you get an A+. When you do it in a court of law, it's perjury. If you're caught, it's a felony. If you're not caught, innocent men are convicted of something they didn't do. And innocent men are executed because of the lies."

Montgomery paused, gazing at the jury. Cocking his head to the side, he let his face sag for a moment. "Now it's up to you. That's what the prosecutor told you. That it's up to you. She's right, it is. It's up to you to decide whether you will trust liars, cheats, thieves and convicted murderers. Gangsters who have been paid thirty pieces of silver for their fabrications. Bought and paid for!"

Montgomery raised his arms like a high priest about to bless his congregation. "It's up to you. Will you trust your commonsense? Or will you trust people like Skinny Benton—a government informant, a snitch—with a criminal history worse than those of the defendants?"

The jurors' eyes followed Montgomery as he walked to his chair and sat down.

Judge Baxter spent the next fifteen minutes giving the jury detailed instructions, and then he released them to deliberate. US marshals escorted the twelve jurors to the deliberation room, and stood guard outside while they went about their work.

JURY SELECTION had taken place five months earlier, before the start of the trial. Prospective jurors underwent what was called *voir dire*. In the legal system of the United States, *voir dire* was an oath given to a person who might sit on a jury, and required the person to give true answers to questions about topics that might affect the trial.

For example, a potential juror who didn't believe in the death penalty might affect the outcome of this particular trial, given that the government prosecutors were going after the death penalty.

The prospective jurors were questioned in a room down the hall from the courtroom. Seated at a long table were the defense attorneys and prosecutors, along with Judge Baxter, and a court reporter recording everything that was said.

The court clerk escorted a tall, slender man into the room, who sat down in the only empty chair.

"Good morning," said Judge Baxter. "How are you on this fine spring day?"

"Pretty good," replied the man, glancing around nervously. All the serious-looking attorneys made him tense. He felt like he himself was on trial.

"Ever been on a jury before?" asked Judge Baxter.

"No."

"Why don't you tell us about yourself?"

"I'm a systems analyst for a large insurance company. I'm single. Actually, I'm engaged. My fiancée is an interior designer. We're Republicans. Believe in law and order and all that. Although, I admit I used marijuana when I was in college."

"The case at hand is a murder case. Do you think you could be fair to the defendants?"

The guy shrugged. "I guess so." He hesitated. "Although I'm not too sure I like the idea of condemning someone to death."

Judge Baxter dismissed the man. The man left happy. No one wanted to sit on a jury, especially one that would last more than a day or two.

The next person was a well-groomed businessman. Gray hair and a light gray custom tailored suit.

"Nice suit," commented Judge Baxter.

"Thanks." The businessman was all business. He said, "I own and operate ten McDonald's throughout the valley. I employ more than 100 people. I don't have time to sit on a jury."

"I see," said Judge Baxter. "The fact that you're so successful, doesn't that obligate you to support the system that allowed your success? What about civic duty?"

The businessman scowled. "It's an inefficient use of my time. The loss of income alone would—"

Judge Baxter held up a hand, which stopped the businessman. "I think you'll fit in quite well on the jury. We need people who know how to make decisions."

The next person to be questioned was a middle-aged black woman. She sat down in the chair and glared. She didn't want to be on any jury. "I hate the police," she said. "They arrested my two sons. Both of them are doing hard time in prison. And the prison is so far away I can't hardly get up there to visit them."

"So you couldn't be fair?"

"No." She glared.

"Excused."

Prospective juror number four was a thin and waspish woman with a slight accent. "I don't think I'm juror material," she said.

"Why is that?"

"Because I read about this case in the *LA Times*. All those jailbirds murdering each other. I'd be terrified for my very life," she explained, putting a hand to her throat.

"No one would know your name or where you live," said Judge Baxter. "We've never lost a juror yet."

"I should hope not!" exclaimed the woman. She shook her head. "No, no. I just couldn't do it. I'd be so afraid I couldn't be fair."

"I disagree. I think you'd make a great juror," smiled Judge Baxter.

Next up was a muscular black man.

"Tell us about yourself," said Judge Baxter.

The man worked on the docks as a crane operator, and was a union man all the way. "I used to drive a truck but hurt my back. Darndest thing, ya know? But the union took care of me and got me on at the docks. Good job. Good hours. Overtime if you want it, which I do. Got me a little cabin cruiser, ya know? Take her out on the weekends and fish. My brother told me all about this trial. He's a US marshal, only not quite as tall as me."

The defense attorneys shifted uncomfortably in their chairs. Mark Montgomery's eyebrows almost touched his hairline as he looked at Judge Baxter.

"I see," said Judge Baxter. "Thanks for coming in, but you're excused."

The next prospective juror was an executive, the vice-president of marketing for Behr, a multinational company headquartered in Santa Ana. Behr made paint. The executive had a big voice that filled the room. "I know I can be objective," boomed the executive. "That's what I get paid the big bucks for. I organize the data. I analyze the data. I make a decision. Every decision has ramifications that I have to live with."

Judge Baxter gazed at the executive. "I see."

The executive assumed the judge was impressed. "I could organize the jury in no time at all. Come up with a win-win analysis plan. You know, for the evidence. Erase all the hesitancy your average person has about all that legal mumbo-jumbo." He looked at the attorneys and raised his eyebrows, chuckling with cheeriness, as if they all belonged to the same old boys club.

Judge Baxter flashed a questioning look at Mark Montgomery, who returned a small shrug. He had no objections.

The Behr vice-president of marketing found himself on the jury.

The selection process went on for weeks. Both sides—the government prosecutors and the defense attorneys—had frequent objections to one person after another. The prosecutors wanted staunch conservatives, people who believed in law and order and 'an eye for an eye' justice. In other words, people who would vote for the death penalty. The defense attorneys, on the other hand, were seeking bleeding-heart liberals, the kind of people who demonstrated outside animal shelters, who couldn't stand the thought of dogs and cats being put to sleep, much less condemn a human being to lethal injection.

On his part, Judge Baxter was a fair-minded man who wanted a fair-minded jury. One that listened to the evidence, weighed it in the balance and came up with a just verdict. He believed in commonsense and the court system. Judge Baxter enjoyed the selection process. This was the fun part in his opinion. People fascinated him, what with all their different backgrounds, perspectives and lifestyles.

In the end, they seated a jury of nine men and three women. After the jury was sworn in, the jurors voted the Behr executive their foreman.

FOR TWO WEEKS, the jury sat in the deliberation room and deliberated. The question was simple. Had Barry Mills and Tyler Bingham conspired to commit, or committed any of the seventeen murders laid at their door?

The Behr executive was as good as his word. He organized all the evidence into categories. Keeping it simple, he named the categories 'possible,' 'probable,' 'certain,' 'not possible,' 'improbable' and 'uncertain,' and assigned evidence to each category. Witnesses were assigned to only two categories, 'believable' or 'unbelievable.' Twelve copies of everything were made and each juror received their copy, which was neatly tabbed for easy reference.

After the copies were passed out, the Behr executive addressed his fellow jurors. "Okay," he said. "As you can see, I have assigned each piece of evidence to a category. And each witness is either believable or unbelievable."

Questioning frowns appeared on the jurors faces. The executive held up his hand. "I admit the assignments are arbitrary. They are based on what I think. I don't expect you to agree with me." He glanced around the room. "But it's a place to start. We can discuss each item and either toss it out or re-assign it based on our discussion."

Relieved to learn that they weren't being bullied, the others nodded. "That's a good idea," remarked one of the women.

The Behr executive agreed. "Right. Now, I placed two pieces of evidence in the 'certain' category. It's in our best interests to start there, and work our way backward. That should save some time and make our deliberations more efficient."

Everyone nodded.

"Right. The two most damning pieces of evidence—in my opinion— are the coded message sent to the Aryan Brotherhood members at Lewisburg prison. And the video of the attack at the Florence prison."* He looked around. "Does everyone agree that both these items are certain?"

Hesitant nods around the table. A hand went up. "I have a question about the video."

"Good," said the executive. "Now we're on the right track. What's your question?"

"The video was taken by one of the guards, they said. It lasts for about two or three minutes. And it isn't until the very end that we see any guards responding to the attack." The juror glanced around. "It's just, well... what took them so long?"

---

* Prosecutors had introduced as evidence a video taken by a correctional officer at ADX Florence. The video showed Tyler Bingham attacking another inmate on the yard at the prison.

"I wondered about that, too," said one of the women. "It's almost as if they were allowing it to happen."

Another juror nodded. "Makes you wonder, doesn't it? Like it was set up. Like they wanted the guy to get beat up."

"Right," said the executive. "Good point. But the video does prove that defendant Bingham is violent and attacks other inmates with intent to kill. Can we all agree on that?"

Eleven heads nodded agreement.

"Right. Now, any comments about the coded message? Look in your second folder, where the green tab is. That's a copy of the message. To me, that indicates conspiracy to murder." The Behr executive tapped the folder. "Defendant Mills obviously sent the message. The message was to incite a war against the black gang. And that's what occurred." Glancing around he asked, "Any comments? Don't be shy. If you don't agree, then you need to speak up. That's the only way we can reach a consensus."

"As far as I'm concerned, the guy is guilty," said one juror.

"Me, too," agreed another. "Two gang members died because of that message."

"Yeah, and the witnesses confirmed it," said a juror. Everyone nodded.

"Right. Now we're getting somewhere," declared the executive. "So let me summarize. We're in agreement that the video and especially the coded message prove conspiracy to commit murder?"

"Not just conspiracy to commit murder," protested one of the women jurors. "But murder. It actually happened."

"Right. So I'll amend the summary as follows: The video demonstrates a violent nature. And the message proves murder as the result of a conspiracy to murder. Agreed?"

"Yes," was the reply.

"Anyone disagree?"

No one disagreed.

"Right. Now, if you'll turn to the folders marked witnesses. Let's go through them one by one and see if we can concur on who was telling the truth and who was unreliable. Anybody have any thoughts on the government informants?"

"I don't trust them," said the man who owned the McDonald's franchises.

"Neither do I," added another man, who sported a beard. "To ease their own situations, to get their sentences reduced, they'd say anything."

"I disagree," said the waspish woman with the accent, startled by her own boldness. She glanced around at the others, expecting to be scolded. When no one said anything, she forged ahead. "People can change. That's the reason they're sent to prison, isn't it? To learn the error of their ways?"

Rolling his eyes, the man with the beard said, "Theoretically, yes. But these informants didn't learn the error of their ways and then volunteer to testify. They got something in return—reduced sentences, better living conditions and—don't forget—money. They were paid." He shook his head. "Makes me sick just thinking about it."

The Behr executive turned his hands out, conceding the point. "I admit it is a little questionable. Yet, I can see why they would want something in return for their risk. Like any negotiation, it has to be a win-win situation. Both sides get something they want."

The woman with the accent made another donation to the discussion. "I thought the first one—Mr. Roach they called him— was telling the truth. There was something about him that made me believe him. It was more the way he spoke than what he said." She paused, thinking of how to say what she wanted to say. "Honest. That's it. He seemed to be speaking honestly, from his heart."

"That's because he's had lots of practice lying," snorted the McDonald's guy.

"I don't think so," objected the woman. "He was just doing the right thing."

"Well, let's see a show of hands," suggested the Behr executive. "If you think Mr. Roach was a reliable witness, hold up your hand." Holding up his own hand, he counted the other raised hands. "Ten of us. Which means two don't think his testimony was reliable." He jotted something down on a piece of paper. "Right. We can come back to the subject later. Let's talk about the other witness—Mr. Benton. Any thoughts?"

"The guy went from a sixty-three year sentence to a nine year sentence for a half-hour's worth of testimony," declared the man with the goatee. "He's a convicted murderer. And he'll be back on the streets in no time at all, ready to kill again." He scoffed. "I'd tell 'em what they wanted to hear, too. For that kind of deal."

"In this case, I have to agree," said the thin woman.

"It's about time," mocked the McDonald's guy.

"Let's not squabble," urged the Behr executive. "Say what you think, but don't get personal. Each of us has a right to his or her opinion. If we start belittling each other, we'll be here until Christmas."

The McDonald's guy nodded. "Sorry," he mumbled.

"You're forgiven," smiled the thin woman.

"Right," said the Behr executive. "Another show of hands, please. Anyone who thinks the second witness—Mr. Benton—was unreliable, raise your hand."

Twelve hands went up. The executive made another notation on his piece of paper.

"What about the retired warden? Coombs? Anyone want to say anything about his testimony?" asked the executive.

"That guy was good," spoke up one of the other jurors. "Completely reliable. When he told how those two men were hitting their knives against the floor... well... my spine tingled."

Everyone nodded.

"We're all in agreement there, I see," said the executive. He made a checkmark on his paper. "Right. Now, let's return to the first witness— Mr. Kevin Roach. Let's see if we can't come to some unity about his testimony. But before we do that, I suggest we take a short break, so everyone can re-charge their batteries."

Everyone thought that was a great idea. Beverages and snacks had been provided, as well as meals, delivered by a catering service.

Smoking in the room was not allowed, but a side-door led to a small, secure smoking area. Some went out for a smoke. Others visited the bathroom. Others got something to drink.

For two weeks the Behr executive cajoled, encouraged and guided the jurors in their deliberations. He felt like a choir director, trying to get twelve distinct voices to blend as one. At times, as patience melted away, sharp words were exchanged. Once or twice tempers flared and hurt feelings resulted. Most of the time, though, the discussions were outspoken and to the point. The point, as the executive constantly reminded them, was this: Did the evidence demonstrate—without a doubt—that the defendants committed murder and/or conspired to commit murder?

On July 28, 2006, the foreman of the jury handed a written note to one of the US marshals, who carried it to Judge Baxter. Judge Baxter read the note with pursed lips. Then he spoke with his clerk, who set the wheels in motion. Two hours later, the Nuremberg Room was packed with spectators, members of the press, court reporters, bailiffs, US marshals, attorneys, and artists from various magazines and newspapers, who were there to make a visual record of the proceedings.

The stars of the show entered last. Barry 'the Baron' Mills and Tyler 'the Hulk' Bingham were escorted to the docket. Clinking and clanking as their shackles and handcuffs and waist-chains bickered, the Commissioners of the Aryan Brotherhood took their places. Marshals slipped chains through the ring-bolts in the floor, binding the two men to their seats.

Barry Mills' cheap, black sunglasses stripped him of any humanity, leaving him looking like a pale, bald insect with large murky eyes. Of course, maybe it wasn't the fault of the glasses, maybe Mills wasn't human to begin with.

Eerily enormous, Tyler 'the Hulk' Bingham sat like a brooding walrus, waiting for feeding time at Sea World. The artists, heads popping back and forth as if at a tennis match, sketched rapidly on their portrait pads, trying to capture the moment. The onlookers simply stared at the two villains and wondered what it felt like to be a monster. Then they switched their attention to the jury and wondered what it felt like to hold the power of life and death. What it felt like to pass judgment on monsters.

Judgment was at hand. Not a hollow judgment where someone received a lecture and paid a fine, the type of mini-judgment that took place every day, but a real judgment, one of Biblical proportions. Who would live and who would die. The final judgment. Just thinking about it sent electric shivers up and down the spines of the onlookers.

The government prosecutors were confident the two murderers would be found guilty. On their part, the defense attorneys were confident they had destroyed the government's case by establishing the unreliability of the government informants, who were opportunistic, disreputable and downright wishy-washy. And yet, both the prosecution and the defense harbored uneasiness in the backs of their minds, for no one ever knew, or could predict, what a jury would do.

The moment arrived.

Judge Baxter turned to the jury. "Have you reached a verdict?"

Silence gathered in the air.

The twelve jurors shifted uneasily in their seats. The Behr executive stood up. "Yes, we have," he said. His voice sounded unconvincing, as if he doubted what he was saying. He didn't doubt it, but the enormity of what was taking place had punched him in the stomach, leaving him wobbly.

"And do you have that for me?" asked Judge Baxter.

"Yes," replied the executive.

The court clerk walked over to the executive, and took the sheet of paper from him, handing it in turn to the judge who read its content to himself.

Judge Baxter looked up from the paper. "Mr. Mills and Mr. Bingham, the jury—after due and very careful deliberation—has found you guilty under the Racketeer Influenced and Corrupt Organizations Law of the following: 1.) Guilty of fourteen counts of Violent Crime in Aid of Racketeering. 2.) Guilty of the murder of Frank Joyner. Guilty of the murder of Abdul Salaam. Guilty of the murder of Arva Lee Ray."

Potentially, under the RICO statute, each count carried the death penalty.

Barry Mills and Tyler Bingham sat perfectly still. No flicker of emotion showed on their faces. No anger, no disappointment, no sorrow, no regret, no disbelief. They looked as if they had just heard the judge read off the departure times of cargo ships leaving the port of San Francisco.

On their part, the twelve jurors looked as if they had just received word their favorite pets had been run over by a truck. Faces pale and pinched, their eyes refused to glance in the direction of the two defendants. Instead the jurors peered at the floor, as if they hadn't quite seen it before, or gazed at the walls.

At the government prosecutors' table, the attorneys were stifling an impulse to jump up and dance for joy, pumping their fists. The defense attorneys appeared stunned, then mystified, then angry. They whispered to each other, shaking their heads as their faces grew sharp.

Judge Baxter proceeded with the business at hand. There were formalities to take care of. "I would like to thank the jury for their time and effort in this lengthy and—at times—tedious trial." He nodded politely to the jurors. "Ladies and gentlemen of the jury, you are almost done. You have one more important task before you. The penalty phase. Until that time you are dismissed. However, I caution you not to read anything, listen to anything, or watch anything pertaining to this trial."

Then he looked at the attorneys. "The penalty phase will begin August 15. Please have any motions filed as soon as possible. If you have any questions or concerns, contact the clerk."

Judge Baxter glanced at the marshals, who were beginning to look restless. "The prisoners are remanded to custody. Please remove them and take all necessary security measures."

Glancing around the court, he added, "This court is adjourned until August 15, 2006."

From beginning to end, judgment took fifteen minutes, no longer than the drive-through at McDonald's. The golden arches of justice were fast and efficient.

OUTSIDE THE COURTROOM, defense attorney Mark Montgomery paused to speak with reporters.

"What did you think about the verdict?" asked a reporter.

"We're disappointed and now we move on to the next phase," replied Montgomery. Frank Sansoni, who stood next to Montgomery, gave his opinion. "I am shocked. Simply shocked. There was little evidence against Mr. Mills and Mr. Bingham."

"So you don't agree that they're guilty of racketeering and the murder of three men?" asked another reporter.

"The defendants live in prison," said Sansoni. "To survive in that violent world—the world of prison—they were forced to seek membership in a gang."

"What about the coded message that incited a race war at Lewisburg penitentiary? Are you saying they didn't send that message?"

"We don't deny they sent it," answered Montgomery. "However we disagree with its meaning. The note did not incite violence. Indeed, the note was merely a warning to other gang members that violence was about to erupt. And that they should protect themselves and stay out of any violence that might occur."

With that, the defense attorneys left. Reporters shouted further questions at them, but to no avail.

Penalty and Punishment

WHEN THE PENALTY portion of the trial began, it was August in Southern California. Which meant hot as Hell. And Hell was where the prosecutors wanted to send the Baron and the Hulk. The government prosecutors were seeking the death penalty for Barry Mills and Tyler Bingham.

US Assistant Attorney Rodney Pierce stood in front of the jury. He said: "Unless these two convicted murderers die for their crimes, they will continue to be a danger to other prisoners. As you know, they've already ordered the deaths of seventeen inmates. You found them guilty of those murders.

"Barry Mills and Tyler Bingham," declared Pierce, pointing at the docket and the two killers, looking on and listening while their deaths were urged, "orchestrated the murders of seventeen inmates. All while they were incarcerated in the federal supermax prison in Florence, Colorado."

Pierce turned to the jury, his manner blunt. "The supermax prison in Florence, ladies and gentlemen, is the most secure in the entire prison system. In other words, that's the best we can do. There is no alternative." He paused. "Psychologists and psychiatrists tell us that the best predictor of future behavior is past behavior. In other words, the way I acted last year is probably indicative of how I will act in the future. If that's the truth, then these two men will go on killing and killing and killing, because that's what they've done in the past."

Pierce cocked his head and held up a hand. "Now that doesn't mean people can't change. They can change—if they want to. They can change and the law provides many opportunities for them to change." He gazed flatly at the jury. "Barry Mills and Tyler Bingham have chosen not to change. You have already heard evidence about the choices these men made. And based on what you heard, you decided there was enough evidence to convict them of seventeen cold-blooded murders."

Pierce looked up for effect, pausing, and then made a gun of his right hand, pointing at the jurors. "When Barry Mills and Tyler Bingham made choices—people died!

"I'm asking you to stand up and say 'it's enough!'

"In 1977, a prison guard at San Quentin penitentiary was an eye-witness as Barry Mills leaned over the body of Garland Berry—a fellow inmate—and stabbed him over and over again in the chest and face."

Pierce moved a step closer to the jury, holding up two fingers. "Just two years later, in 1979, Barry Mills was convicted of killing another fellow inmate—John Marzloff. With his own hand, Barry Mills stabbed him to death in the Atlanta federal prison.

"Both men—Barry Mills and Tyler Bingham—have been committed to longer and longer prison sentences. Yet, despite that fact, the evidence shows you these men committed their most violent crimes while serving their prison sentences."

Pierce walked away a few steps, then walked back. "On three different occasions—in 1996 and 1997—Barry Mills tried to introduce cyanide into the federal prison system. He tried to smuggle this extremely lethal poison into prison. This is an example of how the man thinks, how he operates."

Dropping his chin and raising his eyebrows, Pierce said, "These are the reasons that Barry Mills and Tyler Bingham must die. There is no other way to protect people from Barry Mills and Tyler Bingham."

Rodney Pierce walked back to his chair.

Twelve jurors sat stunned. They had never heard anyone publicly endorse, indeed, urge the death of other human beings in such strong language and with such persistence.

Barry Mills' defense attorney stood and approached the jury. As far as H. Dean Sansoni was concerned, the government prosecutor had just done half his job for him—convinced the jury *not* to impose the death penalty. For Prosecutor Pierce had tried to explain *logically* why Mills and Bingham should be executed. Logic never worked when it came to death. Death and the death penalty in American culture were extremely *emotional* subjects. If you slapped them in the face with logic, you made them angry and resentful and stubborn. Their head said yes, while their heart said no. And the heart always won.

"Let's make a deal," said Frank Sansoni with a smile. He watched as the jurors visibly relaxed. Those words—'let's make a deal'—did two things. First, it appealed to their emotions. Second, and just as important, it put them back in control.

Sansoni let his words sink in, then continued. "I'm going to put before you a number of reasons that will suggest why Barry Mills and Tyler Bingham should not be executed. Why they should not receive— as the prosecutor demanded—the death penalty." With the last three words, Sansoni screwed up his face as if he had a bitter taste in his mouth. "And if just two of my reasons appeal to your commonsense, then those two reasons will be enough to cement the deal. You will impose the right and just verdict—life without parole." Sansoni gave the jurors a questioning look that said *that's more than fair, isn't it?*

Sansoni interlaced his fingers under his chin. "In 1977, Barry Mills and Garland Berry entered into conflict. It was a fight. In prison, sadly, fights take place. In this instance, it was mutual combat. You're not going to hear how it started or who did what, because no one really knows. And Mr. Berry is not here to share those details with us."

Sitting at the prosecutors' table, Rodney Pierce rolled his eyes.

"The District Attorney of San Francisco never even prosecuted the case," Sansoni told the jury. "There wasn't enough evidence against Mr. Mills to begin to prosecute. So it's ridiculous to even mention it."

Sansoni paused, thinking, and let his eyes drift over the jury. "Let me tell you a little about Barry Mills, about his life. When he was a teenager, Barry Mills made an error in judgment, as boys sometimes do. It wasn't a big mistake, but it was enough to send him into the cold embrace of the California Youth Authority, which is a euphemism for reform school. The hard truth is this: The California Youth Authority is jail for anyone under the age of eighteen. And the California Youth Authority failed him miserably. They didn't reform him. They did the exact opposite." Sansoni paused for effect. "They prepared him for a lifetime in prison."

Sansoni paced back and forth momentarily. "Yet in spite of his harsh environment as a tender youth, Barry Mills has tried—with all his strength of will—not to become like the inmates around him. He's not like Al Benton, who became an informant—a snitch—and testified against his friends." Sansoni gave the jury a penetrating look. "Let me remind you that when Al Benton sat before you and testified, he declared under oath that it was he—and not Barry Mills— that stabbed and killed one of the men that Barry Mills was accused of killing. Barry Mills didn't do it! Al Benton confessed that he did it!"

Again Sansoni paused, as if composing himself in the face of such dastardly accusations. "And in exchange for his testimony, what did Al Benton receive? They"—Sansoni pointed at the government prosecutors—"let him plead guilty to assault. And that's not all! His previous sentence of sixty-three years was reduced to nine years. Only nine years! If a man like Al Benton—a confessed murderer— is put back on the streets... how can you put these men to death?" Sansoni gave the jury a challenging look.

He walked over to the defense table and picked up some papers. Back in front of the jury, Sansoni held the papers up. "These are the official reports from prison psychologists. The psychologists—who are acknowledged experts—conclude that Barry Mills does not pose a threat to anyone."

From his chair at the prosecutors' table, Rodney Pierce resisted the urge to jump up and pull his hair out. He wanted to ask the jury, if that's true—that he's not a threat to anyone—then why did you just convict him of seventeen counts of murder?

"What these experts are telling you," continued Sansoni, "is that Barry Mills and Tyler Bingham are completely and fully retired from any type of active gang participation. They are old men. Too old for the dangerous and violent world of prison. Prison has broken them."

Sansoni pointed to the docket. "Look at them," he said. He waited while everyone in the courtroom had a good long look. "Up until this trial, Tyler Bingham was scheduled to be released from prison in four years. His debt to society was over in 2010. When he was nine years old, he was picked up and thrown into jail—yes, jail—for petty theft. By the time he was eighteen years old, he was a heroin addict, living on the streets. He committed a robbery because he was starving to death.

"While he was in San Quentin prison—he admits this—he became part of the Aryan Brotherhood. He had to—to survive. Four years later, because of good behavior, he was paroled. He got a job. He got married. He led a productive life. And his only goal now is to do his time and keep out of trouble so he can return to a normal way of life. Tyler Bingham just wants what any old man wants—to live a quiet, peaceful life."

Sansoni looked around the courtroom. He held up the papers in his hand, then lowered his hand as if in defeat. "The just and right verdict for these two men—Barry Mills and Tyler Bingham—is life in prison with parole. Burying them alive is more than enough of a punishment."

ONCE MORE the Behr executive led his fellow jurors into the deliberation room. They were a solemn group. This was serious business, no longer about simple guilt or innocence, now it was about life and death.

Once everybody was seated around the table, the Behr executive looked at the eleven faces. Folding his hands, he leaned forward on his elbows. "Right. They want us to play God. Decide whether two men should die. Two men, I should add, that I believe are guilty as Hell of murdering other men. Or ordering their murders, which is just as bad." He thought about that for a second, then added, "Maybe worse, I don't know."

Unfolding his hands, he leaned back, pushing against the arms of his chair so his back was perfectly straight. "Although I believe they are guilty," he said slowly. "I cannot sentence another human being to die." Embarrassed, he looked out the windows for a moment. "My conscience... I'd never sleep again."

A couple of heads nodded in sympathy. Others stared at him, aghast. What had happened to Mr. Efficiency?

"You heard what the Prosecutor said, didn't you?" asked one of the eleven. "It's up to us. We have to stop this lawlessness. Make a stand."

It was as if someone had opened a valve on a pressurized tank. Pent-up thoughts and emotions came hissing out. Arguments for and against the death penalty filled the air of the deliberation room. Some of the jurors argued with their neighbors. Some argued with everyone. Some argued with no one in particular. They simply argued. Only the Behr executive sat silent. Inside, he was arguing with himself.

After a few minutes, he slapped the table. Boom! Eleven tongues stopped wagging as if by magic. Eleven heads turned and stared in shocked surprise.

The Behr executive had gotten his shit together, at least partially.

"This is getting us nowhere," he announced. "I suggest we take a vote. That way we'll know where we stand. Then we can go around the table, one at a time, and present our reasons as to why we feel the death penalty is justified or not. After each person gives their reasons, we can—calmly—discuss the pros and cons of what they said." He paused and gave them a pleading look. "If we keep arguing, we'll be here for a year and nothing will be decided."

"You're right," a woman's voice agreed. "Who wants to go first?"

FOR THE NEXT five days, the jurors deliberated. Their deliberations consisted of talking, arguing, yelling and even some crying. One or two wept tears of frustration, because they couldn't understand how people could be so stubborn.

At the end of the first week, on Thursday, the jury filed back into the courtroom and informed Judge Baxter that they were deadlocked.

"I appreciate your quandary," said Judge Baxter. "But I'm going to ask you to deliberate for one more day. See if you cannot come to some accord."

The jury filed back to the deliberation room and sat like zombies. Emotionally exhausted and mentally drained, they didn't know what to do. Someone suggested stretching exercises, which were to be followed by a change of seats. "Maybe changing the seating arrangements will give everyone a different perspective."

No one had a better idea.

Lining up in rows as if in a high school gym class, the jurors went through a series of deep breathing exercises, then some basic stretches, including torso twisting and shoulder rolls. "Okay," said the Behr executive, when he'd had enough, "now everyone find a new place to sit."

The twelve people moved cautiously around the table, watching to see who would sit where. No one wanted to change seats, not really. They had grown accustomed to their old seats and felt comfortable. They now felt very uncomfortable.

Once everyone was in a new chair, the Behr executive said, "Okay. Anybody got anything *new* to say?"

A hand went up. "It's obvious that they're guilty..."

It was the same old stuff.

The next day—Friday—the jury filed back into the courtroom, taking their same old places.

"Have you reached unanimity?" asked Judge Baxter.

"No, your Honor, we remain deadlocked," replied the Behr executive. "We are split. Nine of us have voted in favor of and three against the death penalty for Barry Mills."

"And what was the vote in Mr. Bingham's case?" inquired the judge.

"Four in favor of and eight against the death penalty for Tyler Bingham," stated the Behr executive.

Judge Baxter paused, looking around the courtroom. "Then it is my duty to declare a mistrial. Sentencing will take place November 13, 2006. Court is adjourned."

The jury filed out for the last time. They were glad it was over and each one felt as if he or she had done their best. Yet, at the same time, they felt deflated, as if they were walking away from something that was not finished.

Barry 'the Baron' Mills and Tyler 'the Hulk' Bingham, surrounded by black-clad US marshals, were escorted out the back of the courthouse, where they were loaded into vehicles and transported back to jail. They would be held there until the sentencing hearing.

Defense attorneys Frank Sansoni, Mark Montgomery and Michael Parker spoke with reporters outside the courthouse.

"The judge declared a mistrial," said a reporter. "What does that mean for your clients?"

"It means they will receive a default penalty," answered Sansoni.

"What is that?"

"In a federal case where the death penalty has been requested," explained Sansoni, "if the jury cannot reach a unanimous verdict, the defendants are sentenced to life in prison."

"Weren't they already serving life in prison?" asked the reporter.

"They will spend the rest of their lives in maximum-security cells. Barry Mills and Tyler Bingham pose no further threat," stated Sansoni, ignoring the question.

"It's bittersweet," added Michael Parker. "On the one hand, I'm relieved it's not death. On the other hand, I'm sad that Tyler Bingham is going to spend the rest of his life in prison." He shook his head. "What a waste of taxpayer money, asking for the death penalty in a case that obviously wasn't that extreme."

The attorney was right. Millions of dollars had been spent pursuing one goal—the death penalty. A deadlocked jury and a mistrial were more than the government prosecutors had bargained for. To come away without the death penalty for the Baron and the Hulk meant nothing less than dismal failure, a total waste of time. Prior to the trial, Barry 'the Baron' Mills was already going to spend the rest of his life in prison. He would die there. So what good was another life sentence without parole? Wasn't that like beating a dead horse?

Getting the life sentence for Tyler 'the Hulk' Bingham was some consolation. The Hulk had been scheduled for parole in 2010. Now, of course, he was ineligible for parole and would rot in prison along with Mills. But no matter how the prosecutors looked at it, it still wasn't the death penalty.

Thirty feet away, the government prosecutors were talking with a group of newspaper and television reporters. It was time for lots of spin-control.

"We consider this a victory," said Sherry Sikes, "because there is no possibility of parole for either Barry Mills or Tyler Bingham. It sends a message that convicts can't kill other convicts without severe consequences."

"What about the jury's vote?" asked a television reporter. "Nine of the twelve jurors voted for the death penalty for Barry Mills."

Sherry Sikes looked straight at the camera. "Now he knows how close he came. Hopefully, that's something he takes into consideration before he sends a message out to declare another race war."

She sounded confident and victorious as she spoke. But she was playacting, giving the media the party-line. It was part of her job. Government prosecutors had to exude toughness, competence and a triumphant attitude, no matter what happened. Prosecutors never lost or retreated. They regrouped and counterattacked.

Privately, Sherry Sikes regarded the trial as a giant fiasco. Too much of her case had hinged on the testimony of informants, whose credibility was easy to undermine because they never really had any to begin with. If an informant was already a convicted murderer or a drug dealer, looking for a way out of spending the rest of his life in prison, perjury was child's play. He wouldn't even consider it lying, he'd consider it smart. And if, by some chance, he was actually telling the truth, he was still a felon and therefore easy prey for any good defense attorney. All the attorney had to do was list the informant's past crimes and the jury instantly doubted his testimony. No one likes a tattle-tale.

And Mark Montgomery, who had been Barry Mills' defense attorney, was more than good. He was damn good. Clever without being tricky, he had literally skinned the informants alive, in about ninety-nine different ways. And what an actor. In Hollywood, his performance would have won him an Oscar. When it came right down to it, that was where Sherry Sikes had lost the death penalty and the trial. Montgomery's star-quality stole the show.

A FEW DAYS LATER, government prosecutors filed a motion with the court. It was a rare motion, practically unheard of. If the motion was granted, Mills and Binghan would be allowed to communicate only with their attorneys. Other than their attorneys, they would have no human contact. No visitors. No phone calls. No letters. Which meant Mills and Bingham could not have writing paper or pencils in their cells.

The prosecutors felt they had no other option than to make such a request. This was the only way they could—hopefully—keep Mills and Bingham from communicating with other members of the Aryan Brotherhood. In the government's opinion—if they couldn't execute the two criminals—the way to stop wholesale murders in the federal prison system was to totally isolate the two leaders. They had to be bottled up, as if they lived in a vacuum. That way maybe the Aryan Brotherhood would collapse, because its leaders, although not dead, would at least be buried.

When he read the motion, Judge Baxter was astonished. For two reasons: First, as far as he was concerned, this was nothing less than the Department of Justice openly admitting that it could not control two inmates who were already in prison. Which meant the system had failed; the Bureau of Prisons had failed. Second, the motion teetered on the edge of cruel and inhuman punishment, and possibly—probably—violated the first amendment of the US Constitution.

Judge Baxter sat in his chambers for a long time, thinking.

As scheduled, the sentencing hearing convened on November 13, 2006. Judge Baxter didn't waste any time getting to the point. Looking at the federal prosecutor, he held up a sheaf of papers and asked, "Just what the Hell is this motion all about?"

Paul Vaughn stood up. Vaughn was the lead prosecutor in the sentencing phase of the trial, because he was the acknowledged expert on federal sentencing guidelines and the legal precedents that pertained to them. He didn't need to ask the judge what motion he was talking about, Vaughn understood he had opened a can of worms when he filed it.

"It's a motion to restrict the defendants' ability to communicate," said Vaughn. "The intent of the motion is to effectively dismantle the leaders of the Aryan Brotherhood, which is a white supremacist organization that deals drugs and spreads terror throughout the federal prisons. They're terrorists, pure and simple. Terrorists have no right to communicate."

Barry Mills' attorney, Mark Montgomery, rose from his chair and waited for the judge's permission to speak.

"Go ahead, Mr. Montgomery," nodded Judge Baxter.

"Your Honor, the prison conditions proposed by the motion are draconian. They're cruel and unusual in my opinion," protested Montgomery. "It's worse than the death penalty."

"I'm inclined to agree with the defense," said Judge Baxter.

"Other terrorists in the federal prison system have been subject to such restrictions," countered Prosecutor Vaughn. "Ted Kaczynski, also known as the Unabomber. Zacarias Moussaoui, one of the 9/11 terrorists. Ramzi Yousef, the terrorist who masterminded the 1993 bombing of the World Trade Center—" Vaughn paused when Judge Baxter held up his hand.

"Such restrictions are horrendous. And have only been imposed eleven times in the history of the federal prison system," said Judge Baxter. He had checked it out. He leaned forward a little. "If you're really serious about this, the attorney general is going to have to make the specific request of this from the court. Therefore, I am postponing sentencing until November 21."

ON NOVEMBER 21, 2006, there being no further motions from either the defense or the prosecution, Judge Baxter sentenced Barry Mills and Tyler Bingham to life in prison without parole.

"Defendants will have the right to limited visitation, correspondence and phone calls," stated Judge Baxter. "However, only from and to such persons whose names have been previously designated by the defendants. Those names will then be approved by the bureau of prisons."

In theory, this was an attempt to bottle up any communication between Barry Mills, Tyler Bingham and other members of the Aryan Brotherhood. In practice, as long as the Baron and the Hulk had included a name on their lists, they could communicate with 'such persons.'

This partial limitation was the result of a compromise between Judge Baxter, the government prosecutors and the defense attorneys. Judge Baxter wasn't about to impose cruel and inhuman punishment, but agreed that some "degree of limitation seemed in order." The prosecutors argued that if "measures to control communication" were not implemented, contract murders and a reign of terror would continue to be the norm. On their part, the defense attorneys announced that if cruel and inhuman restrictions were instituted, they would file appeals alleging violations of first amendment rights. And they'd take it right to the top—the US Supreme Court. They felt confident the US Supreme Court would eventually rule in their favor. If so, Mills and Bingham would be granted a new trial and things might turn out differently the second time around.

"A new jury might find the parade of perjurers a little hard to swallow," said Montgomery.

Reluctantly, the government prosecutors gave way to the threat of another trial. They agreed to 'partial limitation,' which pleased Judge Baxter. It also pleased the defense attorneys because they knew a 'partial limitation' was a partly closed door: Things still went in and things still came out, just not as fast.

When the compromise was explained to Mills and Bingham, Barry Mills smiled. "Good job," he told his attorneys. The Hulk just nodded.

Once court was dismissed, the US marshals took over. They escorted the Baron and the Hulk to separate vehicles, which whisked them off to the Los Angeles international airport, where Con Air waited.

With their legs confined by two sets of ankle shackles, and their hands triple-cuffed, Barry 'the Baron' Mills and Tyler 'the Hulk' Bingham boarded the plane. Twenty-five marshals, carrying an assortment of weapons and wearing body armor, accompanied them. Their job was to escort the two villains to another world utterly distinct from any other. A world of which most people have no conception. Isolation.

Con Air took off and headed east. Its destination was Florence, Colorado, the US penitentiary Administrative Maximum—supermax—where the Baron and the Hulk would live very lonely lives in very small cells for a very long time—or until they died.

At least, that's what the Department of Justice and the Bureau of Prisons expected to happen.

There was just one little hitch. The Baron and the Hulk had no intention of retiring or doing penance. Sackcloth and ashes weren't for them. They were the High Priests of a brotherhood of warriors, and like warriors they intended to wage war and die fighting.

JOSEPH PRINCIPE sat in solitary confinement, going crazy. Sensory deprivation got to him. He became wild and violent, lashing out at the guards when they escorted him to shower. When Principe resisted and attacked, the guards pepper-sprayed him and dragged him back to his cell. This went on for weeks.

After a while, Principe came to his senses. He realized he had to get his shit together or go mad. If that happened, he'd end up in a prison nut-ward, where they could keep him indefinitely—a thought that scared him more than anything. He didn't want to spend years in a prison psycho-ward doped to the gills on Halodane. So, he re-invented himself, began reading and meditating. He stopped fighting the system, because he knew—in the end—the system would win.

Principe refused to become a snitch. He wouldn't play that game. And at long last, Principe won a small—very small—victory. The Feds offered him a 'global plea agreement.' This was a handy way to settle the cases against a bunch of defendants, all at the same time. The defendants would have to agree to the same deal, plead guilty to a reduced charge, and the Feds would go easy on them by giving them minimum sentences.

"I wanted to go to trial," said Principe. "But my attorney explained to me that the jury would be listening to the informants—Al 'Skinny' Benton and the Roach—and if the jury believed them, I'd be looking at a lot more time. I didn't know what I should do. It was one of the most grueling decisions of my life. I wanted to clear my name, but maybe the wise thing to do was to let it go."

He let it go. Principe pled guilty to one count of conspiracy to commit racketeering, and in return, the Feds recommended his sentence be not longer than fifteen months, and that it could be served concurrently. In effect, he said he was guilty and was sentenced, but he didn't have to serve any more time. It was a sweet deal. A win-win situation. The Feds looked good, and Principe would get to go home when his time was up.

The Feds shipped Principe back to Colorado to do his time at a medium security facility.

SIX

The Council

THE ORGANIZATIONAL CHART of the Aryan Brotherhood was simple. In the federal prison system, the three-man Commission was supreme. They ran things in the federal penitentiaries. No drugs went in or out of any federal pen without the permission of the Commission, and permission implied that a certain percentage of all profits went to the Commission. All murders, all prostitution, all protection services—everything had to be sanctioned by them beforehand. Which was all fine, except that the real action—the big money-making ventures—took place in state prison systems. Theoretically, the Commission controlled things in the state prisons, too. Practically, each state's prison system had a five to nine man council that pulled the strings on the Aryan Brotherhood puppets in its system. In other words, a council in each state ran the show. They deferred to the Commission, but only because they chose to.

The Aryan Brotherhood didn't know it, but from a functional standpoint, they were pretty much like the Roman Catholic Church in America. The cardinals and archbishops, like the Commission, sat at the top of the power pyramid, but the real power resided in the bishops, who were like the councils in the various state prison systems.

In California, a five-man council ran the day to day operations of the Aryan Brotherhood in the thirty-two prisons in the state. The California council had two primary duties, the first being to maintain the reputation of the Aryan Brotherhood as the toughest, meanest, nastiest, most vicious and most violent gang in prison. They were in charge and not to be fucked with. They upheld their reputation by means of terror. Any show of disrespect was punished immediately. And there was only one punishment—death.

The council's second duty was to make money, and the big money-maker for the Aryan Brotherhood was crystal meth—yellowish-white in color and more valuable than gold. The California council had to make sure lots of crystal meth was produced and distributed. Production was the hard part. Production necessitated a lot of chemicals, along with labs, and, most importantly, people with the know-how to make the stuff without blowing themselves up while doing it. After this, distribution was pretty simple. The product was shipped to various locations, where distributors, who were usually Nazi Low Riders mounted on Harley Davidsons, delivered it to the sales team members or drug dealers. The dealers sold the stuff and sent the cash back up the pipeline. Crystal meth went for anywhere between $3,000 and $30,000 a pound.

The money was the second hardest part. It had to be laundered, which meant it had to be funneled into and out of banks, investment houses and businesses without raising suspicion. Money was getting to be one Hell of a problem, because there was one Hell of a lot of it. So much so, in fact, the California council had stopped talking about amounts, like millions of dollars, and started talking about weight, as in how many tons of cash. The amount almost didn't matter anymore. What mattered was how much of it they had to ship and try to launder. There was so much money they were putting it in water-tight, fire-resistant containers and storing it in warehouses.

Of course, some of the cash went back into the production phase, and the people that provided the hundreds of tons of chemicals didn't take checks. Procurement of these chemicals was done by trusted members of the Nazi Low Riders, who were smarter and more organized than the average Nazi Low Rider. These elite members did business with the aristocracy of the underworld and so had to look like respectable businessmen. They were furnished with top of the line German cars, given luxurious homes, and they dressed in Brioni suits. Their work entailed purchasing pseudoephedrine in Hong

Kong or Czechoslovakia, and having it shipped to Long Beach or the docks in Oakland, where many of the unions accepted favors to look the other way and forget where containers had gone.

Thousands of gallons of anhydrous ammonia were purchased from farmers, who used the chemical as fertilizer. The farmers were well-paid for over-ordering and leaving the stuff stacked on pallets next to forklifts. When the pallets mysteriously disappeared in the night, the farmers reported the theft to the local sheriff and claimed on the insurance. The farmers made out like bandits.

Ethanol and tert-Butanol were purchased from legitimate vendors. When offered cash, the vendors forgot to fill out purchase orders. The way the vendors figured it, what the IRS didn't know didn't hurt anyone. The acquisition of potassium was handled in the same manner. Buying two or three hundred thousand pounds of potassium was not illegal, and neither was paying cash. No one ever asked any questions.

Lithium, though, was problematic. One of the NLR elite came up with a handy solution to the problem. He contacted auto junkyards throughout the United States on the pretext that he was recycling old car batteries. Offering top dollar, he cornered the market. Pretty soon semis driven by heavily tattooed, muscular skinheads were crisscrossing the highways and byways of America, all of them hauling trailers brimming with old car batteries back to California.

Truckload upon truckload arrived at the two warehouses located at the Pleasanton Industrial Park, located on the fringe of the East Bay, just east of Oakland. Each truck was packed with chemicals. Pleasanton was the wealthiest mid-size community in the entire United States, according to *Forbes* magazine. Home to well-paid techies, boutique restaurants, cineplexes and vast mega-malls, Pleasanton was a nice place to live. Residents were unaware that it now hosted two superlabs in operation twenty-four hours a day, seven days a week, producing crystalline methamphetamine for the Aryan Brotherhood.

The labs used the Nazi method of synthesizing crystal meth. Based upon a process used by Hitler's scientists in WWII, this was a faster and somewhat safer method than the synthesis process called 'red, white and blue,' which was used by most small-scale labs set up in motels, trailer parks and basements. Small-scale labs were operated by halfwits looking to make a quick buck off of some crank. They tended to blow themselves to smithereens or die from inhaling toxic gases while attempting to cook red phosphorous on a butane stove.

Atop the two warehouses were custom built signs that read HyperChem Industries. Both labs had lots of employees, but were run by one man: Arturo Colano. Tall, slim and very handsome, Colano knew everything there was to know about crystalline methamphetamine.

FROM LAZARO CARDENAS in Mexico, all his life Arturo Colano had been a survivor. On the day he was born, his mother dropped him off at an orphanage. Arturo lived there until his eighth birthday, whereupon he decided he'd had enough and walked out the front door, taking with him only the clothes on his back. To the young Arturo, life on the streets was tough but fun. The hand of starvation was on his shoulder the whole time, but he found the challenge exciting— learning to lie and steal to stay alive. He was quick with his hands and feet, and his good looks gave him an advantage in that people were reluctant to believe such a beautiful child could be bad on the inside. Arturo caused a lot of people to readjust their thinking.

Arturo learned other things. He learned most poor people in Mexico were uneducated and illiterate. Rich people, on the other hand, could read, write and do math. Arturo wanted to be rich, and so stole some books in order to teach himself to read and write. When he could read, he stole some math books. Not only was he good at mathematics, he discovered a happy facility for learning. It was a knack, and he had it.

Age twelve, Arturo applied for a job. He didn't necessarily want to work for a living—he wanted a job to exploit, and got it, working as a cashier at a pharmacy. He handed people their medicine, took their money, gave them their change. He also stole morphine, Ritalin, Adderall, Dexedrine, Vyvanse, Pervitin, and Percodan, which he sold on the black market. Ritalin, Adderall, Dexedrine and Vyvanse were in big demand, and Arturo was making a killing off the drugs. He found out why: Ritalin and the rest were forms of methamphetamine, and Arturo made it his business to learn everything he could about methamphetamine.

Methamphetamine went by many different names: meth, crystal meth, glass, tweek, P, bee itch, tina, rockets, fireworks, crank, speed, junk, smack, yay, dust, shards, fuel, dope and rocks. Sometimes 'the shit' or 'the product.' It looked like little pieces of broken glass. Meth was a psychostimulant, which meant it stimulated the brain by increasing levels of dopamine. Dopamine resulted in a big rush of happiness, making the user feel really good about themselves and life. Naturally, the user wanted to keep feeling happy, which meant they had to keep buying it and doing it over and over, which meant they spent a lot of money on it.

Arturo smiled when he thought about money. Money was good.

Arturo learned that meth from pharmaceutical companies was difficult for drug dealers to come by. Most drug dealers either made the stuff themselves or bought it from someone who made it. These people were not chemists and didn't really know what they were doing, they just wanted to make money. Quality control didn't mean jack shit. These amateur cooks used cheap ingredients and cooked them up in the vague hope there would be some meth in the result. Then they diluted it or 'cut' it with inositol, isopropylbenzylamine or dimethylsulfone.

Arturo didn't know what any of those chemicals were, but he made a note to find out.

The amateur cooks sold their shit to drug dealers, who tested it to make sure it was the real deal. The tool for this test was simplicity itself. They sold it to some idiot tweeker, and if it didn't kill him they figured it was good shit.

If Arturo could produce good quality meth in bulk quantities, he could have a monopoly and make a lot of money. He went back to his library books. He learned that Hitler and the Nazis had used it to keep their soldiers going in WWII. The Japanese had pretty much invented meth, but it wasn't until after the War they found a use for it—getting high. Everybody began shooting it up, and it became such a problem that the Japanese banned it in 1951. It went underground and the Japanese version of the Mafia, the Yakuza, began dealing it.

In the United States, doctors prescribed meth for people with narcolepsy, obesity, depression and alcoholism. It came in tablets called Methedrine. College kids started using it for a buzz, and long-haul truckers used it to stay awake so they could drive more miles and make more money. In 1970, the US government decided meth was getting out of control, and so passed the Controlled Substances Act. As in Japan in the fifties, it went underground. Outlaw motorcycle gangs saw an undeveloped and untapped market niche and filled it. Utilizing the red, white and blue process, these motorcycle gangs started making and distributing crystal meth on the west coast, where meth was very popular.

In the eighties, the Mexican drug cartels woke up and saw the money being made off meth, jumped in and started mass-producing the stuff. The other international crime organizations soon followed. Groups like the Russian Mafia, the Italian Mafia, and the Serbs, had all been dealing cocaine, heroin and marijuana for years, so they knew what they were doing. They knew how to produce it, distribute it and market it. The Czechs saw what was going on and decided they could make a killing supplying the most important raw ingredient for meth: pseudoephedrine. They ramped up their factories and started pumping out thousands of tons of it.

Most of the meth got shipped to San Diego, the meth capital of the USA. Almost everybody was happy. The tweekers were happy because they shot themselves full of meth and felt real good. The manufacturers and dealers were happy because they were getting rich without half-trying.

However, the biker gangs were pissed off. All the foreigners had pulled the rug out from under them, because the bikers couldn't mass produce. They were still using glass beakers and coffee carafes, cooking the stuff in bedrooms, trailer parks and garages. The bikers wanted to get back into the marketplace. They had the distribution channels, but didn't have the technical know-how.

Salvation was at hand in the form of Arturo Colano.

Barry 'the Baron' Mills was halfway through serving twenty years in federal prison for planning the bank robbery in Fresno, California, when the twelve year old Arturo was educating himself in math and chemistry, and making money stealing and selling drugs. This was the first of Arturo's five-year plans. His second five-year plan was simple: attend the best university in the United States, and earn a degree in chemistry.

No one knew it, but the paths of Arturo Colano, the Aryan Brotherhood and the Nazi Low Riders were about to converge in Pleasanton, California.

AGE SEVENTEEN, Arturo was ready to implement phase two. He felt he was ready for college. In fact, Arturo was more than ready, he was equipped in the absolute sense of the word. His English was excellent, if perhaps a little flowery, and with regard to mathematics and chemistry, he was a walking, talking encyclopedia.

Having narrowed his choice of colleges to two—the Massachusetts Institute of Technology and the California Institute of Technology—Arturo opted for California. Whereas MIT was located in the metropolis of Boston and prided itself on being the best technological university in the world, it didn't have beaches and California girls. The kind of girls the Beach Boys sang about.

He filled out the application forms for Cal Tech, and demonstrated his grasp of mathematics with a 10,000 word essay on theoretical physics and higher-dimensional space. It never even crossed his mind to doubt he would be accepted.

Indeed, being from Mexico, and an orphan, and seventeen years old, and self-taught, and—on the basis of his spectacular essay—obviously a prodigy, Cal Tech waived the usual requirement of SAT scores and admitted him. Cal Tech wanted the best and the brightest, and they positively lusted after Arturo.

Arturo shoved everything he owned into a backpack, along with $4,999 cash. An acquaintance had told him that if he brought less than $5,000 cash into the United States, he could fly under the radar of the authorities and avoid detection. Arturo didn't know if the advice was right or wrong, but he decided to play it safe. Two hours later he was on the bus. In his pocket, folded three times, he carried a cashier's check for $150,000, which was all the money he had saved. Crime had been very good to Arturo. Or, as he liked to say, "alternative ventures had proven to be very profitable."

For the next five years Arturo lived with three other roommates in a four-bedroom house in Pasadena, California. He rode a Schwinn ten-speed bike to his classes, where he studiously took notes and listened attentively, afraid he might miss something important. He didn't need to bother. Most of what the professors taught he already knew, having read all his textbooks by the end of the first week.

Arturo was good-looking and pleasant to be with, and made lots of friends. His killer smile, which began and ended with his eyes, captivated both males and females. Which meant Arturo became popular without even trying. He was invited to all the best parties, and knew all the right people. But it was Arturo's opinion that the 'right people' were often the most boring people, and consequently he sought out and became friends with many of the wrong people: those who lived to the left of right.

One evening, sitting with a group of his friends at an alfresco table at the Bronze Rhino, a popular hang-out for Cal Tech wunderkind, half-a-dozen motorcyclists arrived and parked at the curb. Obnoxiously loud, the motorcycles growled and roared, putting a stop to all conversation. The Cal Tech students turned and stared at the six heavily muscled men with shaved heads and tattoos, who had rolled up astride their polished chrome stallions. One of the men nodded and the noise of the V-twin engines shut down. The men dismounted. They all wore white 'wife-beater' undershirts, faded blue jeans and Dr. Martens boots.

"Skinheads," scoffed one of the females at Arturo's table. A pre-med majoring in biology, she had blonde hair and wore $500, skintight designer jeans that were fashionably ripped at the knees.

Everyone returned to their beers and their conversations. Yet their eyes constantly strayed back to the six striking bikers. The muscles, tattoos and shaved heads were a primitive presence difficult to deny.

The skinheads sat down at an empty table. A Bronze Rhino waitress approached to take their orders. "Six Buds," said one of them. He held one hand over his other hand and added, "The big ones."

"Be right back," smiled the waitress.

Arturo looked at the blonde who had scoffed. "Skinheads," she repeated, grimacing. And for the edification of her friends: "White trash Neanderthals who think Hitler was a righteous dude. They ride around on their motorcycles, selling crank to dopeheads." She glanced at the skinheads. "Actually, they're nothing more than ignorant racial bigots."

"Nincompoops," added her companion, a freckled redhead with a profulgent chest.

Arturo nodded. "And what, exactly, does the term 'crank' designate? I mean, what is its precise chemical signature?" he asked the girl.

"Crystal meth," she said.

Intrigued, Arturo looked over at the skinheads. Then he turned back to the girl. "And where to they obtain it? Do they buy it, or steal it? Or manufacture it themselves?"

She shrugged. "How the Hell would I know? If you're so interested, why don't you ask them?"

Arturo thought about her suggestion for a moment. "An excellent idea. I think I will. Please, excuse me for a moment." He rose and walked over to the table where the skinheads were talking and laughing.

"Good evening," said Arturo. The skinheads stopped laughing and stared at him. "My name is Arturo Colano and, if it pleases you, I would like to put a few questions to you."

Exchanging skeptical looks with one other, the skinheads didn't really know what to say. Most people who approached them either wanted to fight them or to buy drugs. No one ever wanted to sit down with them and talk.

One of the skinheads, tattooed with a swastika and two lightning bolts on his shoulder, shrugged. "Why the fuck not?" he said, and reached out to grab an empty chair from a nearby table.

He put the chair next to his own and said, "Have a seat, man."

Arturo sat down.

"Whatcha wanna know, man?"

Arturo paused for a second, framing his question. "One of my friends explained to me that you merchandize crank, which is also known as crystal meth. Is this an accurate proclamation?" Arturo smiled politely and waited patiently for an answer.

His new friends—the skinheads—sat perfectly still. They gazed at Arturo, but didn't really see him. It was more like they were turning him this way and that way in their minds, trying to figure out if he was real or not.

"You a fucking cop?" growled one of them, popping his knuckles.

Arturo threw back his head and laughed. "No, Señor," he answered. "I am a student at Cal Tech, where I study chemical engineering." He glanced around the table. "And I am very interested in how you procure your crank."

The skinheads just stared at him. Arturo interpreted their silence as interest, so he continued. "As I'm sure you know, there are two methods of synthesizing methamphetamine. Birch reduction and the so-called Nazi method. The first method, Birch reduction, is inefficient and dangerous. While the Nazi method, being more efficient, is made onerous because of the necessary constituents, which are difficult to obtain." Arturo paused, looking around the table. "Which method do you utilize?"

One of the skinheads eased back in his chair. His name was Wolf Weiss, and his nickname was Wolfman, because he was large and vicious. "Let me get this straight," Wolfman said slowly. "You're a chemist and you wanna know how we make our shit? That right?"

Arturo grinned. "Yes, yes! Precisely."

"And why would you wanna know that?"

"It is presumptuous of me, I know," explained Arturo. "However, I am of the opinion that I might be able to facilitate your production methods. You see, synthesizing methamphetamine is a specialty of mine."

Wolfman leaned forward. "You mean you wanna help us make the shit?"

"Precisely so," smiled Arturo. "Inspecting your production facilities, I could—perhaps—propound suggestions to increase productivity and reduce volatility. Thereby increasing the potency of your shit, which would result in greater profits for your syndicate." He waved his hand to indicate everyone at the table, as if he was speaking to the board of directors of a Fortune 500 company.

"You're fucking kiddin' me, right?" announced Wolfman.

"No, no. I am quite serious," stated Arturo.

Rubbing a tattoo on his forearm, Wolfman squinted at Arturo. Unless he was to give the Feds credit for being wildly imaginative, which he didn't, Arturo did not conform to the image of an undercover cop. Undercover cops always tried to blend in as much as possible. This guy, Arturo, with his smiling eyes and funny way of talking, stood out like a flower in a butcher shop. Of course, that didn't mean shit either.

Wolfman made his decision. "Look Arturo, we don't know nothing 'bout no crank, either selling it or making it. We're just a bunch of guys who like to ride bikes and hang out, ya know?"

Arturo smiled and nodded. "I comprehend. It is imperative that you be careful. This is to your benefit, and for this you are to be complimented." Arturo paused, flourishing his hands dramatically. "Perhaps, though, you will do me the favor of... what is the phrase?" Arturo put his hand on his forehead. "Ha! Checking me out. Yes. Perhaps you will check me out, see if what I have proposed is not only accurate, but propitious for everyone."

Wolfman raised one eyebrow, then nodded. "Sure dude, we'll check you out." The other skinheads grinned hugely, as if at some inside joke.

"Excellent!" chirped Arturo. "This is satisfactory news indeed." He stood up and performed a small bow to the skinheads. "It has been fascinating to speak with you. I look forward auspiciously to our next conversation and to associating with you." With that, Arturo walked back to his table, where his Cal Tech friends sat staring at him.

Wolfman watched the slim Mexican for a few seconds, then turned and commented, "Jesus H. fucking Christ. You believe that shit?"

The other skinheads shook their heads.

Wolfman made a decision that he would later congratulate himself on. "Let's get this spic checked out," he said. "Work all our sources and find out who this dude is. I wanna know if he's playing some game, or if he's the real deal. Got it?"

Around the table, shaved heads nodded.

WOLFMAN AND THE OTHER SKINHEADS drinking beer at the Bronze Rhino were Nazi Low Riders. A white supremacist motorcycle gang, the Nazi Low Riders patterned themselves after the Hell's Angels motorcycle club. Only the NLR was more extreme and more radical than the Hell's Angels. The NLR was into chaos and anarchy. They ran guns when they could get their hands on them; and transported and sold drugs of any kind, as long as there was profit involved. The NLR had taken identity theft and extortion and made both pursuits into an art form.

What really set the NLR apart from other outlaw motorcycle gangs was violence. They loved it. It was their calling card.

Crystal meth was the NLR's most lucrative business. But meth was hard to come by. Stealing it from legitimate pharmaceutical companies was almost impossible, because of the security measures such companies used. As a result, the NLR had been reduced to making meth in home labs, which didn't produce the drug fast enough to keep up with the demand. They could sell a thousand times more than what was available, but they didn't have it to sell.

What they needed was a superlab.

Superlabs were the wave of the future, which meant an ocean of profit. But superlabs required specialized equipment, massive amounts of chemicals and the technological know-how to put it together. The Nazi Low Riders didn't have that either.

Wolfman wondered if their luck might be changing. If this Arturo Colano was what he said he was, the NLR could go into superlab production of crystal meth. The next day, girlfriends, wives and associates of the Nazi Low Riders ran background checks on Arturo Colano. Two women who worked at Cal Tech in administrative jobs confirmed that Arturo Colano was indeed a student at the school. Not only was he a student, but a stellar student, referred to by one professor as "an Hispanic genius."

Another contact, working as a clerk at the Pasadena Police Department, ran checks on the police computer databases. Her research revealed nothing suspicious. Arturo Colano had no criminal record and had entered the country legally. There were no flags on his record, which would have indicated he was an undercover cop or an informant.

Arturo Colano was nothing more than a student enrolled in chemical engineering at Cal Tech. He was harmless, but would prove very, very valuable.

WHEN ARTURO graduated from Cal Tech he was twenty-two years old. The school awarded him a Doctor of Philosophy degree in chemical engineering. It was a phenomenal accomplishment by any standard, for in less than five years Arturo had done what takes most students seven or eight years.

Exxon, Shell, BP, Monsanto and many other multinational companies recruited Arturo heavily. They tried to tempt him with huge salaries, company cars and luxurious penthouse apartments in New York, San Francisco, London and Hong Kong. The human resource contact for Monsanto wanted to give Arturo the title of vice-president of research and development.

Arturo listened politely to all the offers. Then told them he'd think about it, but in the end he turned them all down, because the jobs were just that. Jobs. And boring. Arturo wanted pizzazz. He wanted to live a thrilling life—like riding an upside-down looping rollercoaster. It wasn't enough for him to simply know he was alive, he wanted to feel alive.

He'd already found his dream job—working with the outlaw motorcycle gang known as the Nazi Low Riders—where his title would be Magus of Methamphetamine. And like Simon Magus in the Bible, Arturo "would practice sorcery in the city and amaze all the people." He, too, would be known as "the Great Power." But Arturo's sorcery wouldn't be based on mumbo-jumbo and black magic. Arturo's power came from science and its manipulation.

Immediately after graduation, Arturo Colano tossed his clothes, books and diploma into the trunk of a brand new, sparkling white Buick LeSabre, which the Nazi Low Riders had bought for him. He drove north to Pleasanton, where a 3,000 square foot house with a pool in the backyard waited for him.

The outlaw bikers wanted to buy him a Ferrari or a Maserati or a Lamborghini, and a 10,000 square foot mansion to park in front of. But Arturo had vetoed the ideas. "Unwarranted attention would prove detrimental to our enterprise," he told Wolfman, who loved attention and really didn't comprehend the finer points of protective coloration.

Wolfman didn't argue about it. He had been told to give Arturo whatever he wanted and needed. Cost was not a consideration.

Wolfman's instructions had come directly from the Aryan Brotherhood, whom he had contacted because the whole superlab thing was too big and required too much planning and too much money for the Nazi Low Riders to pull off themselves. Wolfman and ten other NLR gangbangers had mounted their hogs and blasted up to San Quentin, where Wolfman paid a visit to Samuel Sauter, imprisoned at the 'Q.' Sauter was on the California council of the Aryan Brotherhood.

Wolfman told Sauter what was going down. "We hooked up with a dude from Cal Tech. A real smart dude," he explained. "This dude can ratchet a shitload of crank, if we can set up a lab for him. I mean a big lab. We need money and help to do it."

Sauter thought about it, then asked, "Who's the dude?"

"He's from Mexico, real sleek cat, smarter 'n shit," replied Wolfman.

"You trust him?"

Wolfman nodded. "Yeah. We did 'due diligence,' as my asshole attorney would say. He checks out."

"Okay," said Sauter. "Then fuckin' go for it. But be smart, Wolfie. Let the dude with the brains be the brains. You be the muscle. Ya' got it?"

"Yeah."

"Whatever the smart dude needs or wants, you get it for him. And don't go cheap. Those dudes on TV are right, you gotta pay out money if you wanna make it. Whatever it takes, just get it done." Sauter smiled. "This smells good. I'll tell my banker what's going down. Hook up with him when you need cash."

SO, ARTURO got his Buick and a middle-class house. And two warehouses in Pleasanton, along with all sorts of fancy equipment that he needed for "the process of harmonizing chemical constituents," as Arturo put it. Truckloads of chemicals started arriving, at which time Arturo began training his technicians, or "junior chemists" as Wolfman called them.

Junior chemists weren't hard to come by. There were lots of people in the East Bay area, especially in Oakland, eager to make a lot of money. And they didn't let little words like 'legal' or 'lawful' or 'illegal' interfere with the beauty of the concept. Most of them were either criminals already engaged in various crimes, or bright white-collar workers who had been employed by dotcom companies, then got laid off and now worked as cashiers at convenience stores, where they were wage-slaves and bored out of their minds. They jumped at the chance to make more than twelve dollars an hour. Because they were educated, they were quick-studies and easy to train. Because they didn't want to go back to the living Hell of cashiering, they were reliable. And, later on, if anyone got scruples about what they were doing, one look at the steroid-induced muscles of the Nazi Low Riders, who walked around bristling with weapons and bad attitude, straightened them out in a hurry. Their scruples vanished like the flavor of bubblegum, shriveling into tasteless nothingness after ten minutes of chewing.

IN NO TIME AT ALL, the superlabs known as HyperChem Industries were up and running. And the shit began to flow. Crystal meth poured out in a steady white stream. And just like the Ford Motor Company, "quality was job one." Arturo made sure that HyperChem's product was of the finest quality. Every batch was tested. Once the okay was given, it was cut with inositol, packaged and shipped all over the western United States, where it was sold to enthusiastic end users, who were known by a number of names: tweekers, addicts, meth-heads, dope fiends and junkies.

One of the laws of physics states that for every action there is an opposite and equal reaction. When the shit flowed out (action), money came back (reaction). Lots of money. Millions of dollars per month in cash, which carried its own unique set of problems. The biggest problem was what to do with the actual physical quantity of it? Banks tended to ask questions when someone walked in with 200 pounds of twenty dollar bills in rucksacks, especially when the people trying to deposit the cash were muscular dudes with shaved heads and swastika tattoos.

Which meant the money had to be laundered, that it had to pass through a legitimate business enterprise so that it could be deposited in a bank without attracting attention.

Wolfman didn't know what to do with the money. He could launder a few hundred thousand, but not $100 million. It wasn't $100 million yet, but within a few months it would be that much or even more. While Wolfman wracked his brains trying to figure how to wash literally tons of money, he stored it in a warehouse. Nazi Low Riders wrapped pallets of bundled bills in plastic, and then used a forklift to put the pallets in PODS, which are fireproof and waterproof 'portable-on-demand-storage' containers that Wolfman had rented. These PODS were stacked by a giant forklift designed to lift cars. The Nazi Low Riders called the giant forklift "Goliath."

In desperation, Wolfman went to Arturo.

"Houston, we have a problem," said Wolfman, trying to be funny.

"What happened in Houston?" Arturo didn't get it.

"No, no, you missed it, dude," Wolfman explained. Then he realized Arturo wouldn't get the explanation either. "Never mind what I just said. Look, here's the problemo, dude. I got all this money coming in and I need to find a way to launder it, ya know? And I can't think of what to do." Wolfman looked embarrassed.

"There is no need for anxiety, my friend," smiled Arturo, gesturing lavishly as he spoke. "Together"—he clasped his hands in front of his throat—"we will resolve your dilemma. Let us ponder simultaneously." Arturo closed his eyes, holding his hands inches from either side of his head, as if trying to cradle his thoughts.

Staring woodenly, Wolfman wondered for the millionth time if all Mexicans were so bizarre, or just the supersmart dudes.

"I have it," announced Arturo, opening his eyes. "The duality of our cerebral energies—yours and mine together—has vanquished all adversity. Such is the puissance of sympathetic cognition." Arturo smiled.

"Yeah," agreed Wolfman, who had no clue what the dude was talking about.

Arturo thrust an index finger aloft. "A number of possibilities exist, my friend. I will submit them to you for your analysis. Thus you may select the most efficacious for our immediate needs.

"First, we might invest our resources in enterprises, which accumulate large amounts of cash. Such as bars, car washes, strip clubs and check cashing stores."

Wolfman's eyes began to gleam, as he nodded.

"I myself have seen many of these check cashing stores in the local strip malls. They are popular among a certain economic segment of the population," added Arturo.

"Yeah," said Wolfman. "Poor people."

"Second," continued Arturo, "we should move rapidly to establish our own company—HyperChem Industries—as a viable shell company. I believe that is the correct term for such an entity. In that manner, we may institute financial transactions with our other shell companies." Arturo grinned. "Doing business with ourselves—a pretext of great beauty, don't you agree?"

"Yeah. But we don't have any other shell companies. So I don't get how—"

"You will, my friend, you will," Arturo said. "Third, we establish shell companies at other banks, then make structured deposits into their accounts." Arturo held up a finger of warning. "But be most vigilant, my friend. No deposit may exceed $10,000. Yet you may make an unlimited number of deposits on any given day, as long as it is only $9,999." Arturo raised his eyebrows, looking at Wolfman to see if he grasped the idea.

Wolfman nodded slowly. Then, like the sun rising at dawn, a smile bloomed across his face. "I get it, dude. You the man!" Wolfman pointed his tattooed knuckles at Arturo.

Arturo performed a modest gesture with his head, tilting it to the side. "As always, my friend, it is my pleasure to be of assistance." And he gave Wolfman a small bow.

WOLFMAN USED all three of Arturo's money laundering ideas. The Nazi Low Riders began buying up bars, car washes, strip clubs and check cashing stores all over northern California. They paid cash for the businesses, telling the owners that they worked for NLR Holding Company, which was a group of investors from the midwest who were expanding operations into California. The owners were happy to sell to NLR Holding Company because NLR didn't haggle over price. They paid whatever the owners asked. And in cash, which meant there was no risk involved—the amount of profit the sellers reported was between them and their conscience.

NLR Holding Company had a number of bank accounts. Since NLR's various businesses were cash intensive, no one at the banks cared when cash deposits were made by NLR's accountants. It was just business as usual.

HyperChem Industries, LLC, was set up and it opened an account at a local bank. A series of shell companies were established both in California and Nevada, each shell company having a bank account. Structured deposits of $5,000 to $6,000 were made in the shell companies' accounts. Sometimes as many as five or six deposits each day in each account. This process was known as 'smurfing.' Female smurfs, dressed like business professionals, would show up, deposit the cash, receive their deposit slip and leave. Then they would repeat the process at another bank, and another and another. It was like riding a carousel. They kept going round and round, making deposits. Of course, the female smurfs had ongoing, intimate relationships with members of the Nazi Low Riders.

All of the shell companies began doing a lot of business with HyperChem Industries, LLC. Invoices for services and supplies were sent to HyperChem, which paid promptly. Which meant a lot of cashier's checks and wire transfers for substantial amounts were disbursed.

Wolfman was glad he had solved his laundry problem. In fact, Wolfman was laundering so much money so efficiently that the California council of the Aryan Brotherhood noticed. The Aryan

Brotherhood had a superlab of its own down in San Diego. Profits from the lab were scandalous, but, locked up in prison, the council was having issues laundering their money. Good help was hard to find. The council asked Wolfman how he was doing it. Wolfman spelled it out for them. The council was so impressed they asked Wolfman to take charge of their laundry, too.

The council were so happy they offered Wolfman a five percent middleman's cut off the top for himself. "That's the least we can do," Sauter said. "All this fuckin' money is nothing but a big fuckin' headache."

Wolfman became a millionaire almost overnight.

HyperChem's production of shit, and all the profits from the sale of the shit, and all the shell companies necessary to wash the profits, along with all the money he was washing for the Aryan Brotherhood, meant that this was no longer a bunch of outlaw bikers trying to make some easy money selling some crank, but instead a vast empire with tentacles reaching everywhere. And every so often things started to go wrong. This meant that Wolfman had to put out fires, and the Nazi Low Riders reverted to what they knew best—violence.

For example, farmers were the primary source of anhydrous ammonia, which was vital to the production of crank. The farmers would either get greedy, demanding more money, or they got afraid and wanted out. Either way, Wolfman sent Nazi Low Riders to perform what Wolfman called "attitude adjustments." The threat of violence was usually more than enough to remind the rebellious farmers that to get along they needed to go along. A bunch of tattooed, hairless, steroid-abusing Nazi gorillas riding Harley Davidsons and packing Mac-10s would arrive at the slacker's farmhouse in the middle of the night and drag the farmer out of bed for a pep rally. After the importance of fellowship and brotherhood had been explained, the farmer invariably had a religious experience. He repented and promised to sin no more.

This saddened Wolfman a little bit, because he enjoyed stomping the shit out of people, especially farmers, who were nothing but cloverkicking hypocrites that put on a front of being righteous, law-abiding members of the community, while at the same time doing business with white supremacist bikers and lying to their insurance companies. On the other hand, Wolfman was glad he hadn't had to kill anyone so far. Dead bodies tended to attract cops and media attention like sugar attracted ants, and Wolfman didn't need any more problems right now. Ever since he'd gotten mixed up with superlabs, shell companies and laundering millions of dollars, Wolfman had become more and more cautious, acting like an old woman at a church bazaar.

Some days Wolfman wondered if he wasn't getting soft. All this responsibility shit was stressing him out.

On his part, Arturo was having nothing but fun. His two superlabs were running like a well-oiled machine. Reserve stock of vital chemicals was adequate, crystal meth production was up, the quality was excellent, and distribution was systematic and prompt. The shit flowed.

In his body, mind and soul, Arturo was a scientist, which meant he was nobody's fool. He'd grown up in the slums of Mexico, living from hand to mouth. He knew that the well-oiled machine could suffer a seizure at any moment. Any criminal enterprise was just like an engine. It had a lot of complex, moving parts. If one of the parts failed, the engine blew, spraying oil, black smoke and debris everywhere. When that happened everything came speeding to a stop. It was inevitable that one of the parts would eventually fail, because for the most part criminals were lazy, weak and stupid. Stupidity was their default mode. They always returned to it.

Arturo had made contingency plans. Most of his money was in numbered bank accounts in Switzerland and the Cayman Islands. Both banks were renowned for their reticence and love of privacy. In his office at HyperChem Industries, Arturo had a coat-tree. On the coat-tree, suspended by its velcro strap, hung a fanny pack, which contained his passport and $5,000 in cash. There was another $5,000 in the glove box of his Buick LeSabre, along with a suitcase of clothing in the trunk. At a nearby U-Store-It, he had rented a forty foot storage unit, in which sat a Cadillac CSX with a full tank of gas and another suitcase of clothing. The keys to the Cadillac were in the ignition. And on the off-chance that he could not simply walk to his Buick and drive away from HyperChem, Arturo had both a Yamaha R-6 and a Schwinn bicycle parked at the back of the warehouse near the loading docks.

THE DAY Wolfman spotted the Yamaha, his booming laugh rumbled through the warehouse. "What the fuck is that?" he asked Arturo.

"A motorcycle," replied Arturo.

"Is it yours?"

"Precisely."

"Well," asked Wolfman, grinning like a skunk eating shit, "can you ride it?"

"Naturally, I have familiarized myself with the vehicle's operating principles," Arturo explained.

"Yeah," repeated Wolfman, "but can you ride it?" Once he stopped laughing, Wolfman noticed the look on Arturo's face. "I'm sorry, dude," said Wolfman. "I didn't mean nothin'. But if you wanted a bike, why didn't you tell me? I woulda' got you a real piece of iron, ya know? A Harley or a custom Arlen Ness. Not one a them rice rockets."

Arturo smiled. "I am convinced your advice would prove most prosperous, Wolfman. However, I suspected my level of competence would be incommensurate with the models you have suggested."

Wolfman nodded. "You're probably right, dude. But still..." Wolfman swallowed his laughter and let the matter drop. He didn't want to hurt the guy's feelings. He actually kind of liked Arturo.

WHEN—NOT IF—things went to Hell in a handbasket, Arturo could walk to the parking lot and drive away in his Buick. Or, if he couldn't get to the Buick for some reason, he could ride away on either the motorcycle or the bicycle. If the situation was indeed dire, he would simply walk away from the warehouse. The U-Store-It facility was less than one mile away. Hoofing it to the Cadillac would be easy enough. After that he could drive to the Oakland airport or the San Francisco international airport, where, after parking in the long-term lot, he would purchase a ticket to Dallas. In Dallas, he would purchase another ticket on a different airline and fly to Atlanta, where he would fly to Orlando with all the other tourists. Only Arturo wouldn't visit Disney World. Instead, he would rent an unassuming van under a fictitious name, and drive to Miami, where he would spend a few days, acting like any other businessman trying to de-stress by catching some rays at the beach. Except Arturo would change hotels every night. He'd also return the van to the rental agency's Miami branch, and either walk or take cabs thereafter.

Then Arturo would wait. He would wait to see what happened. If nothing happened, he would remain in Miami, living quietly, doing nothing for a year or two. Otherwise, if he intuited the Feds were looking for him, he'd go to Europe and live in Barcelona, Spain, where he could blend in. Perhaps Namibia, which had no extradition treaty with the United States. Or maybe Brazil or Venezuela, whichever felt right at the time. Arturo believed in following intuition in such circumstances, because only intuition or second sight, as Mexicans called it, swept away the conscious mind and its inculcated flaws, thus allowing the senses to apprehend events and choices purely by instinct. To most Latin Americans second sight was the same thing as 'faith,' knowing something deep inside. Which was why he often said, "The stomach knows the way."

It was because of his stomach that Arturo had decided to author his contingency plan. Because of his stomach, Arturo would not hesitate to abandon any part of his contingency plan. He would dump the whole thing and leave the Buick and the Cadillac, the clothing in the suitcases, the cash in the glove box. None of it was important.

In the meantime, it was business as usual. Arturo and his technicians pumped out crystal meth, and Wolfman washed the profits through his shell companies. The business community of Pleasanton viewed Arturo as a successful entrepreneur. He made lots of new friends, most of who were educated and wealthy. They drove expensive European cars, lived in million dollar homes with well-stocked wine cellars, dined at pretentious restaurants run by snooty chefs and sent their kids to elitist private schools. They invited Arturo to their parties, where he met all the right people. Arturo loved it. He was having fun.

After worrying about money and managing his semi-legitimate businesses all day, Wolfman hung out at sleazy bars and titty clubs with the Nazi Low Riders, and drank too much beer. Hooking up with a stripper named Bambi, he shacked up with her and her cat, a Siamese named Lovey, in a two-bedroom condominium and bought a new Harley, which was black and had silver swastikas on the gas tank. To keep track of his laundromat activities, Wolfman got a computer with Excel software, which was so hard to understand that he bought a copy of *Excel For Idiots* and began reading it in his spare time. He couldn't even understand the book for idiots.

Wolfman was not having any fun. He longed for the old days.

Meanwhile, two members of the California council of the Aryan Brotherhood—Sam Sauter and Henry Janes—weren't having any fun either. Death row was not amusing.

SEVEN

Adios Amigos

SAN QUENTIN STATE PRISON, also known as the 'Q', was named after a Coast Miwok warrior whose name was Quentin. The 'Q' opened for business in 1852, which made it the oldest prison in California. After Alcatraz closed, it became the most famous prison in California. The source of San Quentin's fame was death row, where California housed all male inmates who had been sentenced to die for their crimes. Once it had been hanging, then it was the gas chamber, now lethal injection was the preferred method of capital punishment. There was a droll feel to death row, as if the inmates were waiting to laugh at a joke whose punch line had been blown. Neither was the joke very funny, which left everyone feeling forsaken and foolish.

The humor of death row was this: A bunch of monsters had been condemned to death by the legal system, but that same legal system couldn't bring itself to actually execute the monsters.

Samuel S. Sauter and Henry Janes failed to see anything funny at all in their situation. But then neither had a sense of humor. Not only were they 'made' members of the Aryan Brotherhood, with the tattoos to prove it, they also sat on the California council, which had a total of five councilmen. The other three councilmen were lodged in the SHU—the Security Housing Unit—at Pelican Bay state prison, located in the middle of nowhere in northern California.

Once upon a time, Sam Sauter had owned a landscaping company in the upscale suburb of Alpine, located in the foothills near San Diego. A very macho guy, Sauter had a regular arsenal of handguns and semi-automatic assault rifles. He liked to go out and blast away at beer cans, discarded toilets and anything else that exploded when hit by a hail of bullets. He also had a Harley Davidson motorcycle, which, when he was riding it, made him feel tough and invincible. But the thing that really made Sauter feel godlike was his membership in the Nazi Low Riders. Being in the NLR was like snorting cocaine, taking a big hit of crystal meth, all while having sex. It was the ultimate rush.

Sauter had hooked up with the NLR in 1997. Within a year he had his colors,* which meant he was a full-fledged member of the Nazi Low Riders. Since the NLR did a lot of favors and ran errands for the Aryan Brotherhood, Sauter soon came into contact with the AB. When he realized the Aryan Brotherhood were the real shotcallers, the ones at the top of the food chain, Sauter wanted in and made himself useful. It was easy. He was clever and organized and ran his own business. He told the Aryan Brotherhood that he could launder money for them. Always on the lookout for new talent, the AB gave him a chance and Sauter came through. He funneled $20,000 of Aryan Brotherhood dirty money, which was delivered in a brown paper sack by two Nazi Low Riders, into his landscaping business. A week later, he returned the money, which now smelled like fabric softener—clean and fresh. Impressed, the Aryan Brotherhood made Sauter an associate, which meant he was a sidekick with a certain amount of status and some privileges, but not yet a 'made' member.

Sauter kept a low profile and did whatever the AB asked him to do. When the DEA and the San Diego Police began targeting the Nazi Low Riders, Sauter's low profile paid off. Since he flew under the Feds' radar, he avoided being arrested, and so remained available when the Aryan Brotherhood needed something done. The Brotherhood made him the 'banker' for the San Diego area. Once that happened, Sauter suggested to the Brotherhood that they make him a member. He reasoned that if he was good enough to be their banker, he was

---

* 'Colors' refers to a club's identifying insignia, which is usually worn on the back of a vest or jacket. Ironically, the term comes from legal usage, where it refers to an apparent or *prima facie* right.

good enough to be a made member. The Brotherhood agreed, and in the spring of 1999, Sam Sauter took the oath and received the Brand.*

SEVENTEEN YEAR OLD Pamela Fleck was a senior at West Hills High School when she met Sam Sauter. She ran in the clique known as 'the slackers.' Bored with school and their lives, the slackers hung out together, smoked cigarettes and tried to look cool. Despite being a part of the clique, Pamela Fleck didn't think slacking was all that much fun. She was restless and always searching for something new and exciting. She spent time on chat lines talking to strangers because she enjoyed hearing the opinions and viewpoints and experiences of other people. Pamela found a sense of risky adventure in talking to strangers. Of course, nothing dangerous could ever happen, because no one knew who she was or where she lived. But it was still exciting and fun.

One night she talked to a guy named Sam, who seemed really cool. He was thirty-something, which was old but not so old that he was dull. He rode a Harley and had a cool car and went clubbing. He made Pamela laugh with his crazy sense of humor.

Pretty soon, Pamela and Sam were talking every night. During one of their conversations, Sam said, "I can't talk too long tonight, Pamela. Got places to go, ya know?"

"What? You gotta hot date?" laughed Pamela.

"I wish. No, a friend of mine slipped me a couple of tickets to a show. So I thought I'd trick my loneliness tonight and take myself out. First, the show. Then maybe a late dinner and a beer or two, ya know?"

"What show?" asked Pamela.

"A jazz concert at the Fox Theater in the old part of town. Some guy you probably never heard of, I'm sure. You're too young."

---

* Samuel Sauter, in discussion, San Quentin prison, 2009. This is one of the few instances when the 'blood in, blood out' requirement of the Aryan Brotherhood was waived.

Pamela bristled a little bit. She didn't like being left out and she was rabid about all kinds of music. Music was her thing. She took Sam's words as a challenge. "Who is it?"

"David Sanborn," said Sam. "He plays—"

"Alto saxophone like no one else in the whole world," interrupted Pamela. "He is like the greatest ever! I love his music!"

"Well, too bad you can't come along," put in Sam. "It'd be nice to have someone to enjoy it with."

Pamela hesitated. After a few moments, she said, "Who says I can't come along?"

"Not me," stated Sam. "It's just that... well, you know... we don't know each other and you're kinda young and..."

"And what?"

"Well, your parents might not let you go with some guy my age."

"My parents?" scoffed Pamela. "My dad left a long time ago and my mom couldn't care less what I do and who I do it with."

Sam acquiesced. "You wanna go?"

"Yes, I do," announced Pamela, feeling a little victorious.

"Okay. That's settled. I'll pick you up around seven. Where do you live?"

Pamela gave him the address. Sam knew the place—a trailer park not far from where he lived.

FOR PAMELA, it was the beginning of a whole new life. Sam had a never-ending supply of money. They went places in his convertible corvette. He bought her sexy clothes that she wore to parties at his house. Wild parties—with rivers of alcohol and mountains of pizza and hot wings—attended by really radical looking people, the kind of people Pamela had never even imagined existed. Muscular guys with shaved heads and tattoos, who rode custom motorcycles, carried guns and knives, and whose girlfriends looked like supermodels out of a Ray Bradbury sci-fi novel, what with their nose rings and designer tattoos.

And lots and lots of drugs.

By this time, Sam Sauter was a major tweeker. Mostly cocaine, which he called "nose candy," and crystal meth, which he called "white." His habit, which he referred to as "my part-time flirtation," commanded $10,000 a month.

Sauter introduced Pamela to crystal meth. She loved it. Her search for something new and exciting was over. Meth left her feeling buoyant and successful and triumphant, as if she was the most beautiful and most powerful woman in history, as if she was Cleopatra, Britney Spears and Paris Hilton all rolled up into one.

When Pamela turned eighteen, she told her mother she was dropping out of school.

Debra laughed, thinking she was joking. She was glancing through the garage sale notices in the local newspaper. She tapped the paper with a forefinger. "Here's one that says it's the hugest garage sale ever."

"I mean it, mom," declared Pamela.

The tone of her daughter's voice caused Debra to stop reading. "That's crazy talk," she said. "You only have four months left until you graduate."

"I don't care," shrugged Pamela. "I'm done with school."

Equal parts of fear and anger flared in Debra's eyes. "Oh, and just what kind of job do you think you'll get with no high school diploma?" she demanded.

"I don't need a job, especially one that pays a stinking eight dollars an hour," sneered Pamela.

"Well then how do you expect to support yourself, missie?" Debra fired back. "I'm certainly not going to. And unless I missed something, no one died and left you $1 million."

Pamela gave her mother a rude, crude look. "I'm moving in with Sam," she stated in a flat voice, as she turned and walked away.

"You mean that cradle robber who's been sniffing around here?" flashed Debra. "Over my dead body!"

Pamela stopped to fix her mother a stare for a moment. "Okay, if that's the way you want it," she said and walked out of the trailer.

Helpless, Debra just stood there. She never saw Pamela again.

TRUE TO HER WORDS, Pamela stopped going to school. There was nothing anyone could do about it. She was eighteen and her own person now. The next day, while her mother was at work, Pamela entered the trailer and grabbed a few articles of clothing. Outside, a corvette idled. Sam Sauter sat behind the wheel, listening to the radio. Pamela waltzed out of the trailer, carrying the sum total of eighteen years of life in a trash bag that she tossed behind the seat. She slid into the car, looked at Sam and smiled. "Let's blow this pop stand," she said.

With a laugh, Sam put the car in gear and drove away. As they turned out of the trailer park, Pamela looked back.

LIVING WITH SAM was a blast. He had a white stucco house with a red tile roof. There was a pool in the backyard and a hot-tub and a big barbecue made of stainless steel. Almost every night of the week, they had a party. Which meant a smorgasbord of drugs, booze and food, although very little food was actually eaten. Everyone seemed content with narcotics and alcohol. Surprisingly, very little sexual intercourse took place, because after a few hours of snorting and swallowing and smoking, most of the party-goers were too stupefied to move.

It was great fun. Pamela loved it. Sam did, too.

There was only one problem. Sam was spending money like crazy, but he wasn't making much. Most of the time he was hopped up on meth or coke, which made it hard to function. He just wanted to feel good, and so his landscaping business went to Hell. First the clients bailed, then most of the employees left. And because he needed the landscaping business to wash the money he was laundering for the Aryan Brotherhood, there suddenly was no money coming in, only money going out—for drugs and booze and parties.

Sam woke up to find himself $200,000 in debt to Mexican Mafia gangbangers, who didn't believe in cutting anybody any slack with an installment plan for payments. When they wanted their money, they wanted it now.

Sam was in a box and needed a way out. If he didn't find an exit, the box would become a coffin real fast. As he racked his brains for an escape plan, an idea formed. Every detail was visible. He didn't even have to think about whether it would work or not, it was perfect.

Sam Sauter made a call to his insurance agent. He needed to take out a life insurance policy on one of his employees.

"Why's that?" asked the agent.

"Because this particular employee is vital to my business," explained Sam. "If anything ever happened to her, I'd have a hard time replacing her. Which means my business would suffer."

"Okay," said the agent. "It's a fairly common practice. Of course, the companies that do it are usually a lot bigger than yours, but you'll never get bigger if you don't play it smart. What's the employee's name?"

"Pamela Fleck."

"And what amount did you want to cover her for?"

"Well," hesitated Sam, "what would you suggest?"

"At least enough to cover one year's operating expenses and profits," said the agent. "That way—if, God forbid, anything did happen—you'd have time to find a replacement and train her."

"Yeah, that makes sense," agreed Sam. "That would mean a policy for $500,000."

"Got it," said the agent, and he ran through the particulars with Sam and filled out a form. "The policy will go into effect the first day of next month, unless you want to start sooner. In which case, I'd have to prorate the premium."

"No, the first of next month is fine," said Sam. "I'm sure she'll make it till then." He chuckled.

"Let's hope so," laughed the agent. "Hey, we need to get together one of these days, play a little golf. Whaddaya think?"

"Yeah, sure. Let me check my calendar and get back to you. All work and no play, ya know?"

"You know it, buddy. Friday or Saturday afternoons are best for me. Talk to ya soon."

"Sure thing," said Sam. He hung up and looked out the window. All he had to do now was wait two or three months, so it didn't look too suspicious. And even if it did, it wouldn't mean anything. Coincidences happened all the time. People died all the time—some with life insurance, some without. Besides, the only ones who would know about the insurance would be him and the insurance company. No one would be the wiser. Only two people would know what was really going on: Sam Sauter, who planned it, and Gaspar Gabriel-Portola, who did it.

Gaspar Gabriel-Portola was an illegal alien from Tijuana who worked for Sauter. Gabriel-Portola, who also went by the name Juan de la Torre, had crossed over into California one year ago. Approaching Sauter, he inquired about a job as a laborer. Sauter knew right away that the guy was in the country illegally. But Sauter didn't care. Sauter used illegals whenever he could, because they worked cheap and wanted to be paid in cash, which meant Sauter avoided the paperwork and expenses associated with taxes and unemployment insurance.

Sauter and Gabriel-Portola hit it off. Both men were major tweekers and greedy for money to feed their drug habits. Gabriel-Portola made it clear to Sauter that he was available for any type of work that might come up. He didn't care what it involved, as long as he could make a lot of money quick.

A FEW DAYS AFTER the insurance policy kicked in on Pamela Fleck, Sauter approached Gabriel-Portola.

"What would you say if I told you I needed someone to take care of some business for me?" asked Sauter.

"I'd say you don't need to bother with *someone* when you got me," replied Gabriel-Portola. "What kinda business you talking about?"

Sauter glanced over his shoulder, then looked at Gabriel-Portola bluntly. "A contract," he said.

Gabriel-Portola blinked. "No problem. Only that kind of work is not cheap, ya know what I mean?"

"Yeah, I know," nodded Sauter. "Say $10,000?"

Gabriel-Portola smiled, shaking his head as if he'd just been insulted. "More like $25,000." His dark eyes peered into Sauter's blue eyes. Sauter was the worst type of coward—a swaggering coward. Sauter boasted about how bad he was, how tough, because he was in the Aryan Brotherhood. It was all an act. The truth was that Sauter was a chicken. He paid other people to do his dirty work.

Sauter paused, thinking for a moment, then nodded. "Okay. $5,000 now, the rest when the job is done."

Gabriel-Portola agreed. He raised his index finger and pointed it at Sauter's temple. "No funny stuff, okay?"

"No funny stuff," said Sauter in a voice plump with certainty.

"Good," nodded Gabriel-Portola. "Now tell me about the job."

Sauter moved half a step closer and began talking in a low voice.

THREE MONTHS LATER, Sauter sat in his corvette, which was in the parking lot of a public beach in West San Diego. He smelled the tang of ocean salt in the air, heard seagulls beeping overhead. Taking out his cell phone, he called his house, where Pamela Fleck was lounging by the pool. Pamela answered.

"Hey, babe," said Sauter. "What's happening?"

"Nothing. I'm bored. When are you coming home?"

"Pretty soon, I hope. I'm at a flashy house out near La Jolla, giving a guy a bid on a big job," Sauter lied. "As soon as I'm done, I'll be heading home."

"Well, hurry," complained Pamela. "I'm about to go crazy here all by my lonesome."

"Look, babe," said Sauter, "while you're waiting for me, I need a favor."

"What?"

"One of my crew needs a jump for his car, which stalled out on him not far from the office."

"Why can't you do it? Or one of the others?"

"I need to stay here and sweet talk this client," explained Sauter. "And everybody else is at other job sites. Which is where this guy needs to be as soon as possible. Please, babe. I really need this favor."

"Oh, all right," agreed a listless Pamela. "Where is he?"

"He walked to the office. You can pick him up there and he'll show you where his car is. It's not far from the office, so it won't take you very long. He has jumper cables in the trunk of his car."

"I guess," said Pamela. "Who is it I'm picking up?"

"Gaspar. Gaspar Gabriel-Portola. I'm sure you've seen him around. You'll recognize him when you see him. Thanks, babe. I'll make it up to you. We'll go out tonight, do some partying. I gotta go. Bye."

Pamela threw a sun-dress on over her swimsuit, grabbed her car keys and purse and walked out to her car.

A WHITE FORD MUSTANG screeched to a stop in front of Alpine Landscaping Company, where Gabriel-Portola stood waiting.

"You Gabriel-Portola?" shouted Pamela through the open window of her car. "Jump in. I'm Pamela, Sam's girlfriend. He wants me to take you to your car so you can get it running."

Gabriel-Portola smiled and slid into the passenger's seat. "Thanks," he said.

"No problem," replied Pamela. "Now where to?"

"Straight to the stop sign," pointed the passenger. "Then right. It's about two miles down one of them little roads."

Pamela gunned the Mustang in the direction of the stop sign.

Gabriel-Portola peeked at her out of the corner of his eyes, wondering why Sauter wanted her dead. She was slender and pretty, with dark hair, and very young—only eighteen, Sauter had told him. Gabriel-Portola shrugged.

As the Mustang turned right, Pamela Fleck was as good as dead. Two miles later, the road ended in a cul-de-sac. Pamela brought the car to a stop and turned to look at her passenger. A puzzled expression pinched her face. "Where's your car?" she asked.

Gabriel-Portola pulled a pistol out of his pocket and squared it at Pamela. "Get out," he said.

"What?"

"Get out of the car," repeated Gabriel-Portola.

Anger flared through Pamela. "Look. Is this some kind of robbery or something?"

"Get out!" yelled Gabriel-Portola.

Scared, Pamela got out and Gabriel-Portola followed. "Move to the front of the car," he ordered.

Pamela walked slowly to the front of the car, looking around for help. There was no help, only dry dirt and parched bushes.

Gabriel-Portola walked up to Pamela, put the gun to her head and fired. Her body fluttered like a rag-doll and dropped to the ground. A puff of wind ruffled her hair.

Gabriel-Portola stood looking at the body for a few seconds. He felt nothing. No sorrow, no pity, no sense of accomplishment, no happiness at having just made $25,000. Not anything. Putting the gun back in his pocket, he turned and walked back the way he had just driven with the girl who was now dead.

WHEN GABRIEL-PORTOLA got back to Sauter's office, he called Sauter and told him he had gotten his car started. Sauter smiled, closing his eyes. Goosebumps cascaded down his spine as he realized that this was the real deal. It wasn't a game. He was in the shit.

Sauter waited until the end of the day, then reported Pamela Fleck as missing to the local police. It was a sham, of course. Sauter just wanted to divert any suspicion from himself.

It wasn't until four days later that Pamela's body was discovered. Kids riding dirt bikes almost ran across her and called 911. Three sheriff's patrol cars rolled to a halt behind Pamela's Mustang. It took only one look for the deputies to decide they had a homicide on their hands. Local television crews, who heard the call on their police scanners, arrived on the scene before the forensics people. The deputies busied themselves in keeping the cameramen away from the crime scene, and gave interviews to the television reporters, who asked questions to which the deputies answered flatly: "Until forensics finishes their analysis, we can't release any information."

Sam Sauter sat in his house, watching the live feed on television. Pleased with the way things were going, he felt confident he would get away with murder. As long as Gabriel-Portola didn't do anything stupid, they had it made in the shade. He had already paid Gabriel-Portola off, giving him a BMW, a Chevy Tahoe and a check for $7,000.

Two weeks after Pamela's murder, Sauter did something stupid. He needed money, both to pay off his debt to the Mexican Mafia and to purchase more drugs. So he put in a claim on the life insurance policy he had taken out on Pamela Fleck. Since the police investigation had not yet been completed, the claim was automatically rejected.

Sauter realized that when the police found out about the claim they would begin sniffing around, looking for a connection. As if that wasn't bad enough, the Mexican Mafia had given him an ultimatum, pay up or else. Sauter couldn't pay up. He had no money. He decided to make like a breeze and blow out of town. Contacting Gabriel-Portola, Sauter told him what was going down. Gabriel-Portola agreed that it was time to go. Driving his new BMW over to Sauter's house, Gabriel-Portola picked up Sauter and drove south on I-5, crossing the border into Tijuana, where the two accomplices took up residence in a squalid two bedroom house that belonged to Gabriel-Portola's uncle. The house had lime green trim and three mangy cats that hated Sauter on first sight. Sauter despised them right back and twice tried to poison them.

Since they rarely left the house and were out of the loop, Sauter and Gabriel-Portola didn't know anything about what was going on just across the border in California, where the police investigation continued. Nine months had passed and enough evidence was collected to indict Samuel Sauter and Gaspar Gabriel-Portola on murder and conspiracy charges. Hiding out in Tijuana for a year, the two men simply figured enough time had passed and the heat was probably off, if there ever was any heat. Sauter was bored out of his mind and sick and tired of living like a rat in a hole. Besides, he wanted to get away from the fucking cats. The two men headed out for San Diego, with the intention of hooking up with the Nazi Low Riders and making some money running drugs.

They made it across the border easy enough, passing quickly through US Custom's inspection. One of the custom's agents had considered the vehicle and its occupants suspicious enough to put a call through to the CHP, giving them the car's description and plate numbers. Two miles later, inside California, two CHP cruisers pulled the BMW over and arrested Sauter and Gabriel-Portola.

Gabriel-Portola decided to cut his losses and be smart. When they got to the jail, he spilled the beans to detectives, telling them that Sam Sauter hired him to kill Pamela Fleck.

On March 30, 2004, heavily shackled as he sat in the courtroom, Sauter showed no emotion as Judge B. G. Walton sentenced him to death for the murder of Pamela Fleck.

Sauter's attorneys had filed a motion the day before, asking the judge to lower Sauter's sentence to life in prison. Sauter's crime was indeed horrible, they agreed, but it did not merit capital punishment. According to his attorneys, Sauter's actions were the result of ongoing mental problems and that medication had already proven effective in altering his mental state and his violent behavior.

Judge Walton rejected the motion. "Evidence clearly shows that Mr. Sauter was able to formulate and carry out complex criminal schemes. His motive was greed and the desire for financial gain."

In conclusion, Judge Walton defined Sauter as "a classic sociopath and a cold, calculated murderer."

Within thirty minutes, Samuel Sauter was seated in his own private cage on a bus, headed north to San Quentin state prison and the cell blocks known as death row. Here he was a condemned prisoner, warehoused until it was time for his execution.

ON APRIL 3, 2004, Gaspar Gabriel-Portola entered the courtroom where a few days earlier sentence had been passed on his partner in crime, Samuel Sauter.

He already told the detectives who arrested him that Sauter had hired him to kill Pamela Fleck. He reiterated the same story to the jury, but with one embellishment: "I didn't actually kill Pamela," Gabriel-Portola confessed in court. "I couldn't bring myself to do it. Sam Sauter was the one who murdered her."

A defense attorney milked this testimony for all it was worth. "Mr. Gabriel-Portola's religious upbringing, along with his own conscience, prevented him from committing such a heinous crime," the attorney explained to the jury. "He could not bring himself to take the life of another human being." The attorney paused for a moment, then said in a low, sad voice, "But Samuel Sauter could. And because of that, Samuel Sauter has already been sentenced to death by lethal injection."

Some of the jurors flinched at the jarring words.

The attorney pointed at Gabriel-Portola. "Mr. Gabriel-Portola was under Sauter's diabolical influence. That's the only reason he was there. Mr. Gabriel-Portola didn't realize he was being used and manipulated." Holding up his hands to indicate the importance of his next statement, the attorney looked at the jury. "Another jury of twelve people has sifted the evidence and determined that Samuel Sauter murdered Pamela Fleck. Not Mr. Gabriel-Portola. It is now your duty to sift the evidence presented in this case and determine the fate of Gaspar Gabriel-Portola."

The jury decided that Gabriel-Portola was guilty of conspiracy to murder, but not so guilty that he deserved to die—not so guilty when compared to Sauter anyway—and they recommended a sentence of life in prison without parole.

Judge Walton asked whether the accused would like to make a statement before sentence was passed. Gabriel-Portola stood and said, "I feel bad. I don't see the justice. I think I've been used. I think it's not fair." Then he sat down.

Judge Walton raised his eyebrows and glanced at his court clerk, who gave a little shrug. Judge Walton said, "Mr. Gabriel-Portola, I sentence you to life in prison without the possibility of parole."

Waiting to be transported, Gabriel-Portola was held in the San Diego County Jail for a few days. That's when things got complicated. Mexican authorities—from the Federal Investigations Agency—requested Gabriel-Portola's extradition to Tijuana to testify in a messy murder trial that involved three dead Mexican policemen and the Mexican drug cartels. The Mexican authorities informed the California Department of Corrections (CDC) that Gabriel-Portola's testimony was vital to their case, and that CDC could do whatever they wanted with Gabriel-Portola *after* he had testified.

CDC agreed to loan Gabriel-Portola to the Mexicans, on the condition he would be returned to the US as soon as the Mexicans were done with him. The temporary extradition was cleared with the US State Department, and, after much paper shuffling, Gabriel-Portola found himself at the Mexican border, passing from the company of two corrections officers and two US marshals, into the company of four Mexican Federal Investigators and a squad of Mexican Army soldiers. He was then hustled off to a secret location so that the drug cartels wouldn't kill him before he had a chance to testify against them.

No one bothered to ask Gaspar Gabriel-Portola what he thought of it all. If they had, they would have discovered that Gaspar Gabriel-Portola had no intention of testifying against the drug cartels. He knew that if he did testify, his life would come to an abrupt halt; he would be dead within ten minutes. And for another thing, one of his uncles was a high-ranking member of the Gulf cartel, which was based in Matamoros. There was no way Gabriel-Portola would ever testify against a blood relation.

The drug cartel, of course, knew exactly the secret location of Gabriel-Portola, because most of the Mexican Federal Investigators and all of the soldiers were on the cartel's payroll. A member of the Gulf cartel arrived in a chauffeur-driven Mercedes to find Gabriel-

Portola seated at a table, eating tacos and drinking Pabst Blue Ribbon beer, watching a re-run of *Baywatch* on a big-screen TV. After embracing each other, Gabriel-Portola and the cartel guy smoked some cigarettes. Then it was time to go. Gabriel-Portola shook hands and hugged each of the federal policemen and soldiers, who had lined up to bid him farewell.

The next day, the Mexican authorities informed CDC that Gaspar Gabriel-Portola had escaped. A massive manhunt for the prisoner was ongoing and they expected to capture the fugitive imminently. Embarrassed by the incident, the Mexican authorities assured CDC that no stone would be left unturned. They would keep the Americans advised. In fact, a liaison officer was already on his way across the border.

Gabriel-Portola boarded a plane for Acapulco, where he vacationed at his uncle's villa, regaling his uncle and other family members with stories about the stupid gringos.

SAM SAUTER languished in his small cell on death row. He was granted a few hours exercise every day, and it was during one of these recreation periods he met Henry Janes, who was also on death row and who was also a member of the Aryan Brotherhood. Janes was no ordinary member of the AB. He sat on the California council of the AB. Sauter and Janes became best friends for a number of reasons. They were both part of the Brand; they were both condemned to death; and they both considered themselves mystic-traditional warriors.

Janes recommended Sauter to fill a vacancy on the council, to which the Aryan Brotherhood voted in the affirmative. Almost overnight, Sauter went from a craven murderer, who used hired help to do his dirty deeds, to one of the top dogs in California's prison system. And because Sauter excelled as a big mouthed braggart, constantly telling lies about his knowledge of making and moving crystal meth, he and Janes were entrusted with the narcotics department. Which meant they—a coward and a lunatic—controlled the production and distribution of crystal meth by the AB in the state of California.

Short and squat, Henry Janes looked like a fire hydrant. He was crazy as Hell, an acknowledged king-crimson psychopath, who had been on death row for six years, and, except for the fact that sooner or later he would be executed, he loved the place. Not only did he enjoy the vicious environment, the other inmates respected him because of his ferocity. Respect was something Henry Janes didn't get much of out in the real world. He was from Los Angeles, where only the rich and beautiful and famous got any respect. Henry Janes was none of these things; he was an ugly gangbanger whose only claim to fame was sadistic lunacy.

First-degree murder, torture, kidnapping and other related charges, that's why Henry was on death row.

It happened like this: Henry knew a chick, who had been dating a really attractive guy from Redondo Beach. The guy's name was Adrian Rooms. Adrian Rooms was an actor and had done some television work, mostly small parts in soap operas. But he was considered an up and comer in the biz, because of his sensuous looks and a willingness to work hard.

Adrian Rooms had a tendency to date women for a while—until they began to bore him—and then break the relationship off. In fact, sooner or later pretty much everything and everyone bored Adrian Rooms, which explained his wicked drug habit. Rooms was what was called a "frequent flyer"—high most of the time. Cocaine and crystal meth were his choice of supersonic transport.

That's what happened to this chick that Henry Janes knew. She dated Adrian Rooms and really started to fall for the guy, except Rooms got bored and dumped her. Remember that old adage, "Hell hath no fury like a woman scorned"? Well, that was the chick. She was hurt, angry and wanted revenge, and so called Henry Janes, who was a pal of hers. He was also a member of the Aryan Brotherhood, which meant he liked violence. Janes was a little bit off, and would start bouncing off the walls and foaming at the mouth.

On the phone with Janes, the chick said, "Just beat him up a little. I mean I don't want him hurt bad or anything, you know? I mean I love him, you know?"

"I know what ya mean," said Janes. "Where'd you say this guy lives?"

She gave an address.

"Okay," said Janes, "consider it done."

"Remember," she gushed, "nothin' real bad, okay?"

"Consider it done," repeated Janes.

After he hung up, Janes called a friend, whose name was Billy Williams, who was an Aryan Brotherhood 'associate,' and even more cuckoo than Janes. If that was possible. Billy Williams would do anything Janes asked of him because of his desire to be a full-fledged, branded member of the AB. Williams also had a van.

The next day, September 7, 1996, Henry Janes and Billy Williams drove in Williams' van to Redondo Beach, where Adrian Rooms lived. When they couldn't find the street, they pulled into a 7-Eleven and asked the clerk for directions. They also bought some donuts and two cherry Slurpees. Janes had a sweet tooth of heroic proportions.

Following the directions of the clerk, they located the street and parked in front of Adrian Rooms' condo. Sucking on the straws of their Slurpees, they got out of the van and walked to the front door of the condo. Janes rang the doorbell, then knocked on the door until Adrian Rooms opened up. Confronted with two guys with shaved heads and tattooed forearms, holding Slurpee cups, Rooms thought maybe they were with his yard service.

"You Adrian Rooms?"

"Yeah."

"Okay," nodded the short, puffy guy. "Just wanted to be sure." With that, he pulled out a semi-automatic pistol and pointed it at Rooms' head.

Rooms tried to shut the door, but wasn't fast enough. Thirty seconds later, he was seated in the back of the van, with one Slurpee-sucking guy pointing a gun at him; the other Slurpee-sucking guy driving.

Henry Janes and Billy Williams drove Adrian Rooms to a vacant warehouse in Ventura County, where they hog-tied him to a chair. When Adrian Rooms started yelling, Janes hit him in the head with the gun. Rooms almost passed out, and then started screaming as loud as he could.

"Shit," cursed Janes. "Be quiet, would ya?"

"I'll shut 'im up," said Billy Williams, who picked up a beer bottle and smashed it into pieces. "Keep his mouth open," he told Janes.

Janes jammed the barrel of his gun into Adrian Rooms' mouth, and levered it wide. Williams pushed the chunks of glass into the gaping orifice, stuffing in as much as possible before taping it shut.

Rooms' eyes rolled back in his head as the shards of glass lacerated his tongue and mouth. Forced to swallow to keep from drowning in his own blood, bits of the glass went down his throat. Rooms tried to hold these back with his tongue, but the pain was too much.

Billy Williams looked at Henry Janes. "That's gotta hurt," he said. Janes laughed.

Janes brought a duffel bag from the back of the van, which he opened to reveal a large, industrial staple gun, a propane blowtorch, and an electric prod. The two psychopaths went to work.

They burned various parts of Rooms' body until his flesh was black and curled. When he passed out from the pain, they waited patiently until he regained consciousness, and then tortured him with the electric prod. Henry Janes drove metal staples into Rooms' head, which made a dull thunking sound slamming into his skull.

This insane torment went on for hours, until Adrian Rooms was almost dead. Exhausted from their macabre labor, tittering and drooling, the two sadists finally slept.

The next morning, Janes and Williams tossed the hog-tied Rooms in the van and drove to the Hungry Valley State Recreational Area, where, at a remote spot, they unloaded him, half-conscious and in extreme agony. Rooms was doused in gasoline from a five-gallon can, and set on fire by Janes using a road flare. Henry Janes and Billy Williams stared bug-eyed as Adrian Rooms burned alive.

When they left, all that remained was a lump of blackened and charred flesh.

A week later, two maintenance workers discovered what they thought at first had been a roasted pig over an open pit barbecue. When they started to shovel it into trash bags, they realized they were mistaken. The police were called. Detective Daniel Thompson said the place "smelled like death."

Henry Janes bragged about the murder to his friends. Killing someone boosted his status, proving to others that he was "one bad dude," who was not to be messed with. Janes did not see his behavior as repulsive and sick, the act of a raving psychopath, yet even his friends in the Aryan Brotherhood, as violent and murderous as they were, thought maybe he had gone too far. Warriors engaged in warfare and killed people, but warriors did not torture people and burn them alive.

The braggart Henry Janes was arrested, so too his accomplice Billy Williams. A friend had tipped off the police, because he was "tired of listening to Henry's sicko shit."

Henry Janes pled not guilty at his arraignment hearing. So did Billy Williams, but Williams pled not guilty by reason of insanity, which, according to the psychiatrists and psychologists, was probably true. As one court-appointed psychiatrist said to one of the investigating detectives, "The guy's all fucked up—a real ding-dong." In official jargon, Williams was said to exhibit the "symptomatic behavior of a paranoid schizophrenic with psychopathic tendencies, who has lost touch with reality in all its manifestations."

When Henry Janes discovered that five of his 'friends' were going to testify against him, he didn't waste any time. He sat down in his isolation cell and wrote a letter to his fellow warriors in the Aryan Brotherhood, telling them that "rats will be squealing at my trial. They have to be killed ASAP." Henry didn't know, however, that his outgoing mail was read and photocopied by corrections officers before it left the jail. It was never sent, but instead delivered to the prosecutor's office, where multiple counts of witness intimidation were added to Henry's charges.

On August 24, 1998, after a trial that lasted eight weeks, the jury found Henry Janes guilty of the kidnapping, torture, and murder of Adrian Rooms. In addition, the jury found Janes guilty of three counts of witness intimidation. Without regret or hesitation, the jury recommended a sentence of death.

Janes' defense attorneys immediately stood up and asked the judge to reduce Jane's sentence to life in prison without parole. The prosecutor, Robert Gorsuch, demanded to the contrary: "The circumstances of the crime warrant a death sentence. The jury's recommendation is sound. Mr. Janes should be sent to death row."

Superior Court Judge Zollinger nodded. "Sentencing a man to death is not a decision to be made in haste. Therefore, I'm going to take a recess so I can weigh my decision."

Four hours later, court reconvened. Judge Zollinger gazed out over the courtroom for a few seconds before making his statement. "The defendant's treatment of Adrian Rooms was savage, barbarous, merciless and cruel. Much of the evidence presented indicates that Mr. Janes reveled in the murder of another human being. He enjoyed it." Judge Zollinger looked at Henry Janes. "Mr. Janes displays a depth of depravity which is, fortunately, quite rare. Therefore, I am denying the request to reduce the sentence recommended by the jury."

The defense attorneys requested a new trial. They argued that the evidence against Henry Janes was circumstantial and presumptive, and that the testimony of the witnesses was hearsay, nothing more than rumor and gossip.

Judge Zollinger didn't even consider the request. "Denied," he said. He then sentenced Henry Janes to death, adding the time-honored phrase, "And may God have mercy on your soul."

Not one single person in the courtroom, except for perhaps the judge, believed God's mercy stretched that far.

Four days later, Henry Janes was transported to San Quentin state prison, where he was placed in a cell on death row to await execution.

HENRY JANES MET SAMUEL SAUTER on death row in 2004. Six months after that meeting, Sauter was voted onto the California council of the Aryan Brotherhood. Four weeks after that, Sam Sauter got his first visit from Wolf Weiss, aka Wolfman. Wolfman asked the Aryan Brotherhood for permission to set up a superlab, and said to Sauter he needed financial help in setting up the superlab in Pleasanton.

HyperChem Industries came into existence, and Arturo Colano and his techs cranked out the meth.

EIGHT

Plan B From Mars

Knitting

BARRY MILLS WAS KNITTING in his cement cell, which sat in the control unit of ADX Florence. Using black and white yarn, he clicked and clacked his knitting needles rapidly, creating a clean and tight rib knit. The Baron was making a sweater. He didn't really know why, he just was. It was something to do. A way to kill time as time slowly killed him.

In here, Mills had nothing but time.

His favorite time-killing activities—if they could be called activities (he thought the word was a little pretentious for such sedentary pursuits)—were, in no particular order, knitting, reading, meditating and sleeping. Sleeping, of course, was neither an activity nor a pursuit. It was a result, a side effect.

Meditation was an escape, a way to extend his soul out of his body. Through untold hours of practice, he was now adept at projecting himself out of himself. Leaving his body, he could actually take his soul for a walk, passing through steel doors and cement walls as if they weren't there. It was like floating. He had trekked (his word for soul-walking) all over the thirty-seven acres of the prison complex, entering the cells of his fellow inmates, all 430 of them, watching them as if they were rats in a cage and he was a scientist studying their habits.

The Baron had learned these skills in a book from the prison library called *How Psychic Are You?* It was a simple little book.

The first few chapters taught the reader how to meditate. The rest of the book focused on 'centering' and 'projecting' the soul beyond the boundaries of the body. For the Baron, one of the handy side effects of the book was salvation. Not religious salvation, but literal salvation. The book had saved the Baron from insanity. Over the years of incarceration, most of it in solitary confinement, the Baron had drifted further and further from the continent of sanity, but the book had managed to shuttle him back again, and he stopped taking the mind-numbing drugs the prison shrinks gave him every day. Instead, the Baron took long soul-walks and knitted.

The book had unified the Baron.

Reading was how he educated himself. It kept his mind agile and flexible. Mostly he read non-fiction books. His favorite, which he read many times, pausing over each sentence, was Machiavelli's *The Prince*. He considered it essential reading to being a mystical warrior, along with Robert Greene's *The 48 Laws of Power* and, of course, Nietzsche.

Knitting relaxed him and allowed him to think about things at a subconscious level. When the Baron knitted, he was like a cow chewing its cud—an automatic and organic digestion process that took place without conscious effort. Only in the Baron's case, he wasn't digesting food, he was processing information. By concentrating on something completely mechanical and repetitive—knitting—he freed his mind from the restraints of linear thought, allowing his thoughts to jump, which meant thinking outside the box.

Right now, the Baron was chewing on a vision that had come to him a while back, one involving guns, Mexican drug cartels, power and money. The Mexican cartels were at war with one another. Each cartel wanted to be supreme, wanted to have a monopoly on the drug trade. Whoever held the monopoly got all the business, which meant all the money, which meant all the power that went along with all the money. This kind of ambition led to conflict. To paraphrase Machiavelli, "only the strongest would survive." Each cartel was doing their level best to wipe out the other cartels. At the same time, the cartels were fighting the Mexican Army, which, for moral and political reasons, the Mexican government had tossed into the equation. In effect, there was a civil war going on in Mexico. Everybody was trying to kill everybody else.

To compliment their many guns, the cartels had a vast arsenal of military-grade weapons: rocket-propelled grenade launchers, assault rifles, and tons and tons of ammunition. The mark-up for such weapons was sometimes as much as 1,000 percent. But money wasn't a problem, the problem was sourcing reliable dealers with enough weapons to sell to the cartels.

The Baron smiled to himself, as he dropped a stitch. This was where the Aryan Brotherhood came in. The AB could supply the weapons and make hundreds of millions of dollars in profit. Of course, the Aryan Brotherhood didn't have any weapons to sell.

The Baron laughed out loud in his tiny cell. "Just a technical difficulty," he said, glancing up at the surveillance camera in the corner of the six foot by eight foot cement container.

MONITORING THE PRISONERS on a bank of monitors, picking and choosing cells to listen on and observe, one guard in the ADX surveillance room felt a tingle go up his spine. "Did you see that?" he asked the guard beside him. "The Baron just looked at me and said something. He was smiling right at me."

"Bullshit."

"I'm telling ya the guy was talking to me," protested the guard.

The neighbor smirked. "Yeah. Well, what'd he say?"

"'Just a technical difficulty.'"

"So what? The guy's in a solitary control unit. He don't see no one, he don't talk to no one. Probably losing his mind. Talking to the walls and all. I mean he's a brick short of a load anyway."

"I guess," nodded the guard. He glanced at the monitor. "The guy gives me the willies."

"I know whatcha' mean," agreed the neighbor. "The Baron is spooky."

The Baron went back to his knitting. The technical difficulty—of having no military grade weapons to sell—was easy to fix. All the AB had to do was pay a visit to 'weapon world,' or rather, the United States Army.

The US Army had major munitions storage facilities at Hawthorne in Nevada, Fort Irwin in San Bernadino, California, Fort Carson in Colorado, and Fort Riley in Kansas.

The Baron smiled with the perfect little plan that bloomed in his mind. It was time to put the Nazi Low Riders and the other peckerwood groups to work.

Reaching for a writing tablet, he began composing a letter to Samuel Sauter. The letter would be read and photocopied before it left ADX Florence. If there were the slightest suspicion that the Baron was directing the activities of the Aryan Brotherhood or even hinting at potential plans, the letter would be destroyed, and the Baron's few privileges would be further curtailed as punishment.

The best way to circumvent technological sophistication—in this case sophisticated cryptanalysis—was to use simple communication techniques. Simplicity was the key, because simplicity baffled the complicated algorithmic analyses of computers. The Baron wrote his letter in pencil on lined paper, using a very abecedarian code. The third letter of every word in every third line made up the hidden message. Deciphering the message was easy as pie. All Sauter would have to do, after he got the letter, was circle every third letter of every word in line three, line six, line nine, and so on. By stringing the circled letters into words, Sauter would know what the Baron was really saying.

Sauter would be made aware of the 3/3 sequence with the first two lines of the letter:

Dear Sam Sauter,

How are you?

If the sequence had been 4/4 or 5/6, then the number of words in the first two lines would have mimicked the designated sequence.

Of course, this meant the Baron had to carefully select each and every word in every third line, making sure the right letters appeared in the correct position. Which meant it took some time and Rodale's *Synonym Finder* to accomplish the task. Since the Baron had a lot to say, the letter was a lengthy one.

But the Baron had lots of time. Time and patience were the least of his problems.

The Baron's letter told Sauter that the Aryan Brotherhood was going into the arms business. Nazi Low Riders and associates should join the US Army, specifying their desired military occupational specialty as Quartermaster Corps. Once in, they were to steal weapons and ammunition, funneling the stolen material to a central location. This location should be in southern California, near Tijuana, so there would be easy access to the Mexican drug cartels.

Additionally, Sauter was to recruit Aryan Brotherhood associates—both male and female and those with appropriate skill sets—to apply for civilian positions at the Hawthorne Army Depot. The associates should make application for employment with Day & Zimmermann, the operating contractors of the depot. Since the depot employed over 14,000 civilians, the AB associates should have little trouble landing jobs. Once within the boundaries of the depot, they were to utilize any and all means of stealing munitions, including hijacking.

WHEN THE BARON'S LETTER arrived at San Quentin, Sauter set about decoding it. Reading the hidden message caused Sauter to laugh and shake his head in admiration. Later, he told Henry Janes about the message.

"Damn!" said Janes. "We shoulda thought a that. The Baron's always way ahead a everybody else. Always thinking."

Sauter nodded in agreement. "That's why he's the Baron, my man." Sauter glanced around making sure no one was near. "Now we need to get this enterprise underway. I'm putting you in charge of it."

"Cool," smiled Janes.

Sauter winked. "You'll need a warehouse down south and someone to run the show." He paused, thinking of possible honchos who weren't in prison somewhere. Someone smart and organized. The guy needed to be subtle. This wasn't a job for some rough and ready aggressive moron. This job called for brains.

Sauter raised his eyebrows in a rhapsodic dance, which meant he had a good idea. "Six Fingers," he announced. "Remember him?"

Janes nodded. "Yeah. The egghead."

"Right. Guy's a fuckin' fanatic for computers and numbers and shit like that. This'd be his kinda thing. Low profile, just keeping track a stuff. Where it was, where it's going, when it'll arrive," said Sauter. A shadow of worry crossed his face. "He's not strapped up tight is he?"

"Nah," replied Henry. "Last I heard, he was up north. Portland or Seattle, maybe."

"Good. Put out the word to 'im. Let 'im know what's going down, what you want 'im to do." Sauter made a rolling motion with his hand. "Get it goin', my man. Get it goin'."

WHEN HE GOT WORD Six Fingers was up in Seattle, living near Pike Street Market, doing nothing, trying to stay out of trouble and out of California, where he had a record of internet fraud, and where he was sure there was a warrant out for his arrest—for parole violation. But to arrest him, they'd first have to find him. And Six Fingers had great confidence in his ability to elude the cops.

The Pacific Northwest was a hotbed of supreme white power groups. The region attracted extremist nutcases like moths to a flame. No one really knew why, but once a few supremacists arrived, the others quickly followed. So there were lots of Nazi Low Riders.

One day, five NLR dudes showed up on Harleys, and, without bothering to dismount, told Six Fingers somebody wanted to talk to him. He was handed a piece of paper with the name 'John Smith' on it and a number.

Six Fingers didn't know any John Smith, had never even heard of John Smith.

"Call 'im," said one of the bikers. "Dude's got a message for ya. S'pose ta be important."

"Yeah?" frowned Six Fingers, who didn't care for the fact that everybody and his freakin' mother seemed to know where to find him.

The biker blipped his throttle, resulting in a prosperous rumble of engine, and nodded his head at the piece of paper in Six Fingers' hand. "You should call. It's 'bout takin' care a some business."

With that, the five Nazi Low Riders revved their engines and roared off.

Six Fingers got the hint. He went to Walmart and bought a disposable cell phone for $12.95. It came with thirty pre-paid minutes of time, which was twenty-five more than Six Fingers figured he needed. He was right. When he made the call, the voice on the other end asked him to meet at Taco Bell for lunch.

John Smith looked, dressed and talked like he was on the television show *Miami Vice*. He told Six Fingers he was "in banking," which made him a money-man for the Aryan Brotherhood. He handled money that had already been laundered, which meant he was semi-legit, made a lot of money, and took no risks. He wasn't a branded member of the AB. He was an 'associate.'

John Smith proceeded to tell Six Fingers what was going down. He outlined the operation that Barry 'the Baron' Mills had outlined to Sam Sauter, who had given the job to Henry Janes, who was dropping the actual implementation of the job into the lap of Six Fingers. Plop!

"I'm just the delivery boy," emphasized Smith, who didn't want any part of any risk. And this idea sounded risky as Hell. His hands were clean and he meant them to stay that way. "I'm not involved, except to deliver the glad tidings." He took a sip of Dr. Pepper. "You got any questions about what I just said?"

"No," said Six Fingers. "I got it."

"I'm supposed to carry back your answer," explained Smith. "Whether you're willing to do it."

"Tell 'em *yes*," said Six Fingers. "Sounds like fun."

Smith beamed, as if he had just spotted Elvis Presley. After a few seconds, he got up. He knocked twice on the plastic table with his knuckles and cautioned Six Fingers, "Okay. You won't see or hear from me again."

Six Fingers hopped on his Harley Fat Boy and headed south on I-5 all the way to San Diego. In San Diego, he rented a house two blocks from the beach and then went warehouse hunting. A Prudential commercial real estate agent took Six Fingers to some likely prospects. Six Fingers made a decision on a property located in an industrial section near the port of San Diego, which was busy as a beehive with trucks and cargo containers moving all over the place. It had once been a paint and body shop, and consisted of 20,000 square feet of cement pad, and an office area.

Six Fingers leased some forklifts, bought some office furniture, including four state-of-the-art computers, and hung up a sign that made him smile every time he looked at it: Acme Components. Six Fingers was a fan of the Roadrunner cartoons, which regularly featured a variety of unlikely gadgets from a company called Acme.

Six Fingers was the ostensible owner of Acme Components, and he had six employees, all of whom looked like bald versions of Arnold Schwarzenegger in *The Terminator*, right down to the Harleys they rode to work. They wore off-white coveralls that had ACME on the back in big red letters. Steel-toed boots and sunglasses completed their uniforms.

Six Fingers left his Harley Fat Boy at home, choosing to drive a newly purchased white Ford pick-up truck to the office every day. The Ford had an avant-garde ACME logo painted on the doors, while the tailgate provided a telephone number and a jaunty slogan: 'Acme Components—the only part you need.'

The money to pay for this masquerade came from an elite business checking account that Six Fingers had opened at Bank of America with a deposit of $3,000 cash. This, of course, was not nearly enough to even pay the monthly lease on the warehouse.

No problem. Six Fingers merely went back to the office at Acme Components and fired up one of his computers. His fingers flew over the keyboard for thirty minutes, following which he shut the computer down, turned off the lights and went home for a beer.

The next morning, Acme Components' elite business checking account showed a balance of $300,000.

Six Fingers had hacked into the bank's LAN and 'borrowed' the money from other accounts—without leaving a trace. Computer hacking was the special skill set of Six Fingers, and he would later boast—from prison—of being one of the ten best hackers in the world.*

Truckloads of stolen munitions began arriving at Acme Components, where the crates containing military armaments were unloaded by forklifts and stacked neatly in prescribed areas. On the side of each crate were the words 'US Army Ordnance.' This was swiftly obliterated by the employees of Acme Components and replaced using stencils and spray guns with the wording 'John Deere—Tractor Parts.'

An employee then affixed a label to each crate, which in turn was scanned by an employee with a scan gun. This data was downloaded onto one of Six Fingers' computers, and used to track the crates from leaving the warehouse to arriving at their destination. "I know where everything is at all times," explained Six Fingers. "I know where it went and when it arrived. Just like fuckin' FedEx, only our profit margin is more satisfactory."

There were salesmen, of course, but Six Fingers didn't know who they were. He didn't really care. As any good salesmen at any international corporation, they traveled to meet with prospective

---

* This claim—of being one of the ten best hackers in the world—was asserted by Six Fingers. This vaunted status can neither be confirmed nor denied by the author; however, with great certitude, the author can attest to the high-tech wizardry of Six Fingers. The author visited southern California, during which time he tagged along with Six Fingers as Six Fingers ran Acme Components. The author entered the warehouse and witnessed shipments of crates. The author did not examine the contents of the crates and thus had no direct knowledge of unlawful activity.

clients—in this instance, the cartels in Mexico—and, over dinner and drinks, advised what products were available and how much the products cost. The laws of supply and demand prevailed. There were no discounts and no negotiations. Basically, it was take it or leave it, because the salesmen knew they had a corner on the market. There wasn't really any place for the cartels to go to shop around, because the competition was unreliable and suffered constant supply problems. In other words, you couldn't trust them. The AB, on the other hand, "took care of business."

In turn, the cartels placed their orders and made immediate payment in full. Payment was by wire transfer, which, to the untutored, might appear risky. But, as Six Fingers explained, "I would never accept an electronic transfer directly from any cartel's bank. That would be suicidal. The Feds'd be all over that kinda rinky-dink shit." He held up his hand, which meant wisdom was about to be dispensed. "But it doesn't happen that way. What happens is this: The cartel wires the money to Banco Mexicana, which is the mother of all banks in Mexico City. And they—the Banco Mexicana—wire it to me." He smiled. "Once it leaves Banco Mexicana, it's clean, baby. Laundered, fluffed and folded."

After the wire transfer was received, the order would be quickly and efficiently filled. The forklifts went into action, loading the requested items into the fifty-three foot trailer. The last three rows of crates loaded were filled with real John Deere Tractor Parts, just in case any border agents got industrious and decided to poke around.

The trailers and the semis that pulled them had been painted bright yellow, carrying the John Deere name and logo in six foot green letters. "Attention to details is what makes or breaks any business," explained Six Fingers, gazing proudly at the big yellow trucks.

Driving south, the yellow trucks stopped at the border crossing, where they presented their paperwork—all forged—and then continued onward. The Mexican customs officers barely glanced at the paperwork. Once delivery had been made, the trucks returned to base.

Every so often, Six Fingers would get a strange feeling, "Like being zapped with a ray gun." When that happened, he intuitively painted the trucks a different color and gave them different insignia. Sometimes the trucks turned royal blue with 'Sony' in big white letters; other times the color scheme would be white with red trim, parading 'Zacky Farms' across the trailers.

Six Fingers relied on his intuitive powers. When they spoke, he obeyed. "The last time I didn't pay attention to what my guts were telling me," said Six Fingers. "I ended up doing a nickel in San Quentin state prison. It weren't nothin' nice."

If Acme Components had been a publicly traded company, its stock would have rivaled Google, for Acme's profits were staggering and its potential for continued growth was—in a word—tremendous. Since all its merchandise was stolen, Acme's overhead was negligible. Rent, utilities, truck maintenance, fuel, forklifts, and lots of stencils and spray paint were the only ongoing costs. And salaries, of course. Six Fingers and his skinheads weren't volunteers. They were paid well for their time, effort, technical expertise and risk.

Installed While You Wait

BARRY 'THE BARON' MILLS was using a broom to tidy up his cell.

ADX Florence, like all federal prisons, was highly regulated. All activities happened according to a schedule. Any variation in the holy program was heresy. Once a week, the schedule ordained that all cells were cleaned. Paper towels, disinfectants, and brushes were delivered to the cell blocks. According to the schedule, the occupant of each cell had one hour to clean his cell. At the hour's end, the cleaning supplies were collected. When all items were accounted for, they were moved on to the next cell.

Barry Mills maneuvered the long-handled straw broom deftly under the tray of his bunk, pushing it toward the far corner, which was just out of reach. Dropping to the cement floor, Mills lay on his stomach so he could effectively wield the broom. Crawling forward until his head and shoulders were under the bunk, he rolled on his side. The guards watching the surveillance monitors could see Mills, who was obviously doing a meticulous job cleaning, but in this position they couldn't see what he was doing with his hands.

What Barry Mills was doing was unscrewing the yellow handle of the broom from its threaded yoke on the blade. Once the handle was out, Mills quickly shoved a tightly folded piece of paper into the bottom of the yoke. He screwed the broom handle back into place, and finished sweeping under the bunk.

The Baron was done. His cell was clean for another week. Placing the cleaning supplies and the broom next to the cell door for collection, he sat back down on his bunk and picked up his knitting.

Eventually, as dictated by the schedule, the supplies arrived at the cell occupied by Tyler 'the Hulk' Bingham. The Hulk, too, was under intermittent surveillance. He knew it, as he knew there was a note from the Baron in the broom. So, he dropped his pants and sat on the toilet with the broom across his lap, anticipating that even if the guards were watching, they would look away or, more probably, shift the feed to their monitors to another cell.

He waited for about sixty seconds, then removed the broom handle and extracted the folded piece of paper, which he unfolded and placed between the pages of a book to read later. Then he stood up, pulled up his pants and continued cleaning his cell.

That same evening, the Hulk dropped his pants and sat down with the book in his hands. Taking from its pages, he smoothed out the note and read it. Then he read it again, tore it up and flushed the pieces down the toilet.

The Hulk's reply to the note was 'yes,' which he wrote on a small square of paper that was precisely folded and inserted into the broom handle the following week. As decreed by the cleaning schedule, he knew full well the Baron would have to wait another week before he received it, upon which the Baron would send back a confirmatory note. If not, the Hulk would try again and again and again. Sooner or later, confirmation would arrive.

Confirmation did arrive. The Baron acknowledged that the Hulk knew about, and was in agreement with, his latest scheme. Barry 'the Baron' Mills constantly came up with blueprints for new Aryan Brotherhood enterprises. Superficially, these stratagems were methods for the AB to expand their influence and make money. But the stratagems were a lot more than that. For Barry Mills, the stratagems were about restoration. Mills saw the power of the Aryan Brotherhood shrinking. The Aryan Brotherhood was losing control, not only inside the prisons, but in the wider world as well. Mostly, it was about prestige. The lustre on the brand of the shamrock was fading, being replaced by the radiance of the Mexican Mafia, which had tens of thousands of soldiers at its beck and call. Even the Nazi Low Riders were gaining members, while the Aryan Brotherhood was struggling for respect.

When the Department of Justice chose to use RICO against the Goliath of the Aryan Brotherhood, just like David the shepherd boy in the Bible story, they brought the monster to its knees.

Barry Mills felt emasculated, which ignited a white-hot anger in him. The anger needed to be quenched, and the only thing that would quench it was prestige, status, power and a reputation that made people tremble with fear. But it wasn't happening. Mills was left with an inner frustration that convulsed and thrashed and screamed at its own confinement.

In short, Barry Mills was scared. Scared that he and the Aryan Brotherhood were inconsequential, that they were being left behind. Mills was frantic in his attempts to regain relevance, to catch up. That's why he'd ordered the AB to become arms merchants, so that the AB—and he—could be of consequence once again. To some degree, it had worked. The scheme had proved efficient and the money was rolling in. But he didn't feel the power, not like he once had. He still felt like he had a bit part in a movie about the Mexican Mafia, when it should have been a movie about the Aryan Brotherhood, starring Barry 'the Baron' Mills.

Mills redoubled his efforts. He would buff and polish the Brand until it gleamed. That was why he had sent the message to the Hulk. Another project was about to be launched, and through it, perhaps, the Aryan Brotherhood would be restored to prominence.

The project had the potential to transform the Aryan Brotherhood from a purely criminal enterprise into a semi-legitimate syndicate, which, if successful, would open the door into a whole new realm of wealth and power. The Aryan Brotherhood was about to become a corporation.

The Baron should have foreseen and done it a long time ago. It was what the Mexican Mafia needed to do, but couldn't. The Mexican Mafia was growing at a geometric pace, but only horizontally. It increased in number every day, but all these soldiers did was run more guns and distribute more drugs, bringing in more money. As long as their territory and wealth increased, the shotcallers were happy. Sooner or later, though, the market would be saturated. Then what?

Barry Mills had the answer—grow vertically. Move into legitimate businesses, using them to launder money and distribute drugs. That's what the Mafia had done and that's why they had been international in scope at one time. And that's what the Aryan Brotherhood was going to do.

In his cell, Barry Mills composed another coded letter to Samuel Sauter, outlining the plan.

SAUTER FOUND HIMSELF holding his breath. The sheer magnificence of the scheme blew him away. It was so simple, yet so wonderfully sensible. Later, Sauter explained it Henry Janes.

"The Baron wants us to go legit," said Sauter.

"Whaddaya mean?"

"Park our money in cars and motorcycles."

Janes glanced at Sauter. "I don't getcha."

Sauter sighed. He loved Janes like a brother, but the guy was as weak-minded as Simple Simon. "Think about it. We buy car and bike dealerships and run 'em as legit businesses."

"Why?" asked Janes. He still didn't get it.

"So we can hide a bunch of our money and launder it at the same time, my man," explained Sauter. "I mean think about it. Any car dealership has millions of dollars in property and buildings, and a few million in new cars that are sittin' on the lot, right?"

Janes nodded.

"Each dealership has a bank account. A legitimate bank account," Sauter continued. "Our dirty money goes into the cars and into the bank. When it comes back out, it's squeaky clean. And," Sauter held out his hands, "when a car sells, we make a profit. We're making money on our dirty money."

"Damn! Tha's pretty good," chimed Janes.

"Damn right, it is."

"What about the bikes?"

Sauter grinned. "I'm glad ya asked." He held up a finger. "We buy Harley shops. You know those great big fancy ones that cater to all the rich dudes. Doctors and lawyers and engineers an' shit. Where they serve wine an' little faggoty foods on Saturday afternoons to get the suckers and their old ladies ta come in. Makes 'em feel like they're part of the cool crowd. You know all that leather and chrome and shit." Sauter laughed. "We sell 'em hogs with saddlebags and windshields, and helmets with walkie-talkies. You know all that panty-liner shit they like."

"Yeah," chuckled Janes, shaking his head.

Sauter leaned in. "While all the fluff 'n' puff foo-foo shit is goin' on in the showroom, the peckerwoods are moving meth out the back door. The place'll be a regular pipeline, distributing shit everywhere."

Janes exposed a twisted grin.

"It's fuckin' perfect," said Sauter. He was thinking ahead, planning. Sauter realized that 'going legit' required a whole new paradigm. He couldn't simply tell some dude from the Aryan Brotherhood to go buy some car dealerships. Going legit meant using the talents and skills of legit professionals, professionals who were willing to associate with the AB. Which meant professionals that weren't squeaky clean.

Sauter looked at Janes. "We need a righteous business dude to handle this little venture," he said. "Know anybody who knows anybody who wears a suit, knows his way around the business sector tha's lookin' to make some easy money?"

Janes nodded. "Yeah. Brenda Jo Riley."

This took Sauter by surprise. "You mean Grizzly's old lady?" he asked.

"Yeah. She was strapped up in Chowchilla for a couple a years. But she got out a while back."

Janes was referring to the Federal Bureau of Prison's facility for women, which was located near Chowchilla, California. Brenda Jo Riley, the wife of AB member Elliott Scot Grizzle (aka Grizzly), had been sentenced to twenty-one months for acting as a messenger for the Aryan Brotherhood. She carried verbal and written messages from AB members in jail to those on the outside, denoting the names of witnesses who would be testifying against brothers in jail. These witnesses were summarily located and threatened, and their families threatened. The intimidation worked and most witnesses refused to testify. A few testified anyway, telling the court of death threats, which is how Brenda Jo Riley was arrested. Her attorney got her a plea bargain.* She did her time and in 2006 was released from prison. Meaner than ever, she immediately hooked up with known associates of the Aryan Brotherhood.

"I remember hearing about her," said Sauter. "Who's she know?"

"Her sister-in-law's brother is some kinda ambulance chaser. You know, penny-ante shit like personal injury, where somebody falls off

---

* Brenda Jo Riley did not cooperate with the government. Although Riley's attorney, W. Michael Mayock, stated that prosecutors had "painted a big bull's-eye on her back."

a ladder at work and decides ta go for the throat. Sues the company for big bucks."

"How you know all this?"

Janes shrugged. "I don't know. I hear stuff."

Sauter's eyes narrowed. "Well, can you get in touch with her? Tell 'er we need a visit?"

Janes shook his head. "Shit man, they're not gonna let her in for a fuckin' visit. Known felon an' AB assoshit. No way."

Sauter nodded, pursing his lips. "Yeah. You're right. Write 'er a letter, tell 'er ta contact this dude, see if he'll make a visit."

"Tha' I can do, man," said Janes.

THE VISTOR'S NAME was Chris George, attorney at law. He flashed his card at the reception desk and told the officer he was here to visit Samuel Sauter. The officer assumed he was another asshole attorney involved in Sauter's ongoing stay of execution. "Sign here, please," said the officer, pointing at a clipboard.

George was ushered to a private room, where he could meet with his client. A few minutes later, he was joined by Samuel Sauter, dressed in an orange jumpsuit. The two men shook hands and sat down. Sauter started talking. He talked for ninety minutes, pausing only to answer his attorney's frequent questions.

At the end of their exchange, Chris George knocked on the room of the door. "We're done," he said to the guard who opened it.

At the reception desk, he signed out and walked to his car. He smiled. He was going to make a lot of money and he didn't have to break any laws. Contrary, he had received strict instructions not to even bend the law. Everything was to be done by the book.*

---

* Chris George, in discussion, 2007. The precise contents of the conversation between Sauter and Chris George remain unknown. However, based on subsequent events, it is apparent that Chris George was kidding himself about not breaking any laws.

THERE WASN'T MUCH to say about Chris George, except that he was ambitious. He was a run-of-the-mill attorney, the product of a second-rate law school in Pasadena, California. Brown-eyed, pale, fidgety, with the gift of the gab, he came across as haughty, overbearing, and too big for his britches. He had no friends other than his secretary and a couple of equally arrogant and mediocre attorneys, who were his drinking buddies. He had become an attorney because he saw it as an avenue to money, and by long and hard hours of unending study, he passed the Bar exams and opened his one-man law firm. Taking out a full-page ad in the Yellow Pages, handing out thousands of business cards, and plastering his name on the back of city buses—'Chris George, he's in your corner'—had led to numerous minor league clients, and an income of over $200,000 per year. Most of his clients were looking to score vast quantities of money by means of frivolous lawsuits against big companies. More often than not, the big companies settled out of court. He drove a late model Jaguar, didn't smoke, exercised regularly and drank in moderation only after hours. In short, he was a total bore. He would have made an ideal corporate attorney for a large insurance company, had he not been so intent on being rich.

FOLLOWING HIS MEETING with Samuel Sauter at San Quentin state prison, Chris George set up a holding company, which he named Phoenix Corporation. He chose the name Phoenix because he liked the idea of the mythical bird, misinterpreting it as one that rises from its ashes and conquers the world. According to the papers of incorporation, Phoenix Corp. was a small company located in Carson City, Nevada. It invested in commercial real estate and other commercial management. Chris George was listed as the CEO. In fact, he was the only real person named—all the other officers of Phoenix were fictitious. Technically, this was a violation of Nevada's state laws, but it was a common practice and Chris George didn't see it as breaking the law. Everybody did it.

With the business up and running, all that was required was business to conduct. Chris George went shopping, and within one month the Aryan Brotherhood owned a chain of car and motorcycle dealerships, staffed by drug-dealing Nazi Low Riders, and perfect for laundering money. It was the Brotherhood's first brush with legitimacy.

Making Bank

SOME OF THE GUARDS said that knitting was the Baron's new religion. That he was no longer a warrior. That now he was just "another old lady, trying to find meaning in making shit out of yarn." The guards laughed as they said it.

The Baron pretended it didn't bother him. But it did. He remembered how it used to be before they excommunicated him to the living Hell called supermax. The Baron remembered how he used to rule over an empire of crime that included bank robberies and drugs and money laundering. This line of thought tickled an idea in his brain. He'd been reading a book about Meyer Lansky—the Mafia's magician of money. Lansky was the Mob's banker, who thought outside the box. The book made Mills realize that robbing banks was for amateurs. Instead of robbing banks, the Aryan Brotherhood needed to own the banks. The guys who owned the banks had the real money. He picked up his writing tablet and wrote a letter, which he passed to the guard that delivered his lunch, who in turn gave the letter to the mail-room, where it was read and photocopied. Every inmate had the right to communicate with his attorney, and since the Baron's letter simply requested a conference with his attorney, the letter was mailed.

Two weeks later, Charles 'Chuck' Rollingshaven arrived at ADX Florence. Rollingshaven was an attorney at law. His specialty was criminal defense, at which he was a whiz. Rollingshaven was fifty years old, and decidedly chubby. He smoked too many cigarettes, ate too much fast-food and drank too much beer. After his third wife divorced him, Rollingshaven gave up on matrimony. Asked whether he was married, he would reply, "Yeah, to my job."

Most of Rollingshaven's clients were 'lifers,' which meant they were either already in prison for life or were awaiting trial, which would result in a life sentence. Rollingshaven had no illusions about his clients, most of who were murderers: They were uneducated, violent riffraff, and if not imprisoned, most would probably run wild on a kill-spree. But they had the right to competent, legal representation, and it was his job to provide it.

One of his high-profile clients was Barry 'the Baron' Mills. Just thinking about the man sent goosebumps careening up and down the attorney's flesh. In Rollingshaven's opinion, a pyre of dry wood as tall as a mountain should be erected and set ablaze, with Barry Mills placed at the top of it, while the London Symphony Orchestra played Mozart's Mass in C-Minor and the spectacle broadcast on CNN. At that point, the justice system would have fulfilled its function.

Until that time, Rollingshaven swallowed his fear and did his job. To the very best of his ability, he defended Barry 'the Baron' Mills. At the present time, this involved a pending appeal regarding Mills' life sentences, which argued that all testimony presented by the prosecutors was either hearsay or the result of blatant fabrication by government informants. Since the appeal would not be heard for at least a year, Rollingshaven had no clue as to why Mills had requested a face-to-face meeting. One thing Barry Mills was not was a whiner, so Rollingshaven doubted it was about the quality of supermax food or the amount of rec-time Mills was receiving. Rollingshaven was curious to find out what Mills wanted.

There was also another reason Rollingshaven zealously defended his clients. Not only did Rollingshaven believe in truth, justice and the American way of life, which included the rights of criminals, he also believed in the free market system, especially the part about profit. He loved money, and criminals like Barry Mills were willing to pay lots of it for his services. Rollingshaven interpreted the phrase "defend to the best of my ability" to mean doing whatever was necessary. And he was not averse to bending the rules a little.

But if Rollingshaven was corrupt, he was not stupid. He never let his greed make him foolish. He would incorporate front companies, launder money, falsify financial records, tamper with witnesses, prep witnesses, and twist the truth like a pretzel—but only if he thought he could get away with it. He carefully examined each and every situation before he acted, and if it wasn't feasible, he didn't delude himself or his client.

Face-to-face meetings at ADX Florence took place in a divided room. The attorney sat on one side of the divider, the inmate sat on the other side. Reinforced one-inch steel bars formed the divider.

As Rollingshaven waited, the door on the other side of the room opened and a massive figure, with a shaved head and a walrus mustache, filled the doorway. The hair on the back of Rollingshaven's head stood on end. Barry Mills stepped into the room. His cuffed hands were attached to a waist-chain and ankle shackles rattled as he walked to his chair. Three guards followed him, examining the room carefully out of habit.

One of the guards looked through the bars at the attorney. "We'll be outside." He then gave the attorney a warning look and nodded at the red button on the wall. "If you need anything just press the button."

Rollingshaven nodded. "Thank you."

Barry Mills' laugh was a rumbling sound like distant thunder. He looked at the guard and shrugged. "What? Like I'm going to inconvenience my own attorney?"

"Have a seat, Baron," said the guard. The three guards then left the room with a thud of the heavy door.

"Nice to see you again, Counselor," said Barry Mills.

Rollingshaven shifted in his chair. "Your letter and your request for a conference took me by surprise."

The Baron's dark eyes focused on the attorney. A shiver rolled up Rollingshaven's spine. Dropping his eyes, he reached for his briefcase and opened it, taking out a legal tablet. He took a pen from his shirt pocket and clicked it open. Still unable to look at Mills, he jotted the date on the tablet. "What seems to be the problem?"

"There's no problem, Counselor," the Baron began. "At least not the kind you're referring to. I asked you to come so I could make a request. Actually, now that I think about it, it's more of an inquiry." He paused. "Of a special nature."

Even the man's style of speaking gave Rollingshaven the heebie-jeebies. Speak, stop, speak, stop. His diction and intellect were disconcerting, and quite unlike the majority of Rollingshaven's other clients, who had the vocabulary of the average first or second grader.

Rollingshaven forced himself to look up. A subterranean energy emanated from Mills' eyes. It was like looking into the face of the Angel of Death.

"What's the inquiry about?" asked Rollingshaven.

"Banks."

"Banks?"

"Yeah. You know the institutions where they keep the money. They make loans, accept deposits from customers, make wire transfers, provide financial services." The Baron paused, then added, "Sometimes they get robbed." His walrus mustache flared and twitched as he smiled.

Rollingshaven nodded. "Of course, banks. What is it specifically about banks that interests you?"

The mustache twitched again. "I'm thinking about buying one."

Rollingshaven frowned. "I'm afraid I don't understand."

Barry Mills cocked his head. "Meyer Lansky—you know, the Mafia's money-man—the one who started Vegas with Bugsy Siegel?"

Rollingshaven nodded. "I've heard of him. What about him?"

"He bought a bank in Switzerland so he could launder the Mob's money. Meyer Lansky had vision and imagination. Pure genius. That's what I want. I want to own a bank. And I want you to find a way to make it happen."

Rollingshaven pursed his lips, considering the idea. "Well," he said, "I have to say that my initial response is that you're out of your mind. The regulation of banks is strictly administered." Rollingshaven noted his client's expression and held up a hand. "But the idea might have some merit. Especially in Florida."

"Florida?"

"Yes," said Rollingshaven. "Based on what I've heard and what I know, many of the banks in Florida, especially those in and around Miami, are involved in laundering drug money. It's so prevalent they even have a name for it. They call 'em Coin-O-Washers."

Barry Mills lifted his eyebrows. "The cartels own them?"

"Some of them," replied Rollingshaven. "They have to wash billions of dollars a year, and they're big believers in the old adage that if you want something done right, there's no substitute for doing it yourself."

"What about the strict regulation you mentioned?" asked Mills.

"That's on the surface," explained the attorney. "The reality of the situation is that the regulators either cannot or do not enforce the regulations. At a guess, probably because they don't have the manpower to do so. It's also no secret that the regulations, in effect, serve to regulate the regulators more than the banks. In other words, the Coin-O-Wash banks are protected by the very complexity of the regulations."

"So it's possible?" asked Barry Mills.

"Yes," nodded Rollingshaven. "All one would have to do—hypothetically, of course—is set up a shell company, with a board of directors, and have the company purchase an existing bank. Legitimate shell companies are sold on the open market, so that poses no obstacle. After that it's simply a process of creating a maze of intermediary money stops between the shell company and the bank, which make it next to impossible to trace the flow of money into and out of the bank."

"Sounds easy," said Mills.

"In one sense, yes, it is easy. In another sense, it has to be done in a careful and systematic manner. For example, the Bank Secrecy Act states that cash deposits of $10,000 or more have to be reported."

"How do you get around that?" asked Mills.

"Any number of ways," replied the attorney. "One, simply don't report them. Two, delay reporting them until the money is long gone. Three, the banks don't have to report large cash deposits from cash-intensive businesses, such as retailers. So it's merely a matter of funneling money through such businesses into the bank." He smiled through the steel bars of the divider at Barry Mills. "But if you own the bank, the easiest way is the first—just don't report 'em."

"Don't the regulators become suspicious?" asked Mills.

"Only if they have a reason to match the bank's cash surplus to the bank's cash transaction reports."

"And if they do have a reason?"

"They won't if the bank isn't reporting them," replied Rollingshaven.

"But what about the bank's cash surplus? Isn't that a dead give away?"

"No," smiled Rollingshaven, "not if the bank keeps a very low cash surplus, one that raises no flags."

"And how is that accomplished if the bank is laundering large amounts of cash?" asked the shotcaller.

"You're very perceptive," acknowledged Rollingshaven. "Again, there are a number of ways. One of the easiest is to have the bank's loan department accept the cash deposits, recording the cash as the bank's own money," explained the attorney with a shrug. "No harm, no foul. Then the bank issues cashier's checks, because they're safer and more portable than cash." Rollingshaven paused. "Did you know that $3.5 million in twenty dollar bills weighs about 300 pounds? You can carry that in through the doors of the bank or you can carry a cashier's check that weighs—oh, two or three ounces. And the cashier's check is harder to trace because it doesn't have to have the recipient's name on it or his address. The money can be cycled through dozens of stops before it comes back to the bank. And when it does finally come back, it is completely clean." The attorney shook his head in appreciation of the beauty of the thing.

Barry Mills' mustache twitched. "Absolutely scandalous."

"Of course, this is all hypothetical," said Rollingshaven.

"I understand," nodded Barry Mills. "Just idle talk about what could happen if someone was to buy a bank in Florida." Then he bared his teeth in a mischievous smile. "By the way, how do you come to know so much about the subject?"

"I'm a criminal defense attorney. In the pursuit of my profession I have on occasion defended a few unscrupulous bankers."

Mills nodded. "Let's translate the hypothetical into actuality," he said. "Let's explore the availability of suitable banks in Florida. And when you find a likely candidate, purchase a shell company, which can purchase the bank. Get the ball rolling, so to speak."

Rollingshaven thought about it for a moment. There was a lot of wiggle room in banking. "It'll take a lot of money," he said.

"How much?"

"Two or three million for starters," answered the attorney.

"Not a problem," replied the shotcaller.

Rollingshaven gave a single nod. Then he left.

INSTEAD OF FLYING BACK to Los Angeles, Rollingshaven booked a first-class seat on a flight to Miami. Waiting at Denver airport, he made a number of calls. He called his personal assistant, Claire. He told her to clear his schedule for the next week. If something couldn't be postponed and re-scheduled, such as a court hearing, she was to send in one of the subs he kept on retainer. The sub could make an appearance and request a continuation.

"And call the Sisterhood," he told her. "Tell them I will be out of pocket for a while. So they'll have to handle all their emergencies by themselves for a few days." The 'Sisterhood' was how he referred to his three ex-wives when he was in a good mood. When he was in a bad mood, he called them the 'Weird Sisters,' or the 'Three Fates.'

His next call was to a crony from way back: Henri Auber. Auber was from France, but lived in Colombia, where he was head of a financial conglomerate called National Financial Group, which owned a number of large, private banks in Colombia and Brazil, along with others in major European cities. In 1995, Auber purchased the Republic Bank of Miami, through a company in the Netherlands Antilles, owned by National Financial Group. Soon afterwards, the Republic Bank of Miami changed its name to National Bank of Miami, and the building was totally refurbished inside and out at a cost estimated to be around $75 million. Auber shifted control of the National Bank of Miami to the Bank of Grand Cayman in the Cayman Islands, where Auber's financial conglomerate had recently invested heavily in commercial properties.

No one questioned Auber's acumen or international banking experience. What they questioned was how his conglomerate made its money. Colombian banking authorities investigated National Financial Group for alleged manipulation of the stock market. And if that cloud of suspicion wasn't enough, along came another one: National Financial Group was accused of laundering large amounts of money—billions of dollars—for the Colombian drug cartels.

Auber was reading about himself in the newspapers every day. He knew what was coming, and so hired the best defense attorneys money could buy. One of those attorneys was Charles Rollingshaven, whose reputation was that of "take no prisoners." He did whatever needed to be done to win, believing that the end justified the means.

The Colombian government brought criminal charges against Auber and some of National Financial Group's highest executives. When the case came to court in Bogota, Auber's legal team ostensibly attempted to bribe two presiding judges. However, the attempt could not be proved. The whole episode smacked of Rollingshaven and his easy rider shenanigans. While the defense attorneys and the Colombian prosecutors bickered back and forth about whom had done what, the court case quickly degenerated into a circus sideshow. In the end, due to a lack of hard evidence against anyone, the case was dismissed. Embarrassed by their seeming ineptitude, the authorities decided to try and save face. They ordered the arrest of three National Financial Group executives, who, when finally they came to trial, were acquitted in record time. Henri Auber was ordered not to leave the country, because he was still "a person of interest."

Meanwhile, the Florida State Banking Regulatory Agency was still processing the transfer of ownership of the Republic Bank of Miami/National Bank of Miami to Auber's Bank of Grand Cayman. Due to the legal fiasco being covered by the media in Bogota, the Colombian government sent official messages to the Florida State Banking Regulatory Agency, which urged the regulators to stop the transfer of ownership or at least defer it until the Colombian government could get its act together. When Rollingshaven learned of the messages, he immediately boarded one of National Financial Group's private jets and made a beeline for Miami. Upon his arrival, a limousine whisked him to a private meeting with the Florida State Banking Regulatory Agency, where Rollingshaven presented Auber's case to the regulators. He pointed out that they pretty much had to approve the change in ownership, because they didn't have a good reason not to. There was no evidence of any wrongdoing. Otherwise the Colombian government wouldn't be stalling for time like they were, but would, instead, be in court convicting the perpetrators. They had no evidence, which meant they had no case.

Impressed by Rollingshaven and by his presentation, the regulators made their decision. They paid no heed to the request of the Colombian government. They approved the transfer of ownership.

Simply because they had no alternative, the Colombian government backed down. Auber was granted permission to leave the country and, once again, it was business as usual for his conglomerate.

When later asked if Auber's National Financial Group was indeed laundering Colombian drug money, Rollingshaven replied, "It's not really up to bankers to become investigators of customers."

WHEN CHARLES ROLLINGSHAVEN made his call from the Denver airport, Auber was in Miami, visiting his investments in the area. Auber smiled when he put his cell phone to his ear. "Speak of the Devil and up he pops," he said.

"No wonder my ears were burning," replied Rollingshaven. "If you're talking about me, you must be trying to impress someone. What's her name?" He laughed. "And is she young and good-looking? Or old, fat and rich?"

"You know me too well, my friend. To what do I owe the honor of this call?"

"I'm about to get on a plane to Miami," said Rollingshaven. "A client of mine wants to get into banking. He wants me to locate likely prospects. I don't suppose you happen to know of any?"

"I'm in Miami right now," said Auber. "There's a bank on every corner and most of them are for sale, if the price is right. Miami is the only place in the world where people walk in off the street, locate the bank manager and offer to buy the bank." He then asked, "Why does your client need a bank? A bank can be a real pain in the ass, tell him."

"He's a major supplier of luxury items for buyers," explained Rollingshaven "who feels that if he owned his own bank, he could avoid some of the cash flow problems he experiences every now and then."

Auber recognized the tone of Rollingshaven's voice. It was code and Auber deciphered the criminal element between the lines.

"Yes," said Auber. "I can see where a bank would alleviate your client's difficulties. I don't suppose your client would consider allowing me to act as his banker? I could guarantee unlimited credit, which would resolve any cash flow dilemma. That way he could focus on what he does best, which is supply. And I could do what I do best, which is banking."

"I'll mention it to him," said Rollingshaven. "But it is doubtful he will consider it. He's a self-reliant individual and somewhat stubborn about his independence."

Auber understood. More code: The guy was an asshole, who didn't trust anybody outside his own organization. And he was prone to violence. The violence aspect didn't particularly bother Auber; all the drug cartels rolled the same way. If anything or anyone got in the way, their default reaction was to blow it away. What did bother Auber was the element of distrust. It was a sticky problem for any banker in the laundry business, because it meant the customers—who were notably agitated under the best of circumstances—were constantly suspicious and nervous. Auber would have his work cut out simply holding their hands, reassuring them everything was okay. He didn't have time for such nonsense.

"I understand what you're saying," stated Auber. "It sounds like we would not be simpatico. But you can't blame a guy for trying."

"Of course not," said Rollingshaven. "So. You say there are banks available?"

"Yes. Take your pick. There are prestigious banks on Brickell Avenue or you can go over to Coral Gables, where the chic Latin-American banks congregate. And there are many, many jackleg banks available for a mere pittance."

"What's a jackleg bank?" asked Rollingshaven. He'd never heard the term before.

"Jackleg banks open one day and close the next. Here-today-gone-tomorrow sort of thing. Very risky. You're better off putting your money under your mattress than in a jackleg bank."

"Okay. Well, I don't think I want one of those." Rollingshaven paused. "Are they legit at all?"

"Supposedly they are insured by the FDIC just like the others. At least that's what they claim. But I don't know anyone who wants to find out the hard way. I suspect most of them are only state-chartered, which means they are definitely not insured by the FDIC."

"I hear you," said Rollingshaven. "I was just thinking—that if they're legit—well, it might be an easy way to get a foot in the door."

"Only for the truly desperate," Auber advised. "Your client doesn't sound desperate. No. My advice is Coral Gables or something close by. That way you get an FDIC insured state bank, but avoid having to deal with the Federal Reserve Board, which is a very deep swamp to navigate. It can be done, but it's complicated."

"You're the expert," said the attorney. "Coral Gables it is."

TEN DAYS LATER Rollingshaven was back in Colorado, sitting across from Barry 'the Baron' Mills in the dividing room.

"Success?" asked Mills, who wore a pair of cheap sunglasses made of flimsy black plastic. The sunglasses had no metal or moving parts, which could be used in the manufacture of weapons.

"Yes, very much so," replied Rollingshaven. "Three Palms Community Bank, which is an FDIC-insured and state-regulated bank, is available. It is the one I recommend, if you're still in the market?"

"Yep," said Mills. He touched the rim of his sunglasses. "What's the asking price for Three Palms Community Bank?"

"Four million dollars. Plus, the cost of the shell company, which will be in the neighborhood of $300,000. And relevant attorney fees. We can engage the services of a Miami law firm, which comes highly recommended." Rollingshaven saw his face darkly reflected in the sunglasses. "And my fee, of course."

"Of course," agreed Mills. "Which is?"

"One million dollars," declared Rollingshaven, stiffening.

The Baron sat motionless. Seconds ticked by. He nodded. "Okay."

Rollingshaven breathed a sigh of relief.

"I thought maybe you'd want a piece of the action," said the Baron.

"No. No, thank you."

"Why not?"

Rollingshaven hesitated, then he smiled and said, "You want the truth or the party-line?"

The Baron shrugged. "Whichever makes you feel the most comfortable, Counselor."

Rollingshaven gave the Baron a heartfelt look. "I always underestimate you, Barry. And for that I apologize, because you may be the smartest person I know." He cleared his throat. "The truth is it's too risky. You could do it without any difficulty at all. But you're stuck in here, where your ability to communicate is circumscribed. Even if it wasn't, and you could communicate freely, your underlings are nowhere near your caliber. They're unreliable. And I only bet on sure things."

The Baron nodded. "Okay then. What's next?"

"I'll locate and purchase an appropriate shell company. It needs to be listed. Once that's done, the attorneys will move on the application for a transfer of ownership. Then we wait. If it's approved, and I have no reason to believe it won't be, you'll be in business. You need to find someone to run the business."

The Baron nodded. "I'll take care of it. And I'll have the funds delivered to you."

"I'll be in LA. The money needs to be clean. That goes without saying, right?"

The Baron's mustache twitched as he smiled his invisible smile. "Of course."

Rollingshaven sat forward. "Just be sure that your delivery person knows that."

"*Fait accompli*," said the Baron.

NINE

Wrap Up

IT ONLY TAKES ONE. Dion 'Bugsy' Milam, who was already serving life without parole and had just come into even more trouble, decided it was the right time to cut a deal. He told the prosecutor he had valuable information about an ongoing criminal conspiracy, which involved the Nazi Low Riders and the Aryan Brotherhood. "It's big," Milam insisted. "Not just Mickey Mouse shit."

"Yeah? Give me a hint."

"A superlab," smiled Milam.

The prosecutor frowned. "Yeah? Where's it located?"

"Over in the Bay," replied Milam. "The East Bay."

"You've actually seen it?"

"Well, no. But it's there," Milam observed smugly. "Couple of dudes told all about it—two NLR dudes who work there. An' I seen the shit they makin' there. High-grade shit. Place's run by some savvy Super Spic, who's the head cook."

The prosecutor was interested. "Okay. Tell me everything you know about it."

"Shee-it, man. How stupid ya think I am?" scoffed Milam. "I ain't sayin' nothin' 'till we got deal."

The prosecutor excused himself. After making a call on his cell phone, he returned. "Okay," he told Milam. "If what you tell me checks out, we'll drop the charges you're currently facing—conspiracy to commit murder and robbery."

Milam laughed. "That ain't a deal, man. Tha's a fuck you. Lookit, I'm already doing forever and never. Life without parole. Ya unnerstan'? Ya need to take a little off the top is what I'm sayin'."

The prosecutor pretended to think about it. He nodded. "Okay. If your information proves efficacious, you'll be eligible for parole. But not for a long time. And even then, all I'm promising is eligibility. There's no guarantee of parole." He stared at Milam. "That's it. Take it or leave it."

Milam grinned. "I'll take it."

The DEA was called in and Dion 'Bugsy' Milam proceeded to tell everything he knew about crystal meth and superlabs in the Bay Area. What he knew wasn't much really, but it was enough, because he knew two pertinent pieces of information: What the place was called and its location. Milam told the DEA agents to look for HyperChem Industries in the Pleasanton Industrial Park, which was in Pleasanton, California.

Electrified by what they heard, the DEA agents got excited. Everybody started making calls on their cell phones and before long DEA agents from all over the western United States were converging on San Francisco, where a DEA command post was established. The Special Agent in Charge decided to adopt a soft attitude toward raiding HyperChem Industries. A 'soft attitude' meant the DEA would probe and observe the target before they descended en masse, surrounded the area and arrested everyone in sight. By reconnoitering the target, they could determine how many perpetrators were involved in the illicit operation, possibly identifying some of them, and discern the routine of the superlab. Knowing the routine of the criminals might enable the DEA to catch more of the bad guys, because the agents would know when most of them were in the building.

The DEA referred to the probe and observe phase as the Dragon's Tongue. The next phase—the actual seizure of the facility and everybody in it—was called Operation Blue Dragon.

In the early hours of the morning, four undercover DEA agents drove to Dublin, California, a few miles west of the city of Pleasanton. A forward command post had been set up in an office building in Dublin, where a small army of DEA agents were already waiting. Heavily armed and eager, they were ready to roll at a moment's notice.

When the four agents arrived, they received a final briefing, which revolved around a detailed street map of the Pleasanton Industrial Park. The layout was a confusing maze of access roads, turnoffs and rear-accesss alleyways. In short, the industrial park was a tactical nightmare because there were dozens of routes into and out of it. Which meant lots of escape routes.

Each of the undercover agents left the forward command post driving a bright yellow DHL delivery van. Their instructions were to locate, identify and observe the target building. Exactly how they accomplished this was up to them. They would have to rely on their innate intuition and inventiveness. The agents, who were old hands at undercover and surveillance work, exuded confidence. Rule number one of any covert action was never rouse suspicion, which in practice meant don't stand out.

The Dragon's Tongue was active.

AT TEN O'CLOCK in the morning, HyperChem Industries was a busy place. The loading dock doors were open. Forklifts were performing a delicate, mechanical dance, as they unloaded two trailers, which had been carefully backed into place. Palettes stacked with bags of chemicals were levitated and moved to a receiving area, where two men armed with scanner guns methodically flicked a ribbon of light over barcodes.

Arturo Colano stood watching the activity. As an intricate machine, each part moved efficiently within a larger part, all the parts forming a magnificent whole. It was wonderful to behold. As he enjoyed the harmony of motion, something caught his eye. Turning a little to get a better view, he gazed out one of the bay doors. A yellow DHL van was parked outside. The driver of the van had climbed out and was talking to one of the Nazi Low Riders. From the man's body language, he was asking for directions. Arturo shrugged. It was easy to get lost in the industrial park, because there was no rhyme or reason to the labyrinth of the streets. A lost DHL driver was nothing to worry about.

On his way back to the office, Arturo observed another yellow DHL van. This one was moving along the street out front. By itself, this wasn't unusual either. DHL made constant deliveries to businesses in the industrial park. Except they always zipped around at breakneck-speed, because the drivers were in a hurry to make their deliveries. The sooner they finished, the sooner they got to go home. The van driving by out front was barely moving. And the driver was staring at the façade of the building. Arturo recalled the quaint provincialism he'd heard Wolfman employ many times, when Wolfman noticed someone staring at his tattoos. "Next time take a picture, asshole. It'll last longer."

Arturo watched the slow moving vehicle until it rounded the curve and was out of sight. Then he turned and gazed at the parked DHL van, whose puzzled driver was speaking to the Nazi Low Rider. The driver was walking back to his van. When he reached it, he didn't hop in and zoom off, he looked back at the Nazi Low Rider. It was a look of appraisal.

Without hesitation, Arturo walked briskly to his office, where he removed the fanny pack, which hung, always and forever, from the coat tree. The fanny pack was his emergency first-aid kit. Only instead of bandages and disinfectants, it contained his passport and $5,000 cash. He had placed it on the coat tree for just such a contingency—the moment when everything ruptured. That moment was here. He fastened the fanny pack around his hips.

Moving to his computer, Arturo clicked through a couple of files, typed in a command and pressed 'Enter.' Within a few minutes the hard-drive would be wiped clean. Arturo was aware that experts—with luck and infinite patience—might partially restore the data, but he didn't have time to do more.

Leaving his office, he strolled to the rear of the building and the Yamaha motorcycle and Schwinn bicycle parked next to the back doors. Arturo glanced at the motorcycle, then shrugged. He put on the bicycle helmet, and threw his leg over the bike. Pulling out his cell phone, he hit speed dial.

"Yeah?" answered the Wolfman.

"Wolfman, it is I, Arturo."

"What's happening, dude?" Wolfman was sitting on the edge of his bed in his underwear.

"My friend," said Arturo, "the moment of dread has arrived."

"What the fuck are you talking about?" asked Wolfman. He liked Arturo, but they guy spoke like a fucking faggot college professor.

"The cusp of transition," explained Arturo. "It has descended upon us. We must withdraw from the field like vanquished warriors of old."

"Arturo, Arturo," implored Wolfman. "Can ya put that in plain English, dude? What're ya tryin' to say?"

"I'm afraid the authorities have discovered our whereabouts," said Arturo.

"The fuck you say? How do ya know?"

Arturo explained what had occurred and what he had observed.

Wolfman sighed. "I think you're right, dude. Ya better get the fuck outta there. An' I mean right now."

"I am already implementing your advice," replied Arturo. "And what about you, my friend. What will you do?"

Wolfman laughed. "Shower, shave the old skull, and eat some breakfast. Then I'm headin' south to LA for a long vacation."

"I pray that safety is your guardian, my friend. I will communicate with you in the future. It has been my tremendous joy and a premium pleasure to have known you."

Wolfman put his head back and roared with laughter. "Fuckin' A, dude. Fuckin' A. Be seein' ya. An' don't forget to write." Wolfman hung up, tossed the phone on the bed, and walked toward the shower.

Arturo let the Schwinn accelerate down the narrow ramp next to the stairs, turned left and, using the network of alleys in the industrial park, pedaled the ten blocks to U-Store-It. Braking to a halt in front of storage unit C-10, Arturo took a key from his fanny pack and inserted it into the master lock securing the door. Ten seconds later, he had the door open and was gratified to behold his getaway car—a Cadillac CSX. Parking the bicycle inside the unit, he opened the driver's side door of the Caddy and slipped into the seat. The new car smell of the leather interior nuzzled his nose. Running his hands along the textured surface of the steering wheel, Arturo smiled at his clairvoyance and prudent preparations for today's events. His survival instincts, which had been honed as a street urchin in Mexico, had served him well.

He turned the key in the ignition and the Cadillac came to life. A soft white towel, carefully folded, sat waiting on the passenger's seat. Arturo picked up the towel and exited the car. Moving quickly, he used the towel to wipe away the thin layer of dust that had settled on the vehicle. He was taking no chances. He didn't want to be pulled over by a police officer, wondering why an obviously new car looked like it had just come from storage. When the Cadillac was dust-free, he put the towel in the trunk and drove the car out of the storage unit. He lowered the door of the storage unit behind him and locked it. Then he drove away.

Once out of the industrial park, Arturo breathed a little easier. He steered the Cadillac onto the freeway, heading west to San Francisco. An hour later, he turned into the long-term parking lot at San Francisco international airport. He parked up, removed his suitcase from the trunk of the vehicle and walked into the terminal, where he bought a first-class round-trip ticket to Orlando. He was only going one-way, but a round-trip ticket was less conspicuous, especially if the authorities questioned the ticket agent later.

Upon arriving in Orlando, Arturo would purchase another first-class ticket to somewhere, probably Rio de Janeiro or Sao Paulo. Some vast metropolis, where he would be swallowed up, just another human being immersed in the mundanities of getting and spending. He would wait a few months, then come back. He liked San Francisco. Besides he would like to see his friend Wolfman again.

He sipped a beer and watched CNN at the bar. An hour later, he boarded his flight, which departed on time.

WOLFMAN WAS SEATED in a booth at the Silver Dollar Saloon, which sat on the corner of Shaw and Blackstone Boulevard in Fresno, California. Wolfman was on his way to Los Angeles, but had stopped for lunch because he was starving. And he was starving because he had skipped breakfast at International House of Pancakes, deciding it might be best to get out of town while the getting was good. Now he was wondering if he should have at least warned everybody at HyperChem of what was going down. Guilt was getting to him. Which explained why his cell phone was on the table in front of him.

Rolling his eyeballs at the ceiling, he picked up the phone and punched in a number.

"Yo, Wolfman. How's it hangin', dude?" answered Mike Bergdorf aka Mongol.

Wolfman shook his head, wishing for the good old days when there was no such thing as Caller ID. All these high-tech gizmos were sucking the fun right out of life. "Swingin' low, dude," replied Wolfman.

"What's up?"

"Where you at?" asked Wolfman.

"In the warehouse, dude. Why? Where 'm I sposta be?"

"Everything cool? I mean any problems or anything?"

"Cool as ice, dude. Course ya'd know that if ya ever got your ass outta bed," laughed Mongol.

"Yeah. Listen, somep'n's come up. Super-Mex thinks maybe it's time for everybody to take a vacation, ya know what I sayin'? He thinks certain people are takin' an interest in what's going on there. Government type people, if ya get my drift?"

Mongol made a sucking noise. "I hear ya. Whatcha want me ta do?"

"Nice 'n' easy, I wancha to drop a word to everybody. Tell 'em it's time ta make like a tree and leave. Just walk away. Ya know what I'm sayin'?"

"No doubt, dude. I'm on it."

"Nice 'n' easy, Mongol. Nice 'n' easy," cautioned Wolfman.

"Gotcha," said Mongol and hung up.

TWO DAYS LATER, Operation Blue Dragon went into action. An army of DEA agents converged on HyperChem Industries. Every street, access road and alley approaching the building was blocked by vehicles from the DEA, the sheriff's department, the Pleasanton Police Department and the Dublin Police Department. The officers manning the blockades were expecting to confront, pursue and capture persons engaged in criminal activity as they attempted to escape. Nothing happened.

The DEA agents who approached the HyperChem warehouses expected to encounter resistance, up to and including a raging gunfight with a hail of bullets from automatic weapons. Nazi Low Riders had the reputation of real rock 'n' rollas in such situations. So the DEA advanced slowly in combat formation, using all available cover. Each agent wore body armor and carried a fully automatic assault rifle at the ready.

Nothing happened.

Anticipating an ambush, a five-man entry team moved to the front doors of HyperChem Industries. Covered by the weapons of thirty other agents, they entered the building. Two minutes later, the 'all clear' was broadcast from within. The Special Agent in Charge, along with another five-man team followed into the building. They were greeted by stacks of chemicals in bags on palettes, forklifts parked in a neat row, and tight packages of crystal meth ready and waiting to be shipped. The only thing missing was people. There was not one living soul in the building.

When the DEA entered the second warehouse, which housed the lab, the situation was the same. The room was full of chemical synthesizing equipment, constituent chemicals and computers. But no people.

Operation Blue Dragon was a bust. The Special Agent in Charge was fit to be tied. "Get some trucks in here and load up all this equipment," he ordered. "Everything. And get the techs going on those computers. I want to know what's on 'em." He turned to his second in command, the Assistant Special Agent in Charge, and said, "Mostly I want to know what the fuck went wrong!"

SAM SAUTER HEARD HyperChem was out of business from Henry Janes, who heard about it from Chalkie, who was one of the Nazi Low Riders, who, until a few days ago, worked at HyperChem. Chalkie tried to get over to San Quentin to visit Janes every few months because they were buddies from way back. When Mongol had put out the word, telling everybody at HyperChem to take a permanent vacation, Chalkie didn't need to be told twice. He'd slip-slided out the door, mounted his Arlen Ness motorcycle and jelly-rolled on out of there, heading for Richmond where his sister lived in a double-wide in a trailer park. After a few days of hanging out, Chalkie had gotten antsy and decided to jelly-roll over to the 'Q,' where he was hoping Janes might tell him what to do. Chalkie didn't have a clue. He didn't know whether to run, hide, stay put or quit.

After his visit with Janes, Chalkie still didn't know what to do, because Janes didn't even know what had gone down. Janes simply looked dizzy, like he thought Chalkie was fucking with him.

"No shit, dude," said Chalkie. "Once Mongol put the word out, the place was a ghost town in about ten minutes. Even the fuckin' bugs vamoosed."

"They just up 'n' left?"

Chalkie shrugged. "Nothin' else ta do, dude. Good thing, too. Cuz two days later'n the Feds showed up—a shitload of 'em—and put a stranglehold on the place."

"Ya seen 'em?" asked Janes.

"Shit no, man. I wadn't anywhere near the place. But I heard about it from some dudes."

"Fuck," muttered Janes.

Chalkie realized right then that it was time for him to be gone. What Chalkie had always suspected was now confirmed: Janes—who was a shotcaller in California—didn't know jack-shit, and was probably looney tunes. Chalkie decided to head south, which was more than likely where Wolfman was. Wolfman would know what to do.

"Where's Wolfman?" asked Janes.

"I don' know, man," replied Chalkie. "Not hangin' roun' here, tha's for sure."

"When ya see 'im, tell'm ta give me a visit. We need ta talk."

Chalkie gave him a nod.

"Whaddaya gonna do?"

"I'll be aroun', dude," said Chalkie, and stood up. "Be seein' ya', dude."

Janes didn't reply. He was too busy chewing his lip.

Chalkie walked out of the 'Q,' straddled his bike, fired it up and roared away. Taking highway 101, he worked his way over to I-5 and turned south, passing the sign that read Los Angeles 365 miles.

El Pimero

SOME EXPERTS thought the days of the Aryan Brotherhood's domination ended with the Department of Justice's 2002 indictment and the subsequent trials that took place between 2004 and 2006. These experts believed that the Aryan Brotherhood was broken. They still existed, but they were not what they used to be.

Others believed the Aryan Brotherhood were never as dominant as everyone seemed to assume. Terry Rearick, an experienced investigator, felt the supposition was overstated. "You got a bunch of dysfunctional dope fiends, and the government's theory is that they became this well-oiled killing machine. These guys are a bunch of brokedick convicts. Mills can't tell them what to do. I mean, they get two fifteen-minute phone calls a month at best, all their mail gets copied and read—and they're running the prison system? Come on."

Still other experts differed with both accounts. These experts believed the Aryan Brotherhood remained not only a historical reality, but also a terrible actuality, one that was awash in blood.

The Aryan Brotherhood was still a formidable power to be reckoned with, simply because of the larger-than-life figures of the Baron, the Hulk and Terrible Tom. Not only were these three men living legends with vast influence and authority, but the Aryan Brotherhood of Texas, the Aryan Brotherhood of Arizona, the Aryan Brotherhood of New Mexico and the Aryan Brotherhood of Florida were growing in numbers and activity. AB membership in these regions was younger, more reckless and more prone to spontaneous violence. They also tended to be white supremacist in outlook, which made them more fanatical and more reactionary than their brethren. In other words, their agenda was motivated by political and philosophical beliefs as well as mere common criminality. Fascism and Nazism were their political guiding lights. Philosophically, they subscribed to the belief that only the strong survive. Which meant brute force was the deciding factor. For a few, there was even a religious element, that of the Christian Identity movement, which asserted people of Aryan pedigree or white people were God's chosen people. This injection of religion into certain segments of the Brotherhood translated into a scary volatility, because these 'racial purist' members lost sight of the criminal goals of power, domination and profit. They were disorganized, undisciplined, hysterical, ignorant simpletons, who had no respect for anyone and wouldn't take orders. They didn't know how to take care of business. Instead, they got drunk and took a few hits of meth, working themselves into a lather and then rode off to rape, pillage and plunder. Which was not the way the Aryan Brotherhood—mystical warriors—did things. Warriors took orders, killing when instructed to do so. Warriors didn't do things willy-nilly.

Fortunately, there weren't many of the racial purists. Yet. But things were changing.

THE BIG THREE—the Federal Commissioners—sat in their cells at ADX Florence. Terrible Tom, consumed with his own secret musings and his meditations, like a great pale beast of the sea, moved through the watery abyss of self. The Aryan Brotherhood held little interest for him now.

The two mystical warriors—the Baron and the Hulk—liked prison. It was a jungle they knew well, and they were kings of the jungle. Most of their lives had been dedicated to staying in prison, where they were celebrities, famous for their prowess in mortal combat. In prison, they got respect because of their reputation. And if they didn't get respect, they got revenge. In their own eyes, they were warriors who depended on their wits and their physical strength to get what they wanted. And what they wanted was supremacy, which was the reward of true warriors. They engaged in mystical warfare, abolishing disorder and establishing order out of the chaos of the jungle.

This was the way they thought of themselves.

And they could prove it was the truth. The Aryan Brotherhood owned a bank in Miami. It controlled the production and distribution of crystal meth in much of the United States, supplied stolen arms to the Mexican drug cartels, owned car and motorcycle dealerships in California, and were responsible for extensive amounts of identity theft in the western United States. And they had an army of 15,000 warriors—inside and outside prisons—who obeyed their commands. Beholding all this, they were impressed. They even quoted the Book of Job: "In my flesh I shall see the gods."

That's what they thought. That's how they perceived themselves— as mystical warriors, demigods.

Contemporary civilized society saw them as psychotic sociopaths, brutal killers, who had nothing to do and nowhere to go. They lived in poured-cement caves, guarded by zookeepers, segregated from civilized society, which had all but forgotten about them. Condemned as monsters, they were locked away in an alien world, the supermax, where their contact with other human beings and the outside world was severely restricted, because if it was not, the tentacles of their influence and power would soon reach right back into the real world.

That's what society thought of them. That's how the penal system perceived them. Not as warriors or demigods, but as belligerent archfiends who were less than human—sub humanoids.

When this author encountered them—the Aryan Brotherhood and the Nazi Low Riders—his reaction was ambivalent, betwixt and between. It was one of astonishment and horror, curiosity and disgust, admiration and recognition. To meet human beings totally devoid of conscience was like coming face-to-face with creatures from outer space or the burning bush. It was as if Death had assumed human form and walked the earth. When he talked with them and listened to their stories, their explanations of why they did what they did, he realized they occupied a different kingdom. Their kingdom was without borders, without rules, yet it was always changing and never entirely fixed. It was a fluctuating kingdom, which can only be described as insane or warped, simply because it made no sense. It was not a reasonable kingdom.

THE WHOLE THING WAS ABSURD. The Aryan Brotherhood controlled millions of dollars in dirty drug money and owned a shell company that owned a bank. Yet there was no one to run the shell company. Additionally, the Aryan Brotherhood's production and distribution of crystal methamphetamine had come to a screeching halt, because a tattooed curiosity named Dion 'Bugsy' Milam, who wasn't even really part of the program, decided to make a deal to save his own skin. He knew just enough to mess everything up. And so, like a blind Samson chained between the pillars, he brought the whole shebang tumbling down.

The three car dealerships and the three motorcycle dealerships, which were owned by the front company called Phoenix, which in turn was owned and funded by the Aryan Brotherhood, were being investigated by agents of the DEA and the FBI, who were also nosing around Phoenix, Inc. If that wasn't bad enough, the attorney who had been running Phoenix, Inc. had been whacked because of an idiotic order given by the same lying death row ding-a-ling who was holding up the bank scheme.

What's more, all three federal shotcallers—the Commission—were sitting in solitary cells in ADX Florence, where they weren't getting any younger. Most of their lieutenants were in similar situations, locked up in Security Housing Units in maximum-security prisons somewhere. The only vitality remaining in the Aryan Brotherhood resided in its up-and-coming members—those in Arizona, New Mexico, Texas and Florida—who were pretty much zippy nihilistic mutant commie-mafioso thugs. Which meant they were as reliable as grasshoppers tripping on cocaine.

The violent empire of the Aryan Brotherhood was still alive and well, but it was a woeful mess.

Twilight of the Commission

BARRY 'THE BARON' MILLS turned sixty in 2009. He was still incarcerated in the ADX penitentiary—the federal supermax prison— in Florence, Colorado. Unless a miracle of Biblical proportions occurred—something along the lines of the parting of the Red Sea—the Baron will remain there until he dies. For he was serving multiple life sentences, without the opportunity for parole. He was a mythical figure in the underworld, especially to those with a 'white' philosophy—Nazi Low Riders, Public Enemy No. 1, the Dirty White Boys, Norcal Woods, and the Aryan Brotherhood. Even within the closed society of the supermax, which housed the upper echelon— the 'celebrities'—of the criminal abyss, he commanded respect for his notoriety.

In 2009, Tyler 'the Hulk' Bingham celebrated his sixty-first birthday in the supermax prison. The Hulk had spent more than half his life in prison. And what life was left to him would be spent there as well. Thomas 'Terrible Tom' Silverstein turned fifty-seven in 2009. He will be eligible for parole in eighty-six years.

For all intents and purposes, they were a brotherhood buried alive.

All three men—the Commission—were fading away. Murder, drugs, money laundering, theft, gun running, terrorism and a brooding absorption with secret ideas defined their lives. All in all, except for their very savagery, they were sad, colorless creatures, who lived and continue to live remarkably drab lives. In the end, they achieved nothing but a lackluster infamy. The only thing interesting about them was their abundant arrogance and opulent narcissism.

A sociological perspective asserted they were the products of their environment. They came from broken homes where violence was not only tolerated but was condoned and utilized. In short, the energy of violence achieved the desired results. Fear made people do what the fear-giver wanted them to do. Terror became an efficient tool of control. When these same men were locked away in prison with other violent men, the end result was an even more intense form of brutality, because, in the jungle, ferocity equals survival. Of course, this explanation denied the fact that people often produced their own environment. In other words, prison was savage not because of environmental factors but because the inmates wanted it that way. They liked savagery.

All arguments and reasons and excuses were moot. For in the end, cold-blooded murder was unacceptable. Society would not tolerate it. The simple and terrible lesson of the Aryan Brotherhood was this: Crime did not pay.

WOLF WEISS AKA WOLFMAN, Mongol and Chalkie ended up in Los Angeles, where they dealt drugs and guns on a small scale. Considered 'old gangsters'—or 'O.G.'—by the SoCal NLR, they didn't really fit in anywhere. Wolfman contemplated a move to Europe. He thought Greece sounded like a good place to live. He still had a lot of the money he made while involved with HyperChem Industries. If he chose to, he could retire and live like a king. The problem was that he was addicted to the outlaw lifestyle.

Isaac Goldfarb aka Six Fingers was around somewhere, probably hacking into a branch of the Bank of America. Arturo Colano was alleged to have gone to Namibia or Venezuela. He was even rumored to be in Colombia, working for the drug cartels there.

Charles Rollingshaven continued to practice law in Los Angeles. Because there was no lack of criminals, his business was booming. Sam Sauter and Henry Janes were still on death row at the 'Q,' waiting for their numbers to be called. When it was their turn, they'd make the dead man's walk to the chamber and receive the dreaded three-drug cocktail.

Tyler Bingham
#03325-091
Florence ADMAX US Penitentiary
PO Box 8500
Florence, Colorado81226
USA

Barry Mills
#14559-116
Florence ADMAX US Penitentiary
PO Box 8500
Florence, Colorado81226
USA

Thomas Silverstein
#14634-116
Florence ADMAX US Penitentiary
PO Box 8500
Florence, Colorado81226
USA

APPENDIX

The Violent Timeline of the Aryan Brotherhood

January 16, 1967 Nazi prison gang associate Robert Holderman is stabbed and then battered to death by Black Guerilla Family gang members at San Quentin.

January 17, 1967 1,800 black inmates and 1,000 white inmates clash on the main yard at San Quentin over the death of Robert Holderman. Prison guards break up the brawl by firing shots into the mass. Five inmates are wounded by the shots. One inmate suffers severe head trauma from the beating he receives from opposing gang members. Two other inmates suffer non-fatal heart attacks.

August 27, 1967 Nineteen year old Barry Byron Mills is arrested in Ventura, California, and held for transfer to Sonoma County, where there is an arrest warrant in his name for grand theft auto.

December 12, 1967 Barry Mills requests and is denied probation. Instead he is sentenced to one year in the Sonoma County Jail.

January 29, 1968 Barry Mills and Buddy Coleman escape from the Sonoma County Honor Farm.

February 17, 1968 Barry Mills is arrested in Windsor, California.

March 12, 1968 Barry Mills is sentenced to one year and one day in prison for escape without force from the Sonoma County Jail.

March 13, 1969 Barry Mills is released from prison.

January 13, 1970 Soledad state prison Aryan Brotherhood leader Buzzard Harris, along with fellow Aryan Brotherhood members Smiley Hoyle, Harpo Harper and Chuko Wendekier, and Mexican

Mafia members Colorado Joe Ariaz, John Fanene, and Raymond Guerrero battle with Black Guerilla Family gang members on the exercise yard at Soledad prison. Tower guard Opie Miller opens fire with his high-powered rifle, killing Black Guerilla leader W. L. Nolen, Cleveland Edwards and Alvin Miller. Aryan Brotherhood leader Buzzard Harris is wounded in the groin by a rifle bullet.

January 30, 1970 Barry Mills and William Hackworth are arrested after robbing a Stewarts Point convenience store.

February 3, 1970 Barry Mills is convicted of first-degree armed robbery after codefendant William Hackworth testifies for the prosecution. Barry Mills is sentenced to five years to life in prison.

April 21, 1972 Aryan Brotherhood members Fred Mendrin and Donald Hale murder Fred Castillo by stabbing him to death at the Chino Institute for Men. Castillo was the leader of the Nuestra Familia gang. The Aryan Brotherhood murder Castillo as part of a contract with the Mexican Mafia.

December 15, 1972 Aryan Brotherhood members Fred Mendrin and Donald Hale are sentenced to life in prison for the murder of Fred Castillo.

1973 The Aryan Brotherhood is officially formed in the federal prison system.

October 18, 1977 Aryan Brotherhood member Little Joe O'Rourke engages in a vicious gun battle with campus police at El Camino community college. The gun battle erupts when the police, as part of a routine check, ask Little Joe for his student ID. Little Joe is wounded and arrested.

November 25, 1977 Aryan Brotherhood members David Owens and 'New York' Crane rob the Bank of America in Agoura, California. They get away with $9,000.

December 2, 1977 'New York' Crane is named as the prime suspect in the murder of fellow Aryan Brotherhood member Hogjaw Cochran.

December 29, 1977 Barry Mills is released from San Quentin state prison.

January 11, 1978 Aryan Brotherhood member David Owens is arrested and charged with robbing the Bank of America in Agoura, California. Owens has $3,844 on him when arrested.

March 13, 1978 David Owens is convicted of bank robbery and sentenced to federal prison. His codefendant 'New York' Crane is held over in Orange County Jail and charged with the murder of Hogjaw Cochran.

March 31, 1978 Little Joe O'Rourke is sentenced to seven years in prison for opening fire on the El Camino community college campus.

June 1978 Barry Mills is sentenced to twenty years in federal prison for planning a bank robbery in Fresno, California. The bank was robbed by the Aryan Brotherhood in June 1976. Barry Mills did not participate in the robbery, but provided the blueprint for it.

May 20, 1979 Barry Mills murders Aryan Brotherhood associate John Sherman Marzloff in the United States prison Atlanta, Georgia.

1980 The Aryan Brotherhood sets up a Commission to run the operations of all Aryan Brotherhood members in the federal prison system. The Commission is composed of three men. Barry Mills assumes command of the Commission.

June 8, 1980 Aryan Brotherhood associate Robert Hogan is murdered. The order to kill him comes from Barry Mills.

September 27, 1982 Aryan Brotherhood Commissioner Thomas 'Terrible Tom' Silverstein murders Cadillac Smith, leader of the DC Blacks, at the United States prison, Marion, Illinois.

December 9, 1982 Aryan Brotherhood member Neil Baumgarten is murdered by members of the DC Blacks. Baumgarten's murder is payback for the murder of Cadillac Smith.

January 13, 1983 Aryan Brotherhood member Blinky Griffen is convicted of the murder of T-Bone Gibson.

February 13, 1983 Aryan Brotherhood member Richard Barnes is murdered. The order to kill Barnes comes from Aryan Brotherhood councilman McKool Slocum.

September 23, 1983 Aryan Brotherhood associate Gregory Keefer is stabbed to death by another Aryan Brotherhood associate. The hit is ordered by Mills, to whom Keefer owes tax money from drug sales.

October 6, 1983 Aryan Brotherhood member Richard 'Rhino' Andreasen provides information to the Feds about a bank robbery in Santa Ana, California. For this transgression, Barry Mills orders Rhino killed. An Aryan Brother stabs him to death at the United States penitentiary Leavenworth, Kansas.

October 6, 1983 At the United States penitentiary Marion, Illinois, Aryan Brotherhood Commissioner Thomas Silverstein, aka 'Terrible Tom,' stabs Officer Eugene Clutts forty times for "disrespecting him." Officer Clutts dies. A few hours later, Officer Bob Hoffman is stabbed thirty-five times by Aryan Brother Clayton Fountain, who "didn't want Terrible Tom to have a higher body count than me." Officer Hoffman dies.

January 30, 1984 An Aryan Brotherhood associate stabs and kills Officer Boyd Spikerman at the Federal Correctional Institution, Oxford, Wisconsin.

February 7, 1984 Aryan Brotherhood member Robert Scully assaults a fellow inmate at San Quentin, because Scully is in a bad mood and "the bastard pissed me off."

March 13, 1984 Aryan Brotherhood member Rick Rose defects. His name is placed 'in the hat.'

April 12, 1984 Aryan Brotherhood member Jesse Brun sets fire to a black inmate at Folsom prison. The victim suffers burns over twenty-five percent of his body.

April 27, 1984 Aryan Brotherhood member Robert Scully is once again in a bad mood. He attacks and tries to stab a prison guard.

April 28, 1984 Robert Scully gases two guards at San Quentin. No charges are filed. No disciplinary action is taken.

May 1, 1984 Robert Scully stabs a guard at San Quentin. Scully is held and searched. Three hacksaw blades are discovered in his rectum and two .22 caliber bullets, which Scully had swallowed, are discovered in his stomach. All charges against Scully are dismissed.

May 29, 1985 Robert Scully assaults another inmate at San Quentin with a shank. He is charged with possession of a deadly weapon and receives six additional years for assault.

September 1985 Tyler 'the Hulk' Bingham is officially named as part of the three-man Federal Commission.

October 10, 1987 Aryan Brotherhood member Rodney Ross stabs and kills thirty-three year old Gordon Gaskill at Folsom prison.

June 22, 1987 Aryan Brotherhood member Art Ruffo attacks and tries to murder a black inmate. Officer David Pitts thwarts Ruffo's attempt by shooting Ruffo in the hip. At the same time, Aryan Brotherhood member Cornfed Schneider attacks another black inmate. The attacks are planned and orchestrated as part of a hit on the DC Blacks at Folsom prison. The hits are ordered by Blue Norris, an Aryan Brotherhood Councilman. This is the beginning of "Hell Week" at Folsom prison.

July 7, 1987 During a strip search, Cornfed Schneider stabs Officer Carl Kropp in the throat. Councilman Blue Norris orders the hit on Officer Kropp as payback for the shooting of Aryan Brotherhood member Art Ruffo. Officer David Pitts, who shot Art Ruffo, is wounded by a shotgun blast as he drives to his home in West Sacramento.

October 10, 1987 Relocated to Tehachapi prison, Aryan Brotherhood member Robert Scully—who is usually in a bad mood—is charged with possession of a deadly weapon. The charge is later dropped.

November 25, 1987 Judith Box is arrested by authorities. Box is the girlfriend of Wildman Fortman, a member of the Aryan Brotherhood. Box is charged with providing the Aryan Brotherhood with the home addresses of prison guards, information she obtains through her job at the Franchise Tax Board.

March 15, 1988 Aryan Brotherhood member Robert Rowland defects, providing authorities with information about a plot to murder prison guards. Rowland's name goes 'into the hat.'

August 28, 1988 Judith Box is convicted of identity theft and conspiring to commit assault.

February 15, 1989 Judith Box is sentenced to three years in prison.

June 5, 1989 Aryan Brotherhood member Marvin Stanton is assaulted and shot with a 37mm block-gun, while fighting with a member of Nuestra Familia. The battle occurs on one of the exercise yards at Corcoran state prison.

June 14, 1989 During his trial, Aryan Brotherhood member Cornfed Schneider testifies that he stabbed Officer Kropp in the throat because he thought the guards were coming to attack him.

July 24, 1989 The jurors, who are terrified, fail to find Cornfed Schneider guilty of attempted murder. Cornfed Schneider is sentenced to an additional five years in prison for possession of a deadly weapon. Cornfed Schneider stabs his attorney Phillip Couzens four times while the two men are talking in the hallway of the Sacramento county courthouse.

April 18, 1990 Aryan Brotherhood member Todd Ashker is convicted of second-degree murder in the death of a Folsom inmate. The hit is ordered by the Commission. Ashker is sentenced to twenty-one years to life in prison.

December 13, 1990 The bad attitude of Aryan Brotherhood member Robert Scully results in a transfer to the new maximum-security prison at Pelican Bay.

December 16, 1992 Aryan Brotherhood member Victor Carrafa, who has just been paroled, is arrested in Stockton, California. He has a six-inch Buck Knife and a .38 caliber semi-automatic pistol on his person.

March 14, 1993 Aryan Brotherhood member Termite Kennedy shoots and kills Glenn Chambers of Oregon. Chambers had been supplying the Aryan Brotherhood with chemicals for the manufacture of crystal meth.

May 11, 1993 While being escorted to the dentist, Aryan Brotherhood member Victor Carrafa escapes from the custody of the Sacramento County Sheriff's department, shooting Deputy Steve Fonbuena in the face and stomach. The escape had been planned with the help of Aryan Brotherhood member Gerard Gallant.

February 26, 1994 Robert Scully is released from Pelican Bay prison. Scully's parole stipulates drug and alcohol testing. It also prohibits him from associating with members of the Aryan Brotherhood or any other known felons.

March 24, 1994 Robert Scully is arrested in Newport Beach. He is carrying a .25 caliber pistol and displays false identification. Scully is sent back to Pelican Bay prison for one year.

June 1, 1994 Aryan Brotherhood member Joseph Barrett assaults a prison officer who has confiscated a television from his cell.

March 23, 1995 Robert Scully is released from Pelican Bay prison. Brenda Moore, who was the girlfriend of Cornfed Schneider, picks him up in front of the prison.

March 26, 1995 Robert Scully and Brenda Moore murder Frank Trejo, a deputy with the Sonoma County Sheriff's department. The murder takes place in the parking lot of a bar in Sebastopol, California.

1996 Barry Mills proposes that the Aryan Brotherhood absorb the prison gang known as the Dirty White Boys.

February 7, 1996 Aryan Brotherhood member Art Ruffo is strangled by his cellmate Brian Healy, an Aryan Brotherhood member. The murder takes place at Pelican Bay prison and is ordered by the Commission.

April 9, 1996 Aryan Brotherhood member Joseph Barrett, incarcerated at Calipatria prison, receives a message from the Commission. The message instructs Barrett to "squeeze and hug his cellmate," Aryan Brotherhood member Thomas Richmond. Barrett obeys the instruction and kills Richmond.

November 1, 1997 As a favor to the Mexican Mafia, the Commission orders a hit on Pelican Bay inmate Felipe Cruz. Cruz is strangled by Aryan Brotherhood member James Ellrod.

February 22, 1998 Aryan Brotherhood member Brian Healey tells the Feds he is willing to testify against the Aryan Brotherhood.

February 23, 1998 In an ordered hit, Pelican Bay inmate Timothy Waldron is strangled by Aryan Brotherhood member Steve Olivares.

March 10, 1998 Aryan Brotherhood member William Stanton is stabbed to death by two inmates. The murder takes place on Pelican Bay prison's A yard.

February 2, 2000 Aryan Brotherhood member Joseph Barrett is strip searched at Tehachapi state prison. A shank and six razor blades are found in his rectum.

January 30, 2001 Aryan Brotherhood members Cornfed Schneider and Dale Bretches, both incarcerated at Pelican Bay, are discovered to be running a dogfighting ring on the outside. Two of their pitbulls kill Dianne Whipple of San Francisco.

September 5, 2001 The northern California office of the US District Attorney announces it is indicting six members of the Aryan Brotherhood and one associate.

October 16, 2002 A federal indictment unsealed in Los Angeles charges forty members and associates of the Aryan Brotherhood with several RICO violations, including murder. The indictment includes Rafael Gonzalez-Munoz, a high-ranking member of the Mexican Mafia, and Joseph Principe, a federal correctional officer.

April 7, 2003 Aryan Brotherhood member Blue Norris is found stabbed to death at Calipatria state prison. He had defected from the Aryan Brotherhood and provided information to prison officials. His murder is ordered by the Commission.

September 4, 2003 Aryan Brotherhood member Cornfed Schneider pleads guilty to conspiracy, racketeering and smuggling. He is sentenced to life in prison. This is his third life sentence.

April 4, 2004 Brenda Jo Riley, the wife of an Aryan Brotherhood member, is sentenced to serve twenty-one months in prison for acting as a message courier for the Aryan Brotherhood.

November 29, 2004 Aryan Brotherhood member Wade Shiflett is shot and killed by a prison guard on B yard at Sacramento state prison. Shiflett was attempting to murder another member of the Aryan Brotherhood who had defected and was going to testify against the Aryan Brotherhood. The hit was ordered by the Commission

July 22, 2005 US District Judge David Baxter sets a date for the federal trial against the Aryan Brotherhood. Judge Baxter rules defense attorneys could call Thomas 'Terrible Tom' Silverstein as a defense witness, but that he is to remain shackled in court.

The Indictment

Specific crimes cited in the indictment against Barry Mills, Tyler Bingham and Thomas Silverstein. The murders of:

John Marzloff in prison in Atlanta, Georgia.
Robert Hogan in Illinois.
Richard Barnes in California.
Gregory Keefer in Illinois.
Richard Andreasen in California.
Thomas Lamb in Illinois.
Arva Lee Ray in California.
William McKinney in California.
Charles Leger in Kansas.
Arthur Ruffo in California.
Aaron Nash in California.
Frank Joyner in Pennsylvania.
Abdul Salaam in Pennsylvania.
Terry Walker in Illinois.

NOTES AND SOURCES

1 THE BARON AND THE HULK

US vs. Barry Byron Mills, et al., United States District Court for the Central District of California, February 2002, Grand Jury.

Duerstein, Matthew. 'Who'll Stop the Reign?' *Los Angeles Weekly.* 2005.

Grann, David. 'The Brand,' *The New Yorker*, February 16 and 23, 2004, 157-171.

California vs. Mills, 21 Cal. 2d 746 (1967).

Barry Mills, interview by Roger Poppen, February 2006, interview 3, transcript, Los Angeles, CA.

Tyler Bingham, interview by Roger Poppen, February 2006, interview 1, recording, Los Angeles, CA.

2 CON AIR

Prendergast, Alan, 'The Caged Life,' *Westword*, August 2007.

US vs. Thomas Silverstein, transcript, 1975.

US Bureau of Prisons, *Medical Examiner's Official Report*, date illegible.

Summers, Chris, 'America's Most Dangerous Prisoner?' *BBC News*, undated.

Roberto Messia, in discussion with Roger Poppen, transcript, 2007.

Earley, Pete. *The Hot House: Life Inside Leavenworth Prison.* Bantam, 1993.

Thomas Silverstein, interview by Roger Poppen, 2006, transcript.

3 RINGLEADERS AND RATS

Richards, Tori. 'Heavy Security Set for Aryan Brotherhood Trial,' *Red Orbit*, July 2005.

Grann, David, 'The Brand,' *The New Yorker*, February 16 and 23, 2004.

Prendergast, Alan, 'Bringing Down the Brotherhood,' *Westword*, May 2005.

US vs. Barry Byron Mills, et al., court transcript, 2006.

Danny Weeks, interview by Roger Poppen, transcript, 2005, Los Angeles, CA.

5 THE VERDICT

US vs Barry Byron Mills, et al., court transcript, 2006.

US District Court for the Central District of California, court records and transcripts.

CBS News, July 28, 2006.

Goffard, Christopher, 'Aryan Brotherhood Leaders Get Life Terms,' *Los Angeles Times*, 2006.

Flaccus, Gillian, 'Judge Postpones Gang Leaders' Sentencing,' *Associated Press/Fox News*, November 2006.

Prendergast, Alan, 'Bringing Down the Brotherhood,' *Westword*, May 2005.

7 ADIOS AMIGOS

Jones, Harry, 'Man Who Hired Out Killing of Fiancée Gets Death,' *San Diego Union Tribune*, March 2004.

Soto, Onell, 'Man Hired by Boss to Kill Fiancee Gets Life,' *San Diego Tribune*, April 2004.

Associated Press, *Daily News*, June 1998.

California vs. William Williams, court medical report, 1998.

Wilson, Tracy, 'Death Penalty Ordered in Torture Case,' *LA Times*, August 1998.

8 PLAN B FROM MARS

Krasnowski, Matt, 'Woman Sentenced in Aryan Crackdown,' *The San Diego Tribune*, April 2004.

9 WRAP UP

Prendergast, Alan, 'Bringing Down the Brotherhood,' *Westword*, May 2005.

Holthouse, David, 'Smashing the Shamrock,' *Southern Poverty Law Center: Intelligence Report*, 2008.

Tyler Bingham, interview by Roger Poppen, 'Deadliest Prison Gang,' Electricsky Productions, 2009.

Gallagher, Mike. 'Aryan Brotherhood Expanding in New Mexico and Texas,' *Albuquerque Journal*, August 2007.

'Arrests of Alleged Members of Aryan Brotherhood,' *Anti-Defamation League*, July 2008.

ACKNOWLEDGMENTS

THE ACCURACY of the narrative of this book relies on interviews with primary sources whenever possible, reconstructing events and dialogue according to their memories.

Numerous legal documents such as court transcripts and law enforcement reports provided invaluable information. Historical and contextual material was obtained from books, newspaper articles, and interviews, and are noted elsewhere in this book.

For their dialogue and cooperation, the author extends his thanks to US Marshal Clarence Sugar, Buddy Coleman, William Hackworth, Robert Pearson aka Bully Boy, Moose Forbes, Albert Benton, Frank Sansoni, Danny Holliday, Wolf Weiss aka Wolfman, Gaspar Gabriel-Portola, Henry Janes, Isaac Goldfarb aka Six Fingers, Correctional Officer David Pitts, and Chris George.

Many other people were interviewed, but their names have been withheld by mutual consent. Among these are police officers, DEA agents, officers of court, federal correctional officers, health care workers, and various gang members, including those of the Aryan Brotherhood, for whom confidentiality was the tariff for edification. In many other cases, not only were the names of people changed, but also places and identifying characteristics. This was done to protect the innocent and the guilty.

The company names HyperChem and Acme Components are pseudonyms. Arturo Colano is a fictitious name. Samuel Sauter is a fictitious name. Pamela and Debra Fleck are fictitious names. Charles Rollingshaven is a fictitious name.

The account of the jury in chapter five comes courtesy of a juror, whose detailed, handwritten notes of the trial were invaluable.

A HEADPRESS BOOK
First published by Headpress in May 2011. Revised September 2011.

Headpress, Suite 306, The Colourworks
2a Abbot Street, London, E8 3DP, UK
[tel] 0845 330 1844
[email] headoffice@headpress.com
[web] www.worldheadpress.com

BLOOD IN, BLOOD OUT
The Violent Empire Of the Aryan Brotherhood

Text copyright © John Lee Brook
This volume copyright © Headpress 2011
Cover art & design: Sean Fannin & Ganymede Foley
Headpress diaspora: David Kerekes, Thomas McGrath, Caleb Selah, David,
Giuseppe

The moral rights of the author have been asserted.

A CIP catalogue record for this book is available from the British Library

ISBN 9781900486774

WWW.WORLDHEADPRESS.COM
the gospel according to unpopular culture